The Jew In American Politics

I am indebted to David I. Lichtman for research assistance and to Mrs. Genevieve Linebarger, Professor William F. Marina, Theodore Lit and my beloved wife, Sylvia Castleton Weyl, for invaluable aid in editing the manuscript.

THE JEW

IN

AMERICAN POLITICS

BY

NATHANIEL WEYL

ARLINGTON HOUSE • *New Rochelle, N. Y.*

Second Printing, May 1969

Library of Congress Catalog Card Number 68-13314

MANUFACTURED IN THE UNITED STATES OF AMERICA

ACKNOWLEDGMENTS

I wish to express gratitude to the following for having given me permission to quote from published works: Doubleday and Company, Inc., *The Hero*, by Kenneth S. Davis and *The American Dissent*, by Jeffrey Hart; Dr. Ives Hendrick, *Statesmen of the Lost Cause*, by Burton J. Hendrick, published by Little, Brown & Company; Princeton University Press, *The Structure of Spanish History*, by Américo Castro (translated by Edmund L. King, copyright 1954 by Princeton University Press); Holt, Rinehart and Winston, Inc., *The Legend of Henry Ford*, by Keith Sward; the Macmillan Company, *The Quest for the Dream*, by John P. Roche (copyright by Anti-Defamation League of B'nai B'rith, 1963); Harper & Row, Publishers, Inc., *Dynamics of Prejudice*, by Bruno Bettelheim and Morris Janowitz; Sheed and Ward, Inc., *A Jew in Christian America*, by Rabbi Arthur Gilbert; Frederick A. Praeger, Inc., *From Lenin to Khrushchev*, by Hugh Seton-Watson; World Publishing Company, *A Little Girl Is Dead*, by Harry Golden; the *American Jewish Year Book*, numerous items; *New York Times Magazine*, November 29, 1964 (copyright 1964 by The New York Times Company), "The Negro Is Prejudiced Against Himself," by Eric Hoffer; *National Review*, 150 East 35 St., New York, N.Y. 10016, "A Little Known Chapter in American History," by Max Geltman, October 5, 1965; *Commentary*, "An Anatomy of the Klan," by Seymour Martin Lipset, October 1965; *Good Housekeeping*, "Why Did They Do It?," by William Peters, June 1962; and *Harvard Business Review*, "The Ethics of Executive Selection," by Lewis B. Ward, March–April 1965.

CONTENTS

1. Problem and Paradox 1
2. Jewry and Intellectual Aristocracy 10
3. From Spain to the New World 20
4. American Beginnings 30
5. The Civil War 49
6. The Gilded Age 61
7. The Fight against Anti-Semitism: 1880–1914 77
8. From World War to Depression 93
9. Socialism, Communism and the Far Left 110
10. Fascist and Pro-Nazi Movements 124
11. The Anti-Defamation League and the Right 142
12. Jewish Voting Behavior: 1932–1967 159
13. Economic, Social and Intellectual Elites 172
14. Under Czars and Commissars 189
15. The Ordeals of Soviet Jewry 212
16. Aspects of American Anti-Semitism 232
17. Jews, Negroes and Civil Rights 248
18. Israel, Zionism and Assimilation 291

viii   CONTENTS

19. Church and State   304
20. American Jews and the Conservative Movement   327
     Notes   339
     Index   369

CHAPTER 1

Problem and Paradox

AMERICAN JEWISH POLITICAL BEHAVIOR is an anomaly and
a contradiction. The American Jewish community is overwhelmingly middle class and upper middle class. American
Jews are more highly educated than any other national or
religious group in the U.S. population. They are concentrated in entrepreneurial, professional, scientific and aes-
thetically creative occupations. Their income is much higher
than the national average. Their contribution to the economic, political and creative leadership of the nation is
much greater than their numerical strength would indicate.

Yet in their political attitudes, they are overwhelmingly
liberal-to-radical and this despite the general rule of political behavior that the higher a group stands in status, income
and education, the more it tends to prefer a conservative to
a liberal philosophy. Thus, despite the fact that the intellectual community in the United States has in recent years

tended to be preponderantly liberal, a majority of college graduates has consistently supported the Republican Party and taken a conservative stance on most controversial domestic issues. This was partially confirmed, as far as education is concerned, in the wake of Senator Goldwater's 1964 presidential defeat, one that gave the Republican Party a smaller proportion of the total popular vote than it had obtained in any of the previous six presidential contests. Even after this massive setback, one segment of the population remained loyal to the GOP according to the evidence of public opinion polls. That last steadfast group was the college-bred, the element which William James considered the only true American aristocracy.

Two years later, a Gallup Poll revealed that 59% of the college-trained had supported Republican candidates in the 1966 elections as against 41% who voted Democratic. By contrast, of those with less than a grade-school education, 61% backed Democratic, and only 39% Republican, candidates. The Republicans had the support of 58% of the business and professional voters, 52% of the white-collar workers and 50% of the farmers, but only 39% of the manual workers.[1]

A positive correlation apparently exists between wealth, income, education and status, on the one hand, and conservatism, on the other. This is not equivalent to asserting that the richer people become and the more education they absorb, the farther they gravitate to the right. The term "right wing" is in itself variously defined, meaning different things to different people at different times and places. The Nazis in Germany were known as *Rechtsradicale*, or radicals of the right. Like various small hate groups in the United States which ape them, the Nazis had greater affinity to Communism than to the forces of democracy. Both Nazis and Communists engineered major social revolutions in which the upper classes were ousted from power and their institutions perverted or destroyed. Both wage relentless war on individualism and on freedom. Both seek to destroy institutions which protect the rights of minorities and of the individual. Both are destructive movements, spurred forward by resentment and hatred. Both are devoid of moral standards which might inhibit them from committing heinous crimes against humanity.

To some people, the litmus test of whether movements and individuals are "right wing" or "left wing" is their attitude toward Communism. This is an inadequate standard. The Nazis were motivated by a virulent hatred of Communism. This hatred, however, was not so much the reflection of a fundamental conflict of principle as of the fact that both movements were rivals for total world power. The victory of either involved the extermination of the other.

One of the most vital aspects of a genuine conservative outlook is deep respect for tradition and history. The conservative regards the institutions of Western civilization as towers of social strength and forces for good. He considers their continuity to be necessary to the preservation of law and order based upon the consent of the people. He believes that those who deride authority and recklessly destroy traditional institutions are leading society into chaos and retrogression. As a champion of law and tradition, the true conservative cannot have any alliance or rapport with those "radicals of the right" who are dedicated to the destruction of fundamental freedoms and institutions. The radicals of the right are not the fellow travelers of conservatism. Together with the radicals of the left, they are its mortal enemies. Indeed, the terms "left" and "right" lose descriptive meaning when applied to totalitarian movements.

The fact that the conservative emphasizes institutional continuity does not mean that he opposes all change. If he did, if he were frozen in contemplation of a dead past (as some pseudo-conservatives are), he would be merely a fossil, living in a theoretical world irrelevant to the problems of the age. He would be incapable of devising intelligent solutions to new problems.

Liberalism in the American Context

The United States was born in a struggle against British Tory restrictions on economic and political freedom. The basic document which defined the structure and course of the nascent republic, the Constitution of 1787, was primarily concerned with *conserving* the freedom of the individual and the rights of dissenting minorities against powerful central government and tyrannical political majorities.

Thus, the spirit of the Constitution was one of conservatism and also of liberalism (in its dictionary sense of protection of liberty). It was not accidental that the American Constitution should have been hailed as the most perfect political system ever devised by the same Lord Acton who wrote: "Power tends to corrupt and absolute power corrupts absolutely."

The French Revolution at first seemed to Jefferson and others to be part of the worldwide movement toward human freedom which they thought they discerned on the horizon. However, it derived much of its philosophy from Jean Jacques Rousseau's notions of an all-powerful general will. Rousseau's philosophy was basically contrary to the liberal current and contained the germs of future totalitarian systems—whether Nazi, Communist or the bacterial nationalism of backward peoples. Implicitly, Rousseau and his disciples denied the importance of individual freedom. If

the French Revolution led to a reign of terror and a centralized bureaucracy with police-state features, whereas the
American Revolution led to a free and orderly society, the
difference between the philosophies of Rousseau and Locke
had much to do with the matter.

As the twentieth century advanced the concept of liberalism changed. Today, American liberalism is, in many
respects, the very antithesis of the traditional liberal philosophy. In essence, it is social democracy of a non-doctrinaire
sort. It believes in the continual, and apparently unlimited,
expansion of the powers of the federal government to advance whatever it considers to be conducive to the general
welfare. It sees no contradiction between individual freedom and the expanding spider's web of governmental controls. It applauds Supreme Court decisions which do
violence to the language and meaning of the Constitution.
It considers tradition a millstone around the neck of reform,
states' rights an anachronism, and such concepts as equality
of opportunity pernicious wherever they give the more intelligent, hard-working and self-reliant elements in the nation
a competitive advantage over the stupid, lazy and dependent ones.

The liberalism of today is dedicated to the concept of
human equality, not in the original American sense of
equality of opportunity to actualize whatever abilities lie
within one, but in the crude sense of equality of ability.
If we assume biological equality, we must infer that success
is the undeserved result of good fortune and that failure is
the product of misadventure or injustice. We thereby deny
human responsibility and assert by implication that no
man can be better or worse than any other.

This philosophy degrades man to the level of a purely
passive product of external circumstance. It removes, to the

extent that anyone seriously believes in it, the incentive to be creative, productive or responsible—to seek to be, in short, not the common man, but the uncommon one. Among the gifted, it creates guilty reactions to the fact that society is still far enough removed from the madhouse to reward them for their superior gifts—and this masochistic attitude toward success is, as we shall see, at the root of the anomalous Jewish attitude toward American politics.

During the decades in which the connotations of the word "liberalism" were gradually altered so as to apply to an ideology inimical to human freedom, the new liberalism became the dominant political philosophy throughout most of Western civilization. In most countries of the West, liberal parties, dedicated to the indefinite expansion of the executive power of the central government, arose, grew and won majority support. In the name of equality, these parties worked to give special privileges to the least energetic, least intelligent and least productive elements in the population. Simultaneously, they created and maintained large bureaucracies, the members of which were paid attractive salaries to distribute largesse among the poor.

Jewish Liberalism: the Allinsmith Study

The degree of commitment of American Jewry to liberalism is different from the degree of that commitment among other religious groups. The difference is that the Jewish devotion to liberalism is not correlated with economic or educational status. This was demonstrated almost 20 years ago by Wesley and Beverly Allinsmith.[2]

Toward the close of World War II, the Allinsmiths asked 8,820 members of eight religious denominations whether they believed that the most important postwar task of the U.S. Government was to provide opportunity for people to get ahead on their own or "to guarantee every person a decent and steady job and standard of living."[3]

Nationally, 47% of the people questioned preferred security to opportunity. As the percentage of manual workers in each denomination increased, the proportion favoring security rose. Status, education and income were inversely related to the choice of security. As one proceeded from Congregationalists to Presbyterians to Episcopalians to Methodists to Lutherans to Baptists and finally to Catholics, the preference for security steadily increased from 26% to 58%.

The Jews were the only exception to this rule. Although they were a very high status group, ranking first in occupational level, third in educational level and fourth in economic level, 56% of them preferred security to opportunity. This was almost as high as the Catholic preference for security.

Moreover, within each of the eight religious denominations, the preference for opportunity was greatest among those with most education, highest status and best occupational level. Again, the Jews were the only exception.

The 1944 presidential vote also revealed this marked difference between Jewish and Gentile political behavior. The upper-class and upper-middle-class Christian denominations voted heavily against Roosevelt and in favor of Republican standard-bearer Thomas Dewey. Only 31.4% of the Congregationalists, 39.9% of the Presbyterians and 44.6% of the Episcopalians backed Franklin Delano Roosevelt. The more working-class denominations, however, voted heavily for him, particularly the Catholics who were 72.8% in his favor. In terms of their combined educational, occupational and status rank in the Allinsmith survey—that of second place—the Jews might well have been expected to vote Republican. Actually, they were 92.1% for Roosevelt. This overwhelming support was greater than that of any of the Christian denominations.

It is evident that the massive Jewish backing for Roosevelt in 1944 cannot be interpreted exclusively in terms of liberalism vs. conservatism. American Jews felt immense gratitude to FDR for having pursued a strong anti-Nazi policy in the face of internal and external opposition and for having committed the nation to all-out war which saved the world from domination by Hitler and the Jewish people from total extermination.

However, in the 1952 elections, despite the fact that the Republican presidential candidate, Dwight D. Eisenhower, had led the Western coalition to victory over the Nazis, 75% of the Jewish voters supported Adlai E. Stevenson, a man who had played no role of any importance in World War II. There was no difference in the attitude of the candidates toward Jewry or the state of Israel. The issue was clearly one of moderation vs. liberalism. In a situation where American voters as a whole gave decisive support to Eisenhower, three-fourths of the Jews backed his Democratic opponent. Moreover, interviews in depth of Boston voters showed that only 30% of the Gentiles with high socioeconomic status, as against 60% of those with low socioeconomic status, backed Stevenson. Among Boston Jews, 72% of those with high status voted for Stevenson.[4]

Evidently we are dealing with a political phenomenon that is unique and not explicable in the standard terms of public opinion analysis. The aberrant political behavior of American Jewry has deep roots in the religious, economic and political history of the Jewish people. It is related to their centuries-long struggle to find institutions and socioeconomic forces which would give them equality of opportunity and security from the specter of persecution which has so often haunted them.

This aspect of the political behavior of American Jews is not, I believe, realistically related to their experience in the United States. Attitudes have been absorbed from their heritage in Czarist Russia, from their relationship to the revolutionary movements against Czarism and, more recently, from the holocaust which European Jewry suffered under the Nazis. A Jewish syndrome has arisen in America and elsewhere, which magnifies minor slights and injuries from conservative groups, while largely overlooking the global threat to Israel and to Western civilization posed by Soviet and Chinese Communism and by the strident, racist nationalisms of the new, impoverished states of the Asian and African world. Above all, Jews in general have refused to recognize themselves as an elite group with an immense stake in the existing social order and a great political role to play in the orderly evolution of the world toward the institutions of Western civilization, institutions which have alone thus far given man both order and freedom.

CHAPTER 2

Jewry and Intellectual Aristocracy

THROUGHOUT HISTORY, one encounters peoples, castes, classes and religious communities which constantly manifest superior all-round ability and greater intellectual distinction than their neighbors. The Puritans and their descendants are an outstanding example of this state of affairs. The Jews are another.

As I have pointed out elsewhere,[1] the intellectual eminence of the Jews is the result of a two-thousand-year process of selective breeding for intelligence. Prior to the modern scientific age, the calling which was most attractive to scholars and to men who wished to lead the life of the mind was the priesthood. In Catholic lands, this priesthood was generally celibate and hence a significant proportion of the most able and creative people in Catholic societies was, in effect, debarred from reproduction.

It is well to remember that there were cogent reasons for the steadfast refusal of the Church to compromise on the issue of sacerdotal celibacy. The fact that the clergy were not permitted to marry lessened the ever-present danger of nepotism, a malpractice which involved the bestowal of Church offices and property to aggrandize the wealth of particular families and build up dynastic power within the ecclesiastical hierarchy. Where it was effectively enforced, clerical celibacy tended to favor the bestowal of Church offices on the basis of merit, on priests who themselves had no heirs to take care of and hence few axes to grind. Clerical celibacy helped to set the Church apart from and above the familial struggles for power and wealth in the Middle Ages and to make the priesthood a calling open to the suitable regardless of family and class origin. Nevertheless, an inescapable genetic consequence of clerical celibacy was that a large part of the most intellectually gifted element in Catholic society failed to reproduce. The genetic heritage of Catholic countries has to this extent suffered.

The most important *biological* consequence of the Reformation was that it enabled the priesthood of Protestant countries to marry and raise families. A variety of studies has shown the prodigious fertility of this Protestant clergy and the astounding extent to which clergymen's sons provided the leadership and the brain power that brought their countries to positions of hegemony. As Possony and I wrote in 1963:

"An analysis of influential men in English history showed that 1,270 were sons of ministers, 510 sons of lawyers, 350 sons of physicians. One in every six of the foreign members of the prestigious Royal Academy was a parson's son."[2]

If the abolition of priestly celibacy gave Protestant countries a genetic advantage over Catholic ones in respect to brain power, similar institutional factors gave Jews a genetic advantage over Christians.

The Jewish priesthood, or rabbinate, was never celibate. While the Jews esteemed virginity in young girls, they regarded marriage and motherhood as the fulfillment of women. Believing that a bachelor was not a complete man, they imposed social pressures on their young scholars and intellectual leaders to marry and procreate.

Moreover, from approximately the beginning of the Christian era, Jewish education was free or nearly so and obligatory for all male children. This educational system was a highly competitive field for the winnowing out of the untalented, whose formal studies would normally terminate after a few years, and for the selection of an intellectual elite. Since the Jews were outside the feudal system and, under most conditions, had no landed estates or titles of nobility, they tended to vest leadership over the Jewish communities in this aristocracy of intellect.

Jewish education was primarily religious, but it concentrated on logical reasoning much as did Christian scholasticism. Thus, it was an excellent vehicle for the discovery and training of brilliant minds, irrespective of whether the religious premises from which these minds reasoned were true or false.

The rewards for this Jewish intellectual aristocracy were prestige, power within the community and the contracting of advantageous marriage alliances. There was keen competition to secure gifted scholars as sons-in-law or to secure their sisters as daughters-in-law. Intermarriage with families of noted rabbinical scholars had the same sort of social attraction as marriage into the nobility among Christians. Hence, the scholars frequently, if not generally, married the daughters of rich merchants and obtained generous marriage settlements. Because of the intense competition for such alliances, the scholars generally married at an early age.

Like other Jews, they were subject to the Biblical command to be fruitful and multiply. Accordingly, we read in such sources as the autobiography of that strange and tragic genius of the Polish ghettos, Moses Maimon, an account of a fierce competition among parents of eligible daughters to acquire him as a son-in-law. In this case, the scholar was married at eleven and fathered his first child at fourteen.

During most of history, population growth has been checked primarily by high death rates rather than by low birth rates. In other words, human societies have habitually bred up to the limit of their reproductive capacity. However, mortality rates have varied among different castes, classes, occupations, nations, races and geographical areas.

Among the Jews, rabbis, scholars and their progeny enjoyed significant survival advantages. On the average, rabbis and scholars probably married at earlier ages and stayed married longer. The causes of this include the keen competition for scholars—whether bachelors, divorced or widowed—among families with eligible girls. While all Jews were urged to marry as a religious duty, this obligation was emphasized in the case of rabbis. Moreover, not all Jews were able to marry. The records of many Jewish medieval communities refer to funds to provide dowries for poor girls of marriageable age. These funds, which were filled by charitable contributions, were never sufficient to take care of all the poor. Hence, lots would be drawn. The lucky girls would be able to get husbands, but the unlucky ones would have to remain spinsters. Since there was no polyandry in Jewish communities, the existence of women, condemned to spinsterhood by poverty, presupposed the existence of men condemned to bachelorhood for the same reason.

Aside from the question of reproduction, the more important biological advantage enjoyed by the intellectuals and scholars lay in the far superior chances of survival for themselves and their children. Married into well-to-do families, the scholars ate better food, were better clothed and enjoyed superior lodgings. They were not obliged to share the huddled squalor of the poor or the unsanitary conditions which made the latter the prey of every epidemic that scourged medieval man.

In periods of persecution of Jewish populations, the alliance of the merchant and scholarly families brought additional advantages. Better informed as a rule, they would be more likely to foresee impending calamities and hence able to depart threatened areas in ample time. Under conditions of flight, they would travel by horse and bring their possessions in wagons, whereas the poor would have to go on foot with only those necessities they were able to carry on their backs. Jewish communities, facing an influx of refugees, would give first preference to scholars. Non-Jewish authorities would be more favorably disposed to would-be immigrants rich enough to pay bribes. A final factor improving the chances of survival for the families of rabbis and scholars is the close and intimate connection, which has persisted during at least a thousand years of Jewish history, between the rabbi and the physician. It was common for the same man to practice both professions and distinguished theologians and philosophers, such as Maimonides, were also famous doctors of medicine.

Thus, the Jews, like the Protestants, encouraged highly

intelligent priesthoods to marry and raise large families. This process has lasted for only about four centuries in the Protestant case. It has lasted, with some exceptions, for about twenty centuries of Jewish history and consequently must have produced greater genetic effects in the area of brain power.

Recognition of Jewish Intelligence

As far as can be discovered, the Jewish reputation for intellectual brilliance arose during the Middle Ages. In Graeco-Roman times, the Jews were not regarded as mentally outstanding by their neighbors. They were attacked by their enemies for being clannish, but not for being clever. When such Roman writers as Juvenal satirized them on economic grounds, they did not envy them their wealth, but ridiculed them because of their poverty.

By the Middle Ages, the attitude toward the Jews had changed drastically. In his great social and intellectual history of the Spanish people, Américo Castro observes that the belief was widespread that the Jews were of superior intelligence. This view was held both by "the ignorant populace" and by learned scholars. In a book written in 1575, we find the Spanish philosopher, Dr. Juan Huarte, attributing Jewish "sharpness of wit" to the manna their ancestors ate when Moses led them from Egypt to the promised land.[3] Several decades earlier, when Francis I of France fell sick, he begged Charles V of Spain to send him the best Jewish physician in his court. Charles sent a Marrano (that is to say a Jew who, to escape persecution, professed Christianity). But when the latter was heedless enough to say that he was a Christian, the French monarch immediately dismissed him. According to Huarte, Francis then "sent to Constantinople for a Jew, and with nothing but asses' milk the Jew cured him."

It is difficult to get quantitative data on the Jewish contribution to the intellectual life of the medieval world. Long lists of reputedly Jewish inventions and of the outstanding Jewish scholars, philosophers and scientists of the period do not provide a reliable basis for comparison with the achievements of other peoples.

A measuring rod of a sort is provided by the monumental *An Introduction to the History of Science*, which the late Professor George Sarton of Harvard published between 1927 and 1947.[4] A work of immense knowledge and wide-ranging scholarship, it surveys the world panorama of science and metaphysical speculation from 600 B.C. to A.D. 1400. The first volume covers science from the time of Homer to that of Omar Khayyám; the second deals with the period from A.D. 1100 to A.D. 1300, while the third and last volume covers the fourteenth century.

As Possony and I pointed out in *The Geography of Intellect*, an analysis of Sarton's magnum opus reveals a prodigious Jewish contribution to the thought of the medieval world in relation to Jewish numbers. During the first four centuries of the Christian era, 6.1% of the thinkers listed by Sarton were Jews. Then, in the Dark Ages (A.D. 400–A.D. 700), the Jewish contribution declined to 2.6%. Islam dominated important parts of the Western world intellectually from about A.D. 700 to A.D. 1100 and, during these four centuries, Jews furnished 9.1% of the world total of scientists and savants. In the twelfth century, the Jewish share rose to 11.4% of the total and, in the thirteenth century, to 15.0%. In the fourteenth century, when the Jews had been expelled from most of Europe,

Jewry still accounted for 10.9% of the listed philosophers and men of science. For the entire period of 1,400 years, Sarton lists 201 Jewish figures of intellectual importance out of a world total of 1,897 and a European total of perhaps 1,250. The overall Jewish participation works out to 10.6% of the world total and about 15% of the European total. This is quite remarkable when one considers the immense disabilities under which the medieval Jews lived and the fact that they constituted only an estimated 4% to 6% of the population of Europe.

Had Sarton projected his great history into succeeding centuries, he probably would have had to report a substantial decline in Jewish participation during the sixteenth and seventeenth centuries. The religious wars of the Reformation led to drastic restrictions on intercourse between Jew and Gentile. The Jews of Europe were compressed into crowded and insalubrious ghettos. At various times and places, they were obligated to wear distinctive clothes or badges, restricted to such unhealthy and unrewarding occupations as mending and selling old clothes, restricted in their freedom to marry or to enter strange towns and confined to a bare minimum of relationships with non-Jews. The parallel intellectual process was for the Jews of Europe to relapse into religious medievalism, to occupy their minds with the abstruse theological problems that Christian Europe had largely discarded. They combined intellectual decay with the humble bearing and sickly, stunted physique that overcrowding and squalor created.

The emancipation of the Jews of Western Europe and their emergence into the brilliant light of the modern world began with the Enlightenment and was completed under Napoleon. The intellectual acuteness that Juan Huarte had found characteristic of Jewry had long since yielded to the stereotype of the ghetto Jew. Hence, the amazingly swift upward advance—intellectually, economically and even socially and politically—of this people which had been caged for centuries in tiny, isolated quarters caused astonishment and, at times, envy and hatred.

A reaction pattern emerged that would repeat itself through time. The Jews were well received in those societies which had a deeply ingrained tradition of individual freedom and a highly competitive economic system. In such countries as Holland, Britain and the United States, it was assumed that men differed widely in abilities and should therefore be differently rewarded. The outstanding success of the Jews or of any other group was considered, not as grounds for persecution, but as an indication of ability.

The reception of Jewry was likely to be unfriendly in societies which retained many of the elements of feudalism and mercantilism. Here, status was more important than contract. There were strong forces which believed that rewards should not be proportionate to work and ability, but should be based on one's position in the societary hierarchy. From Germany, through Poland and the Balkans to the eastern frontiers of Siberia, the classes and social forces dedicated to the preservation of hierarchic rank opposed the Jews.

This status-conscious political anti-Semitism was parallelled by the radical anti-Semitism of the mob. In both cases, the motivation was opposition to the doctrines of individualism and of political and economic liberty. The radical opposition was not, however, a defense of privilege by an aristocracy which was becoming obsolete. It was an effort by the poor to bring about a society in which they would be protected from the gales of competition. From the revolutionary conspiracies of Babeuf to the Paris

Commune, from the utopian Socialists to the Marxists, from the philosophical anarchism of Proudhon to the violent anarchism of Bakunin, antagonism to Jews was a common note. In time, the Socialist, Anarchist and Communist movements of the West abandoned sharp, overt anti-Semitism primarily because of the large number of Jews who had entered their ranks. The fact that these movements were protests by masses against elites meant, however, that they were inherently anti-Jewish, just as they were inherently anti-upper-class, anti-liberal and anti-intellectual.

Jewish political behavior in America has been strongly conditioned by the underlying factors which I have touched upon. First, there is the outstanding intellectual capacity of Jews of European origin and their ambivalent feelings about it, amounting at times to a simultaneous assertion and denial of its reality, and involving frequently a reaction of guilt. Second, there is the omnipresent Jewish fear of anti-Semitism, a fear that was, however, fading prior to the Nazi holocaust. Coupled with this fear is the illusory belief that social democracy or Communism, or both, are propitious for the abatement of antagonism to Jewry rather than for the reverse. Finally, there is the fact that Jews survive and function best in pluralistic societies with a maximum of freedom and a maximum range of opportunity.

CHAPTER 3

From Spain to the New World

THE COMPLEX HISTORIC BACKGROUND of the Jews of Spain
is relevant to an understanding of the character and social
condition of the first great strand of American Jewry, the
Sephardic, or primarily Iberian, element. We are not dealing here with the stunted and humbled product of the
ghetto, but with a society which had traditionally provided
warriors and statesmen, which stood close to the Iberian
aristocracy in its centuries of power and which shared that
aristocracy's fierce pride in its origin and lineage.

The first Jewish settlement in the North American
colonies, though by no means the first in the New World,
occurred in 1654 when the tiny vessel, "St. Charles," arrived in New Amsterdam carrying in her hold 24 Jewish
refugees from Brazil who had made the long passage in
congestion and squalor, suffering from storms and other
vicissitudes.

These refugees encountered the hostility of the Dutch governor, Peter Stuyvesant. A devout Calvinist, Stuyvesant opposed allowing the Jews to remain in the colony. If this were done, he pointed out in a letter to the Dutch West India Company, "we cannot refuse the Lutherans and Papists."[1] The governor, however, was overruled by his superiors, partly because of the powerful Jewish influence in the Company. The refugees were allowed to remain provided they did not become "a charge upon the deaconry and the Company."

Background of Flight

These two dozen Jews, like thousands of others who would follow them to America in the first two centuries of the existence of the colonies, had originally formed part of Iberian Jewry. The Jews of Spain and Portugal had for many centuries been one of the most intellectually advanced elements in Europe. The distinguished historian, Américo Castro, concluded that only the kings and aristocracy of Spain were their superiors in the intellectual, technical and administrative spheres.[2] In addition, they served as the bridge between Graeco-Roman science and culture (which had been appropriated and expanded by the Arabs), and the nascent learning of Christian Europe. Translating between Arabic, Greek, Hebrew and Latin, they also did original work of significance in metaphysics, medicine, astronomy and cartography. Spanish Jewry, as a whole, was concentrated in the professions, the mercantile and fiscal occupations and the highly skilled trades. It was urban in a world that was rural; enlightened and cosmopolitan in a milieu of bigotry, ignorance and parochialism, and well-fed in the midst of hunger. As late as the sixteenth century, the

Archbishop of Burgos could point out that not only did he himself have Jewish ancestors, "but that almost all the aristocracy of that epoch also had them."[3] Another bishop, Don Pablo de Santa Maria, had been Rabbi Salomon Haleví prior to his conversion. Even Torquemada, the head of the Inquisition and the most relentless persecutor in Spanish history of relapsed converts from Judaism, was partly of Jewish blood.

The Jews occupied a bizarre and contradictory position in Spanish society. They were outsiders, adherents of a strange religion, deniers of Christ and, as such, subject to insult and at times scorned and despised. Yet, they were also essentially part of the upper class. They played a disproportionately great role in everything intellectually creative. For centuries, they provided the doctors for Spanish kings and Moorish caliphs. They served as the foreign ministers and financial advisors for the various principalities into which Spain was divided. In some instances, they were the explorers and conquerors who carried Spanish arms across new frontiers. Thus, Alvar Nuñez Cabeza de Vaca, who landed in Florida in 1527–28 and wandered for eight years until he finally reached the Gulf coast of northern Mexico and who later served as governor of the province of Rio de la Plata (Argentina and Paraguay), was a Jewish convert. Other Jewish conquistadores included Luis de Carvajal y de la Cueva, who captured Hawkins' buccaneers, and Gil González, who discovered Nicaragua in 1519 and massacred a large part of the Indian population of Central America.

The Jews were so inextricably intermixed with the nobility and the higher clergy that very few of either order could boast of *limpieza,* or purity of descent from exclusively Christian stock. The primary reason for this extremely close blood connection between Jewry and aristocracy was that each formed part of the creative elite. Consequently, virulent anti-Semitism in Spain was generally an expression of plebeian intolerance and envy.

As the world entered an era of religious struggle, the position of the Jews became increasingly precarious. Protestants and Catholics alike deemed religious pluralism a threat to man's immortal soul, considered that the state had the duty of protecting the faith and regarded torture as an acceptable means of eliciting testimony.

The specific instrument which destroyed Jewish power and influence in Spain was the Inquisition. In their denunciations of the Jews, both those who clung to their religion and those who professed conversion to Christianity, the Dominican masters of the Inquisition had the consistent support of the masses of the Spanish people. The noted historian and philosopher of history, Henry Thomas Buckle, investigated the nature of the Spanish mind in his *History of Civilization*, published more than a century ago. He expressed constant surprise at the fact that the Inquisition, its torture chambers and autos-da-fé, were consistently supported by the Spanish people, just as they were generally disapproved of by the aristocracy.

The appeal for the conversion or exile of the Jewish population of Spain reached a pitch of intensity toward the close of the fifteenth century. A devout queen, Isabella the Catholic, ruled jointly with her less determined husband, Ferdinand of Aragon. The climactic year for this royal pair was 1492, in which three great events occurred that would have profound consequences for Spain, for Jewry and for the Western World.

In that year, the last Moorish foothold on Spanish soil, Granada, fell to a Christian army. The centuries-long struggle of the *Reconquista* was over and Islam and Africa were finally expelled from western Europe. Spain emerged united, Christian and a nascent world power.

Buoyed by the religious enthusiasm of the *Reconquista*, Ferdinand and Isabella ordered all Jews who refused to adhere to Christianity expelled from their realm. Under conditions of immense hardship and deprivation, 100,000 Jews were forced to sell all they possessed in haste and to embark in small vessels in a hazardous search for new homelands. Of these 100,000, more than half died or were enslaved. Another group (some 50,000), embraced, or pretended to embrace, Christianity and remained in Spain to live under the watchful eye of the Holy Office. Many of these so-called Marranos were later burned at the stake for relapsing into Judaism.

This act of expulsion, which was later characterized by Cardinal Richelieu as "the most barbarous in history," deprived Spain, at the moment when she faced the great tasks and responsibilities of world empire, of perhaps the most intellectually gifted, scientifically creative and financially able element in her society. The blows against the Jews were coupled with the expulsion or forced conversion of the Moors.

The persecution of Spanish Jewry seems to have been primarily an expression of the wrath of the masses. This anger was concentrated against the Jews, rather than the aristocracy as a whole, because the former were much more vulnerable. The high status of the nobility was justified by law, tradition and religion and by its historic function of bearing arms. The Jews also enjoyed high status, but this was unsanctioned and existed despite the fact that they practiced a despised religion and were a people without a fatherland. Hence, it was easy for the masses to believe that the power and wealth of the Jews was due to greed or trickery or usury or to a pact with the devil or to a gigantic conspiracy to subvert the world.

This plebeian movement of resentment was supported by those members of the nobility who felt that they were losing power to the Jews and who resented the rapid advance of the latter. It was also supported by those devout members of the upper classes who felt that the Jewish penetration of the nobility and the ecclesiastical hierarchy endangered the Christian religion.

The Discovery of America

In the long run, the event of 1492 that would have the greatest impact on world history and on the role of the Jews within that history was the discovery of the Americas. The origins and background of Christopher Columbus (or Cristobal Colón) are sufficiently obscure to raise the question of his being the descendant of converted Jews. This view was ably defended by the distinguished Spanish historian and philosopher, Salvador de Madariaga, in his biography of Columbus and by other Spanish historians before him.[4]

Certainly, the name Colombo, or Colón, was not uncommon among Jews. Moreover, Columbus' son, Fernando, asserted that his father descended from the royal blood of Jerusalem, an expression used by Marranos who claimed aristocratic Jewish origin.[5] Columbus' cabalistic signature suggests an Hebraic origin as does his Biblical style and the fact that he left a small legacy to a Portuguese Jew who lived in the Lisbon ghetto.[6]

Columbus' navigation, like that of Vasco da Gama and Magellan, relied upon "Jacob's Staff," a much improved quadrant, invented by Rabbi Levi ben Gershom.[7] Columbus was taught by Abraham Zacuto, was was professor of astronomy at Salamanca and Saragossa until the expulsion of the Jews from Spain forced him to proceed to Lisbon where he became court astronomer. On his voyages, Columbus carried Zacuto's books. His cause was defended before Ferdinand and Isabella by the secret Jews Santangel and Sánchez. These two provided the funds which enabled Columbus to buy and provision his ships and they were the first to be informed of the discovery of America.

Mestre Bernal, Columbus' doctor on the 1492 expedition, was the first European to set foot on American soil (except for the earlier expeditions of Vikings and Irishmen), and also the first white man to smoke tobacco. Bernal had been sentenced by the Inquisition as a relapsed Marrano and had narrowly escaped a grisly death. Luís de Torres, Columbus' interpreter, was a Jew who had been baptized shortly before the expedition sailed. At least three other members of the crew of the first voyage, and perhaps several others, were Jews.[8]

After the expulsion from Spain, thousands of Iberian Jews flocked to neighboring Portugal, which pursued a less intolerant policy. However, in 1497, Portugal followed the Spanish example and deported her Jews, but did not offer them the alternative of conversion to Christianity. Again, an elite element was in effect expropriated and compelled to emigrate.

To be sure, these biological and social forces were far from swift-moving. Ironically, Spain's "golden century" of Cervantes and El Greco occurred after the Jews had been expelled and at a time when the persecution of Protestants was at a peak. In the following century, however, a general cultural, political and economic decline set in which was to continue inexorably for three hundred years.

Tens of thousands of the dispersed Jews found new homes in England, France, Germany and the Netherlands. There they made significant contributions to the intellectual and economic life of northern Europe. They became a real factor in the shift of European power from predominantly Catholic to primarily Protestant lands. In the world of thought, displaced Iberian Jewry contributed such figures as Spinoza, Michel de Montaigne and Jean Bodin—the two last having been half Marrano.

Another part of the emigration turned toward the New World. Prior to the "Mayflower" landing in 1620, this meant either the Spanish or the Portuguese possessions. In Spanish lands, the Inquisition followed on the heels of the conquistadores. As early as 1515, it seized a victim in America and sent him back to Spain to suffer death as a Judaizer. Thirteen years later, one of Cortes' officers was burned at the stake for having relapsed into Judaism and, by the middle of the sixteenth century, autos-da-fé were common in the Spanish overseas territories.

In this as in other matters, the Portuguese were less intolerant. The authorities frequently deported relapsed Marranos to Pernambuco in northern Brazil rather than deliver them over to the pyres of the Inquisition. Between 1580 and 1640, however, Portugal and Spain were united and Spanish methods prevailed in the smaller country. As a result of the fusion, Spain's enemies became Portugal's and the Dutch seized Pernambuco, the sugar capital of Brazil, and took energetic steps to create a great Protestant colony in South America. The Jews of northern Brazil enthusiastically supported the Dutch regime and its stadt-

holder, John Maurice of Nassau, perhaps the ablest statesman in the Netherlands. The disgraced Marranos discarded the mask of Christianity and formed an alliance with
the thriving Jewish community of Amsterdam.

In Dutch Brazil, the Jews enjoyed full civil rights and
equality under the law. Consequently, they served the new
state ably as officials and soldiers. The stadtholder planned
to establish a great tropical empire, based on religious tolera-
tion, limited self-government by the colonists and recon-
ciliation between Dutch, Jews and Portuguese. He imported
artists and scientists from Europe to depict and study the
wonders of Brazil and began building imposing monuments
in the capital, which he renamed Mauritzstadt.

However, the Colony was laid waste in a fierce religious
war. The beleaguered Dutch and Jews faced famine and
every other sort of hardship and finally, in 1654, evacuated
Brazil.

The Jews left by sea. Some found refuge in the British
sugar colonies of Jamaica and Barbados, where they became
rich merchants and slave-owning planters. Naturalized as
British subjects in 1740, the Jews of the sugar islands were
the most important Jewish community in British America
at the time of the outbreak of the American Revolutionary
War.

Others went to Surinam, a Dutch colony in the Guiana
lowlands traversed by the Equator. Here again, they became
sugar planters and merchants, living under conditions of
political and religious tolerance. When vast slave uprisings
shook the colony to its foundations between approximately
1775 and 1790, the Jewish plantations were often the most
vulnerable since they were furthest in the interior and
closest to the ill-defined frontier between the estates and
the jungle. Jewish planters had gone deep into the interior

to escape possible future persecution by the non-Jewish majority, but, in so doing, they had located in an area peculiarly exposed to the ravages of slave revolt, since the Negro insurrectionaries could always retreat into the malaria-infested jungle where white soldiers could follow only with the greatest difficulty and hardship. Today, only a faint trace remains of the Jewish plantations that thrived in the interior four centuries ago. When these estates went up in flames, the illiterate slave insurrectionaries engaged in looting and drunkenness, then retreated into the bush and reverted to their original condition as tribal Africans. They took with them a composite language, which is a pidgin version of the words they had picked up from their Dutch, English, Jewish, Portuguese, Spanish and French masters. When I was in this bush Negro country about fifteen years ago, I found that, when they wanted to indicate that a food was ritually forbidden, they would use the Hebrew word—*trefa*. As far as I could determine, all the other traces of Jewish plantation agriculture had vanished.

The 24 Jews who arrived in New Amsterdam in the hold of the "St. Charles" in 1654 were part of these vast historic dispersions. We can assume that their ancestors had been expelled from Spain in 1492 or from Portugal in 1497. Else they had pretended conversion to Christianity, had been found out and had then been deported to northern Brazil, along with prostitutes and other undesirables, perhaps by some humane Portuguese judge who secretly disapproved of burning heretics. Once in Brazil, they had enthusiastically sided with the Dutch and, in the years of Dutch defeat, had been evacuated so as not to fall into the hands of the Inquisition.

CHAPTER 4

American Beginnings

THERE WAS NEVER A TIME when the Jewish settlers in America suffered from discrimination and disabilities comparable to those prevalent on the European Continent. As Cecil Roth cogently observed, the American development was a gradual and continuous broadening of freedom for Jews and for other minorities.[1]

In this respect, the American colonies followed the practices and institutions of the mother country. Having been expelled from England in A.D. 1290, the Jews began drifting back in the seventeenth century on a more or less surreptitious basis. No formal agreement or treaty defined their rights and duties. Oliver Cromwell merely "connived" at their presence and succeeding British rulers followed his example.

America never had a ghetto. Jews were free to live where they pleased, to dress as they liked, to travel about at will, to worship as they saw fit and to employ non-Jews when they so desired. They were not subjected to the special taxes and degrading oaths prevalent on the Continent.

In the American colonies, the first right the Jews secured was the right to stay there. This was obtained from the Dutch Company governing New Amsterdam in 1655. A generation later, the Jews established their right to serve in the Trainbands, as the voluntary militia which kept the peace in New Amsterdam were called. Before the close of the seventeenth century, the Jews in this Dutch outpost had gained the privilege of having their own burial ground.

To be sure, these rights were offset by the discriminatory rule of 1656 which barred them from opening retail shops or practicing their crafts in New Amsterdam, a restriction which made the distinguished historian of American Jewry, Dr. Jacob Marcus, conclude that they were "second-class burghers . . . citizens with circumscribed economic liberties. . . . ."[2] As long as this regulation remained in effect, New Amsterdam Jews concentrated on wholesale trade and, when the Royal Exchange was reorganized toward the close of the seventeenth century, one-twelfth of its seats were set aside for Jewish brokers.

The achievement of the right to vote was a slower and more difficult process than that of gaining equal economic rights. The mother country denied Catholics the franchise and the view that the electorate should belong to the established religion was widely held. Under the enlightened Charter written for the Proprietors of Carolina by their Secretary, the philosopher and political theorist, John Locke, Jews were permitted to vote in that colony. No serious effort was made to put Locke's Charter into effect,[3] but Jews went to the polls in Carolina as early as 1702. They were, however, disfranchised by the South Carolina legislature in 1759 and this prohibition was subsequently re-affirmed.

No other colony permitted non-Christians to vote and, in some, the franchise was confined to Protestants. New York barred Jews from the ballot box in 1737 on the grounds that they were not entitled to vote in England, but by 1761 they were in fact voting in New York elections.

England permitted the naturalization of foreign-born Jews in the middle of the eighteenth century, native-born ones being automatically British subjects. On this point, the colonies were less liberal. In 1761, Aaron Lopez, one of the great merchants of the day who traded in spermaceti from Newport, applied for Rhode Island citizenship. He was refused on the grounds that the laws of the colony restricted this privilege to Christians.

Jews and Puritans

Meanwhile, other Jewish settlements had followed in the wake of the landing of the "St. Charles" at New Amsterdam. Massachusetts welcomed Jewish settlers in the latter part of the seventeenth century. Indeed, there were intellectual affinities between the Puritans and Jewry.

For one thing, the Massachusetts colonists prided themselves on their scholarship in Hebrew. Of the "Mayflower" settlers, Elder William Brewster and Governor Bradford were accomplished Hebrew linguists. John Eliot, "the apostle to the Indians," Henry Dunster, first president of Harvard, John Cotton and both Cotton Mather and Increase Mather were erudite in that language. "We see even our English women," Cotton Mather wrote, ". . . grown as expert at it [Hebrew] as the ladies whom the Church Father Jerome praises in his works."[4]

Another point of similarity was that the Puritans named their children in accordance with the Old Testament and hence their given names were practically the same as those prevalent among the Jews. One reason for this was a desire to set themselves apart from the Catholics who traditionally gave their children specifically Christian names. Virtually the only New Testament name used by strict Puritans was Nathaniel. The cause of this preference was that Nathaniel was almost the only early follower of Jesus (John 1:45–49) upon whom the Church had not bestowed sainthood, the omission being explained by the conviction of the Church Fathers that Nathaniel and Bartholomew were one and the same person.

Finally, the Puritans avoided the term "church" and instead had "meeting houses," a designation akin to the Hebrew *Beit hakneset*. Like the synagogues, the meeting houses were both houses of worship and centers of community life and were often situated on hilltops. The Puritan elder, like the rabbi, laid no claim to supernatural authority, but qualified for his vocation through piety, wisdom and Biblical learning. Like the rabbi, he was consulted on all political and juridical issues.

Venetian Jews settled in Connecticut. The generally tolerant settlement of Rhode Island, under the leadership of Roger Williams, invited Jews to come there and the Jewish community of Newport soon became one of the wealthiest and most important in the American colonies. Delaware and Pennsylvania were early recipients of Jewish immigration.

When James Oglethorpe started the colonization of Georgia, he offered full liberty of conscience to everyone except Catholics. Consequently, enough Jews settled in the colony so that they soon constituted one-sixth of the population of Savannah. John Wesley, the founder of Methodism, learned Spanish during the two years he was in Georgia "in order to converse with my Jewish parishioners, some of whom seem nearer the mind of Christ than many of those who call him Lord."[5]

On the Verge of the Revolution

At the time of the American Revolution, there were two or three thousand Jews in the colonies, comprising somewhat more than one-tenth of one per cent of the population. They were townspeople rather than farmers, heavily concentrated in mercantile operations, particularly those involving shipping and international trade, areas in which their linguistic ability, international connections, sophistication and intelligence gave them a competitive advantage. Others were petty tradesmen and artisans.

Major factors in the fur trade were the Gratz family of Philadelphia and Hayman Levy (who employed John Jacob Astor and was the most important fur dealer in the colonies). Aaron Levy was a major economic power in the spermaceti candle trade; Moses Lindo of Charleston pioneered in indigo exports; Jacob Franks of New York cut a big figure in the shipping industry.

When the American Revolutionary War broke out, the Jewish community was vitally concerned. A fundamental cause of the struggle was British perseverance in a mercantilist policy designed to place colonial industry, trade and shipping in a strait jacket and to perpetuate England's privileged position. Since the Jews were deeply involved in international trade, they supported the cause of American independence in their large majority and about fifty Jews served as officers in the Continental Army.

These colonial Jews found American society so congenial that they rapidly abandoned clothing and habits that set them apart from Christian society. Most of them shaved regularly, ate pork and took their religion lightly. According to Sachar, almost every Jew who came to Connecticut prior to the Revolution married a non-Jew and raised his children as Christians. Most descendants of colonial Jewry were absorbed into the Gentile world.[6]

Birth of the Republic

The enthusiastic support which the Jews had given to the revolutionary cause was reciprocated by its leaders. In his reply to the expression of support from the Hebrew congregations of Philadelphia, New York, Charleston and Richmond, George Washington wrote: "The affection of such a people is a treasure beyond the reach of calculation. . . ."[7] John Adams wrote Mordecai M. Noah, a somewhat mystic political leader of American Jewry: "I wish your nation may be admitted to all the privileges of citizens in every country of the world. This country has done much. I wish it may do more; and annul every narrow idea in religion, government and commerce."[8] As for Thomas Jefferson, he declared himself "happy in the restoration of the Jews, particularly, to their social rights, and hopes they will be seen taking their seats on the benches of science as preparatory to their doing the same at the board of government."[9]

American independence accelerated the processes which were enlarging the rights and opportunities of the Jewish community. The Northwest Ordinance of 1787 established full religious and political freedom. The Constitution of the United States declared that "no religious Test shall ever be required as a Qualification to any Office or public Trust under the United States."[10] The First Amendment, moreover, denied Congress the right to pass any law "respecting an establishment of religion, or prohibiting the free exercise thereof. . . ."

Neither of the two last provisions guaranteed Jews the right to vote in elections or to be elected to state office. This depended on the laws of the various states. Religious tests were nullified in Virginia in 1786 at the insistence of Jefferson and Madison. Georgia, Virginia and South Carolina followed suit and, in the North, Pennsylvania and New York eliminated religious discrimination. The other states were slower to remove these barriers.

In North Carolina in 1809, the right of a Jew, Jacob Henry, to take the seat in the state House of Commons to which he had been elected was challenged. State law required that officials be Protestants and accept the divine authority of the New, as well as the Old, Testament. Addressing the House in his own defense, Henry made such an eloquent appeal that he was seated, but the same privilege was not extended to other North Carolina Jews until the Reconstruction era.

During these early years, the Jews seem to have been more interested in consular posts and appointments to West Point and Annapolis than in elective politics. The first major consular appointment of a Jew posted Mordecai Manual Noah to Tunis, a hotbed of piracy with which the United States had unfriendly relations. Either because of Moslem protest or for very different reasons, Noah was curtly dismissed by then Secretary of State James Monroe on the grounds that "the Religion which you profess . . . would produce a very unfavourable effect" upon the Tunisians.[11] This seems to foreshadow the twentieth century

State Department practice of not sending Jewish diplomats to posts in Arab League countries in the hope of appeasing the latter.

To the extent that the political activity of American Jews followed any distinctive pattern in these early decades of the Republic, they were Jeffersonians rather than Hamiltonians, Republican-Democrats rather than Federalists. One reason for this preference was the Jeffersonian dedication to low tariffs, international trade and states' rights, planks which appealed to Jewish export and shipping interests. Moreover, the Jewish community was changing from an essentially Iberian to a largely German element. The Jewish immigrants from Germany were often liberal-to-radical political refugees who found the political and social doctrines of the Republican-Democrats attractive.

Generally speaking, Northern Jews, if they had any political affiliation at all, were Democratic during the four decades before Abraham Lincoln's election. In New York City, the rapidly growing and influential Jewish population was powerfully represented in Tammany Hall, which at that time led the more radical faction in the Democratic Party.

To be sure, Mordecai M. Noah, the ousted American consul in Tunis, led the journalistic fight to destroy the power of the so-called Albany Regency, a tight-knit clique of radical politicians under President Martin Van Buren who controlled New York State politics. Despite the protests of Noah, "a substantial majority" of the 15,000 or so American Jews supported the Van Buren Administration— that of probably the most radical President in American history prior to the inauguration of Franklin D. Roosevelt.[12]

In return for this support, or perhaps as a matter of principle, Van Buren supported Jewish protests against the Damascus ritual murder affair of 1840. The Damascus authorities had accused seven Jews of having kidnapped and murdered two Christians so they could secretly drink their blood during Passover services. This charge was supported by forged passages from the Talmud. The Ottoman authorities put the rabbis of Damascus, together with 64 children, in prison, where "after severe Tortures and threats several of them confessed. . . ."[13] Several of the prisoners died under torture, others turned Muslim and 72 were sentenced to be hanged.

John Forsyth, Van Buren's Secretary of State, took a strong stand. He instructed David Porter, the American minister to the Ottoman Empire, "to do everything in your power with the Government of his Imperial Highness, the Sultan to whom you are accredited, consistent with discretion and your diplomatic character, to prevent or mitigate these horrors . . . and, in an especial manner to direct your philanthropic efforts against the employment of torture in order to compel the confession of imputed guilt."[14]

Mass meetings of the Jewish communities of New York, Philadelphia, Richmond, Charleston and other cities sent urgent petitions to the President. At Charleston, a general meeting of all citizens was held, with the support of Mayor Henry L. Pinckney and the Roman Catholic Bishop of the city, to protest the persecution of the Jews in the Ottoman Empire.

American Jews in the Jacksonian Era

In an 1826 memorandum, the Charleston journalist, Isaac Harby, estimated that the largest Jewish community in the United States was that of South Carolina with 1,200 members. He thought New York was in second place with 950 Jews, followed by 400 apiece in Virginia and Georgia, perhaps 350 in New England and the same number in Pennsylvania, 100 in Louisiana and not more than 40 in Florida.

If these figures are accurate, over 55% of American Jewry lived in the South. However, the picture was changing. Harby thought there had been no growth in the Charleston Jewish community for twenty years, while that of New York was rapidly expanding.

"Men who reflect go anywhere in pursuit of happiness," Harby wrote concerning the motivations of the Jewish immigrants. "The immediate ancestors of the most respectable Jews in these United States came, some for the purposes of commerce, others for the more noble love of liberty and the majority for both. . . . As to the descent of the Jews of the United States, they are principally German and English; though South Carolina has a portion of French and Portuguese. My ancestors came originally from Barbary, where my father's father enjoyed a post of honor in the palace of the emperor of Morocco, that of Royal Lapidary."[15]

The Jews were expanding westward and southward. Some who settled in the West farmed, but more were attracted by mercantile opportunities and, in particular, by the fur trade. Letters from Jewish fur dealers in St. Louis and other frontier towns describe their difficulties under heavy burdens of debt and their conflicts with the roistering and often drunk French *voyageurs*. In the South, a similar occupational pattern emerges. There are Jewish planters, but many more Jews are attracted to merchandising, shipping and foreign trade. A few, such as Benjamin Monsanto of Natchez (whose family would later play a major role in the development of the American chemical industry), were in the domestic slave trade.

Arrival of the German Jews

A rapid expansion of population in Germany during the decades of peace following the Napoleonic wars resulted in mass emigration to America. Schedules of vessels departing for the United States were posted even in the most humble German towns and villages. The exodus was so immense that, in the course of barely two weeks, four thousand people left the small state of Baden alone.

German Jews were part of this trek. They were subject to the same forces of overpopulation and economic need as their Christian neighbors. They had the additional goad of rampant discrimination, inability to get licenses as craftsmen and an atmosphere poisoned by anti-Semitism.

The *Leipziger Zeitung* of September 3, 1839 commented as follows on the reasons for the heavy Jewish emigration from Bavaria:

"Conscription remains a thorn in the side of the Israelites. Who can blame a father if he sells out and leaves with his family? The parents are then joined by hundreds of engaged couples, candidates for degrees and physicians, commercial clerks and every sort of people eager for work. Naturally, there is never any talk about purchases in the North American woods, of agriculture, landed estates, etc. One becomes a merchant; i.e., carries on trade in the ever-roaming wagons and steamboats, until one gets a house and established store, or one carries on one, two, three trades, according to what he has derived from others, in addition to what he has, in passing, learned here. A German is gladly accepted as a workingman in America; the German Jew is preferred to any other. Thus, hopelessness at home, a secure future overseas, no pressure or persecution of one or another sort lead the Bavarian Israelite to take up the wanderer's staff."[16]

The emigration was immensely accelerated by the crushing defeat of the liberal 1848 revolutions in Europe and the triumph of reaction. Up to 100,000 German Jews came to the United States in the twelve years between that event and the Civil War.

Jews had taken a prominent part in the leadership of the 1848 uprisings and a large majority of European Jewry had sympathized with them. Thus, Daniele Manin, a Catholic of Jewish ancestry, was the outstanding leader of the Venetian rising of 1848 and two Jews were members of the Cabinet of the short-lived Weimar Republic of that time. The Prussian National Assembly which proclaimed the new liberal constitution of 1848 had several Jews as members and elected one of them, Raphael Kosch, as its vice president. The more important Frankfurt parliament had at one time a Jewish president and a Jewish vice president. In Breslau, Berlin, Mainz, Worms, Cracow and Vienna, Jews were prominent in the 1848 struggle as military leaders, politicians and newspaper editors. In the last category was Karl Marx, the Jew-hating son of an apostate Jew. The Hungarian National Army under Louis Kossuth had no fewer than 20,000 enlisted Jewish soldiers in its ranks.[17]

When the revolution was stifled throughout Europe, its Jewish and non-Jewish adherents turned increasingly toward the United States. Hence, the massive Jewish emigration of the 1840's and 1850's was politically selective.

Moreover, it was overwhelmingly German. Throughout the Northern states, Jews habitually spoke German, lived in or near German communities, often peddled their wares to Germans and either took part in German social and political organizations or created Jewish facsimiles of them. Of these Jewish fraternal organizations, the most important was the Independent Order of B'nai B'rith, founded in

1843. It combined mutual-aid functions with the organizational structure of Masonry and in fact its earliest leaders were Masons of high degree.[18]

Slavery, Abolitionism, Anti-Semitism

As the United States moved toward mid-century, the conflict over slavery began to overshadow all other political issues. The large majority of Jews opposed slavery as immoral and sympathized with the nascent Republican Party. There were, however, dissenting voices. One of them was Rabbi Isaac M. Wise, the eloquent, gifted and organizationally brilliant leader of Reformed Judaism in America. Wise viewed the abolitionist movement with suspicion and strongly opposed any radical solution of the slavery issue. Similarly, Emanuel Hart, perhaps the most influential of Northeastern Jewish politicians, refused to abandon the Democratic Party despite its pro-slavery stand.

In part because it was a coalition of minorities, the Democratic Party had been the traditional political home for American Jews. Its geographical minority was the South; its religious minorities the Catholics and Jews; its ethnic minorities the more recent and less respectable waves of immigrants, of whom the most important were the Irish. While a few American Jews supported the Know-Nothing movement with its hysterical anti-Catholicism, the vast majority viewed the nativists as potential enemies. In fact, their hatred of Catholics and of the newer immigration was already spilling over into anti-Semitism and such prominent leaders of the movement as William G. Brownlow and Henry Wilson were "notorious Jew haters."[19]

The Know-Nothing element in its majority later swung over to the Republican camp and some of its leaders became prominent abolitionists. Among these was the anti-Semitic Henry Wilson, who wrote an enormous, impassioned and prejudiced history of slavery,[20] became Vice President of the United States under Grant and was implicated in the corrupt Crédit Mobilier scandals. An anti-Semite who was even more prominent in the abolitionist movement was Thaddeus Stevens. During a long life, Stevens discharged his venom at one target after another, changing his beliefs and convictions with bewildering speed. At one time, his political career had been based on hatred of the Masons whom he characterized as "a secret, oath-bound, murderous institution that endangers the continuance of Republican government." At other times, he had raged against the banks and the moneyed aristocracy. In his later years, when his power to wound his enemies was greatest, he concentrated the full force of his cold, implacable will on the destruction of the institutions and way of life of the white South.[21]

Utopian Socialism and Anti-Semitism

The abolitionist movement eventually absorbed most of the utopian Socialists who had flourished in America during the first half of the nineteenth century. These movements derived primarily from three European thinkers—Saint-Simon, Fourier and Robert Owen—two of whom were anti-Semitic.

A member of the French nobility who had survived the Reign of Terror, Saint-Simon claimed that he had been visited by the ghost of Charlemagne. He planned a world without war in which property would be held in common and a managerial class would direct labor. This authoritarian society was the very antithesis of the rapidly expanding world capitalist economy and was conceived as an aristocratic reaction against it. Since the Jews seemed to represent the free-market economy which he detested, Saint-Simon became an anti-Semite. He assailed Jews as imbued with "a spirit of greed and cupidity" and as "the very incarnation of the capitalist system of exploitation. . . ."[22]

The second of the great utopian Socialists, Charles Fourier (1772-1837), was a bourgeois who lost his fortune during the French Revolution, failed as a soldier and spent the remainder of his life as a small-time broker. His Socialist scheme consisted of reorganizing human activity in *phalanges* or colonies of 1,620 members. These were to be based on agriculture, with rotation of tasks between members, division of income according to a rigid formula and a close association between rich and poor that would break down the arrogance of the former and the humility of the latter.

Considering the simplicity, indeed the naiveté, of his formula for saving society, it is strange that Fourier should have at any time exerted a major intellectual influence on the world. Yet between 1840 and 1850, in the decade following Fourier's death, his writings had a great vogue and no fewer than 41 *phalanges* were attempted. Fourier's doctrines were introduced into the United States by Albert Brisbane and the most famous of all the *phalanges*, Brook Farm, attracted such superior minds as Ralph Waldo Emerson, Margaret Fuller, William Henry Channing, Theodore Parker and Charles A. Dana.

Like Saint-Simon, and for the same reasons, Fourier was an anti-Semite. "To grant the Jews citizenship," he asserted, was "the most shameful of all the recent vices of contemporary society." The Jews were "parasites, merchants, usurers," who "pillaged the country like pirates and were

guilty of mercantile depravities."[23] Fourier also expressed
the view—one contradicted by the entire past millenium of
Western thought—that the Jews "have achieved nothing in
art and science" and "are distinguished only by a record of
crime and brutality. . . ."[24]

Because of Fourier's eminent reputation, this invective
had considerable impact on American intellectuals of the
day. It was disseminated widely through the strange alliance
of Charles A. Dana with Karl Marx. A frontier boy of
Puritan background, Dana had had to leave Harvard because of failing eyesight and had then joined Brook Farm
to become one of its leaders. "A militant idealist, widely
read in Socialist literature and warmly espousing associa-
tionism as a cure for the evils of competition,"[25] he left
Brook Farm after the *phalange* was burned down, joined
Horace Greeley on the *New York Tribune* and for fifteen
years was one of its directing intelligences.

In 1848, he went to Europe as foreign editor to observe
its epidemic of revolutions. At the age of 39, Dana had run
through Jacksonian radicalism and utopian Socialism and
was eagerly awaiting a new ideology and a new destructive
hero. He met Karl Marx in Cologne in 1848 or 1849 and
shared the opinion of his colleague, Albert Brisbane, that
Marx was "the leader of the people's movement," whose
"star was just in the ascendant" and who possessed, behind
a reserved exterior, "the passionate fire of a daring spirit."

Dana promptly employed Marx as roving correspondent
on foreign affairs for the *Tribune*. This radical newspaper,
which had been established by followers of Fourier, had a
circulation of 200,000, which was probably greater than
that of any other paper in the world at that time. Opposing
autocracy and slavery and favoring free trade, it was critical
of practically every government in Europe.[26]

For over ten years, Marx was able to submit an article a

week to Dana, for which he was paid a pound. When the Civil War broke out, the *Tribune* had to retrench and Greeley urged the dismissal of its cantankerous, ultra-revolutionary and anti-Semitic correspondent. Dana was able to stave off the inevitable for a time, but in 1862 Marx was finally sacked.

Marx probably first acquired his virulent anti-Semitism from his father, who had been a disciple of Voltaire, and from his father-in-law, Ludwig von Westphalen, an ardent follower of Saint-Simon. To trace the pedigree of an obsession is, of course, not the same thing as to explain its underlying rationale. Since Marx was distinctively Jewish in appearance and so dark that he was nicknamed "the Moor," his anti-Semitism was a source of embarrassment to his friends. It must have seemed to them a revelation of his own self-hatred.

Karl Marx and American Anti-Semitism

From the beginning of his connection with the *Tribune*, Marx had used it as a vehicle for his profound hatred of Jews. Describing the political situation in eastern Europe, he observed: ". . . the money lender, the publican, the hawker—a very important man in these thinly populated countries—is very generally a Jew, whose native tongue is a horribly corrupted German."

In 1856, he wrote a long article, inveighing against a loan to the Russian government, launched under the auspices of the Jewish house of Stieglitz. This piece could have been accepted with few editorial changes by the Goebbels Propaganda Ministry had Marx been alive at the time and able to submit it under an Aryan pseudonym.

After harping on his theme that the ruling dynasties of

Europe were sustained by Jewish banking houses, Marx concluded: "Thus we find every tyrant backed by a Jew, as is every Pope by a Jesuit. In truth, the cravings of oppressors would be hopeless, and the practicability of war out of the question, if there were not an army of Jesuits to smother thought and a handful of Jews to ransack pockets."[27]

The article continued with an excoriation of Amsterdam for "harboring many of the worst descendants of the Jews whom Ferdinand and Isabella drove out of Spain. . . ." Marx poured vituperation on the small Jewish traders whom he described as comparable to "the smartest highwayman in the Abruzzi. . . ."

As Geltman points out, this article is not a typical Socialist tirade against capitalism, in which Jews happen to be the targets. Rather it bears the hallmarks of the Nazi theory of history as a sinister Jewish conspiracy. For in discussing the non-Jewish banking house of Hope, which was also involved in the Russian loan, Marx went out of his way, without any evidence, to exonerate it of evil-doing. "The Hopes lend only the prestige of their name," he wrote, "the real work is done by Jews and can only be done by them, as they monopolize the machinery of the loan-mongering mysteries. . . ."[28]

Possibly as a result of Marx's insidious propaganda against his own people even such minds as Emerson's seriously believed that the world was dominated by the Jews, and a writer of the stature of James Russell Lowell could rhetorically ask, perhaps unconsciously plagiarizing one of Marx's diatribes, "Where would a Jew be among a society of primitive men without pockets. . . ?"

The abolitionists fell heir to this unsavory crew of Socialists, utopians, crackpots and anti-Semites. Horace Greeley became increasingly hostile to Jewry as he became more deeply committed to abolitionism, perhaps because of his resentment at the skill with which Secretary of State Judah P. Benjamin was directing the foreign policy of the Confederacy, perhaps for other reasons. Occasionally, one of Marx's disciples, such as the man he termed "our philosopher," Joseph Dietzgen, would voyage to America. Among Dietzgen's philosophic contributions was the equation of Polish Jews with evil spirits. Fourierists, Socialists and the American representatives of the anti-Semitic hate movements which Proudhon, Marx and Bakunin had managed to create plunged into the Civil War and enthusiastically supported the radical wing of abolitionism. Their hope, like that of Marx, was that the end of chattel slavery would sound the funeral dirge for "wage slavery." As America entered her great fratricidal conflict, the seeds had been planted for a significant anti-Semitic movement, not among the majority of Americans of either North or South, but in the minds of a few intellectual radicals and a rabble driven by resentment.

CHAPTER 5

The Civil War

AT THE TIME OF THE CIVIL WAR, there were about 150,000 Jews in the United States among a white population of 27 million. Jews thus constituted slightly more than half of one per cent of the total.

The most influential religious leaders of American Jewry saw the struggle in simple black-and-white terms. Rabbi David Einhorn of Baltimore, for instance, argued that, since Jehovah had liberated the Israelites from Egyptian slavery, it was the duty of their descendants to fight for the emancipation of the black man. This and similar rabbinical efforts helped swell Jewish enrollment in the Union Armies to anywhere from 6,000 to 15,000. Since a total of two and one-half million Americans served with the North, the Jewish contribution was about what could have been expected, given the fact that many Jews were recent immigrants and hence largely indifferent to internal American political issues.

The Jewish contribution to the military effort of the Confederacy may have been proportionately much greater. Confederate War Secretary John Seddon estimated that there were from 10,000 to 12,000 Jews in the Southern ranks.[1] The Confederate Army reached its maximum strength in early 1863, when 700,000 men, or one-tenth the total white population of the South, were under arms.

The intense loyalty of Southern Jews to the Confederacy was to be expected in view of the fact that the South was the first region in the United States to tear down the barriers blocking the political and social advance of Jews. Thus, the first Jew to serve as a state governor was David Emanuel, who, having distinguished himself for valor in the siege of Savannah in the Revolutionary War, was elected Governor of Georgia in 1801. By contrast, the last state to retain discriminatory laws against Jews holding public office was New Hampshire, which did not remove them until 1876.[2]

The first Jew to be elected to the United States Senate was also a Southerner. David Levy Yulee (1810-1886) was elected Florida's first United States Senator in 1845. In Congress, he was vociferous in his opposition to federal restrictions on the introduction of slavery into the territories to be acquired from Mexico.

The second Jew to serve in the Senate was a much more significant figure. Judah Philip Benjamin descended from Spanish Jews who had been expelled from the peninsula and had migrated first to Holland and then to England. Although Benjamin's father was a poor man, who had failed as a London fishmonger in Cheapside before emigrating to the American South, Judah managed to attend

Yale, where he was immensely popular and admired for his brilliance. However, he left Yale under a cloud without graduating,[3] arrived in New Orleans with four dollars in his pocket, married into a distinguished Creole family, became an immensely successful lawyer and planter, and pioneered in the mechanization of sugar cultivation.[4]

The man who was later to be known under the sobriquet of "the brains of the Confederacy," was elected to the Senate for the first time in 1852 and served there continuously until the outbreak of the Civil War and the secession of Louisiana. His reputation for learning and judgment was such that Whig President Zachary Taylor nominated him for Attorney General of the United States and Taylor's successor, Millard Fillmore, offered to submit his name as an Associate Justice of the Supreme Court. Preferring a more active political life where he could better defend the interests of the South as he conceived them, Benjamin declined the honor.

In the Senate, Benjamin was a spokesman for the uncompromising pro-slavery position. Rather than apologize for "the peculiar institution," as did so many of his Southern colleagues, he insisted that it derived from English Common Law and was a necessity in governing "an inferior and servile race."[5]

Senator Ben Wade of Ohio called him "an Israelite with Egyptian principles." Benjamin, however, refused to consider all peoples and races equal. This was quite evident from a retort he was alleged to have made on being characterized as "that Jew from Louisiana" by a fellow Senator.

"It is true that I am a Jew and, when my ancestors were receiving their Ten Commandments from the immediate hand of Deity, amidst the thunderings and lightnings of Mount Sinai, the ancestors of the distinguished gentleman who is opposed to me were herding swine in the forests of Scandinavia."⁶

During the first few months of the Confederacy, William H. Russell, the perceptive correspondent of the London *Times*, journeyed to Richmond and interviewed the members of the Confederate Cabinet. Although Benjamin had been pigeonholed in the comparatively unimportant post of Attorney General, Russell found him the most "brilliant of the Southern orators." After commenting on his "most decidedly Jewish features, with the brightest, large black eyes, one of which is somewhat diverse from the other, and a brisk, lively, agreeable manner, combined with much vivacity of speech and quickness of utterance," the *Times* representative added that Benjamin was "one of the first lawyers or advocates in the United States. . . ." He claimed that Benjamin earned between £8,000 and £10,000 a year, a prodigious sum in those days, but lost most of it periodically at the card tables.⁷

As Hendrick points out, British interest in the Senator from Louisiana was whetted by the fact that another Sephardic Jew, also named Benjamin, was rising toward political power in London. Benjamin Disrali and Judah P. Benjamin provide parallels as well as contrasts. Both were intellectual spokesmen and political leaders of conservatism and imperialism. Both were the descendants of Spanish Jews who had found refuge in England. Where Disraeli was flamboyant, theatrical in manner, a talented novelist and a lover of beautiful women, Benjamin was almost an ascetic and was reserved to a pathological degree.⁸

From his insignificant post in the Confederate Cabinet, Benjamin was advanced to the crucial position of Secretary of War. He was sacrificed for having failed to supply Roanoke with ammunition (the real reason for the failure being that none was then available), thus causing its fall to Union forces. He resigned in disgrace but in the summer of 1861 President Davis named him Secretary of State. Diplomacy was the area in which his abilities could best be called into play. For the next four years, Benjamin discharged the almost hopeless task of obtaining effective foreign support for the South with consummate ability.

Although he had once challenged Jefferson Davis to a duel (one which was never fought because Davis magnanimously apologized), Benjamin became the closest adviser of the Confederate President during their four years in Richmond. After Appomattox, Benjamin made his escape to England where he rebuilt his practice and became one of the most respected figures in English legal circles.

Having risen to the highest office ever held by a Jew in America, Benjamin was subjected to the insinuating criticism of J. B. Jones in his *A Rebel War Clerk's Diary* (1866) and was called "Judas Iscariot Benjamin" by Henry Stuart Foote, who had opposed secession. On the other hand, he was staunchly supported by Jefferson Davis and by those Southerners who dreamed of a southward expansion to the Isthmus of Tehuantepec. The often caustic Mrs. Chestnut regarded him as "a Delphic oracle of the innermost shrine" and the other belles and society matrons of Richmond, including Varina Howell Davis, were his friends and admirers.

Though he was the most eminent Jew serving the Confederate cause, Benjamin was by no means the only one. Edwin Moise served as Speaker of the Louisiana House during the first period of the Civil War. Raphael J. Moses was influential in leading Georgia out of the Union and later, with his three sons, served in the Confederate Army. Henry Hyans, who had been Lieutenant Governor of Louisiana during the four years immediately prior to the birth of the Confederacy, served the latter loyally.[9] A South Carolina doctor named Simon Baruch fought at Gettysburg (as did many other Jews), and later imbued the mind of his son, Bernard Baruch, with emotional dedication to the lost cause of the Confederacy.[10]

Other Jewish figures in the brief history of the Confederacy included Edwin de Leon, whom Benjamin sent to Paris to handle public relations and propaganda for the South. De Leon stupidly put his unflattering opinions of the French on paper. When they were stolen and published, Benjamin recalled him in disgrace.

Perhaps the ablest diplomat of the South was John Slidell, a ruthless and courtly machine politician who had been born in New York City of humble and obscure origins. The son of a candle maker, Slidell was once informed by a lady that he had been "dipped, not moulded into society." Slidell ably represented the Confederacy as its minister to France. Hendrick accepts the general opinion of the day that Slidell was partly Jewish, but this seems based on no stronger evidence than his close friendship for Benjamin and the fact that his niece married August Belmont, a Jewish banker who helped finance the North, while his daughter became the wife of Baron Emile Erlanger, the Jewish banker who financed Confederate operations and built ships for the South.

The prominent role of Jews in the Confederacy is generally either ignored or condensed into shamefaced footnotes by those historians of American Jewry whose opinions conform to the liberal-leftist stereotype. While these writers are happy to expatiate on the deeds of comparatively insignificant Jewish Socialists and needle trades organizers, the most pertinent thing they have to say about Judah P.

Benjamin is that he did not believe in the tenets of Judaism. By this criterion, Benedict Spinoza, Karl Marx, Sigmund Freud and Albert Einstein would also have to be denied inclusion in the ranks of Jewry.

The loyalty of Southern Jews to the thwarted struggle of the Confederacy for nationhood was by no means necessarily in contradiction to the traditional Jewish emphasis on individual freedom. The South believed in weak central government and shared Jefferson's fears of the aggrandizement of federal power. It traditionally fought for and depended upon low tariffs and unrestricted internal trade, whereas the North and West tended to be protectionist. It insisted on asserting states' rights even up to and beyond the point of secession.

The view traditionally promulgated, both by Northern writers of the Simon Legree school and by Southern romanticists of the magnolia-and-old-plantation stamp, is that the South was a caste- and class-conscious aristocracy ruled by the great landed and slave-holding families. Yet, as Burton Hendrick cogently observed, the South of 1861 "was a land of newly acquired wealth, not particularly well-mannered or cultured, but pushing, self-assertive and arrogant," including within its ranks men from New England and New York looking for quick fortunes in cotton. As for the leadership of the Confederacy:

"The President of the Confederate States of America was born in a log cabin. The Vice President spent his early days as a 'corn dropper' on his father's slaveless farm and chore boy in tasks ordinarily assigned to negroes. The Secretary of State—at least the one who filled that office for most of the war—was the son of the keeper of a dried fish shop in London. The Secretary of the Treasury, born in Germany, spent his childhood in a Charleston orphanage. The Secretary of the Navy, son of a Connecticut Yankee, started life as assistant to his widowed mother in running a sailors' boarding house in Key West, Florida. The Postmaster General, son of a tanner, had for a time engaged in an occupation that made any man a social outcast in the South—that of plantation overseer. The Confederacy's ablest diplomat was not Southern in origin; born in New York City, he was the son of a tallow chandler, and had in his early days followed that trade himself. If the cabinet occasionally enlisted men of more pretentious stock, all of these recruits with one exception—Seddon of Virginia—occupied their posts for very brief periods, and all were failures."[11]

To be sure, the Confederacy was not a democracy, in that the Negroes were slaves and disfranchised. But by that criterion, Athens was not a democracy either since the majority of her population, in the age of Pericles and thereafter, consisted of slaves and foreigners. Perhaps a better test of a democracy is not whether it bestows freedom and the franchise on everyone, but whether those whom it defines as citizens enjoy representative government and free institutions. By this criterion, the Confederacy was emphatically democratic.

Jewry and the Union Cause

By 1860, a large majority of American Jews lived north of the Mason and Dixon line and a decided majority of them sympathized with the Republican Party which had been organized in Wisconsin six years previously. In Chicago, four of five organizers of a mass meeting to launch a local Republican Party were Jewish. In Philadelphia and New York, Jews were almost equally prominent in the new party. A Kentucky Jew, Lewis Napthali Dembitz (whose nephew, Louis Dembitz Brandeis would later sit on the Supreme Court), was one of those who placed Abraham Lincoln's name in nomination for the Presidency.[12]

The Northern Jews and the Germans tended to be strongly Republican and anti-slavery both before and during the Civil War. The other great new immigrant group, the Irish, in the main sympathized with the South and was antagonistic toward Negroes. The draft riots which swept New York City in July 1863 were a barometer of the intensity of this feeling. Mobs, largely Irish, threw up barricades, stole carbines, made headlong assaults on the State arsenal, repulsed 2,000 armed police, burned some $5 million worth of property and shot, stoned, trampled, hanged or burned to death some 30 Negroes, hunting others down like rabbits. When the storm in the streets subsided, the North became aware of the power and fury of a primarily Irish proletariat which deeply resented a conscription system bearing down upon the poor and a war seemingly fought to free the Negro slaves.

Union Generals and Jewish Peddlers

As the Union armies advanced into the South, merchants, many of them Jews, proceeded in their wake. Their main interest was in buying cotton from those Southerners whose plantations and warehouses were now behind Union lines and in moving this desperately needed raw material into the normal channels of international trade. To do so meant to violate various military economic regulations and to interfere with the punitive policies of the War Department and the radical anti-Southern element in Washington.

The first to raise the issue of the "Jew peddlers" was

General William Tecumseh Sherman who on July 30, 1862 complained of "swarms of Jews" in a letter to General John A. Rawlins, which Grant read. At about the same time, General Samuel R. Curtis wrote General-in-Chief Henry W. Halleck that his camp was "infested with Jews."[13]

Speculators were also swarming around Grant's headquarters at Holly Springs, Mississippi, and following his forces in search of cotton to be bought as cheaply as possible and sold in the North. Grant complained to Assistant Secretary of War C. P. Wolcott about "Jews and other unprincipled traders" who flouted Treasury regulations, and ordered his commanding officer at Columbus, Kentucky, to deny permits to all Jews who wished to travel South. In other correspondence, he expatiated on his unfavorable opinions of Jewish traders with their "carpet sacks" and "pockets full of gold."[14] When Grant's own father, a leather merchant, came to Holly Springs with some Jewish tradesmen in hopes of making money from the cotton trade, Grant sent him North again and in cold fury issued his notorious General Order 11 of December 17, 1862.[15] This read: "The Jews, as a class violating every regulation of trade established by the Treasury Department and also department orders, are hereby expelled from the department[16] and held in confinement within twenty-four hours from the receipt of their order.

"Post commanders will see that this class of people be furnished passes and required to leave, and anyone returning after such notification will be arrested and held in confinement until an opportunity occurs for sending them out as prisoners."

This discriminatory order aroused a storm of opposition,

not because it took action against war profiteering, but because it singled out Jews as a class for punishment. Jesse Grant claimed that his father had been made a cat's paw. "That Jew order so much harped on in congress," he claimed, "was issued on express instructions from Washington." Bertram Wallace Korn in his *American Jewry and the Civil War*[17] laid the blame for the order on Halleck and called it not accidental and the "logical capstone of a policy of discrimination against Jews."[18]

A Jewish delegation, under a somewhat servile and clownish leader, a certain Cesar Kaskel of Paducah, remonstrated with President Lincoln about Grant's order, claiming that "we have come unto Father Abraham's bosom for protection." Lincoln agreed to rescind General Order 11, whereupon the Jewish delegation thanked him profusely.

On January 21, 1863 General-in-Chief Halleck explained to Grant: "The President has no objection to your expelling traitors and Jew peddlers, which I suppose, was the object of your order; but as it in terms proscribed an entire religious class, some of whom are fighting in our ranks, the President deemed it necessary to revoke it."[19]

The *New York Times* regarded Grant's order as "one of the deepest sensations of the war" and expressed editorial dissatisfaction with both Lincoln and the sycophantic Jewish delegation:

"The order, to be sure, was promptly set aside by the President, but the affront to the Jews conveyed by its issue, was not so easily effaced. A committee of Jews took it upon themselves to *thank* President Lincoln at Washington for so promptly annulling the odious order. Against the conduct of this committee the bulk of the Jews vehemently protest. They say they have no thanks for an act of simple and imperative justice—but grounds for deep and just complaint against the Government, that General Grant has not been dismissed from the service."

The proposal that Lincoln sack his best general on such grounds was unreasonable; the *Times'* belief that the "Jew peddlers" incident was serious was not. It seemed ominous to many American Jews that three of the Union's outstanding generals—Halleck, Sherman and Grant—had singled them out for discriminatory attack. By contrast, the Confederacy never issued any orders which singled out Jews by name. Jefferson Davis considered Grant's conduct an arbitrary abuse of power.

CHAPTER 6

The Gilded Age

THE GERMAN JEWISH IMMIGRATION of the first eight
decades of the nineteenth century did not huddle in New
York and other eastern seaboard cities, but spread westward
and southward. Its economic role was to set up merchandising organizations that linked the nation, bringing the
manufactured goods of the cities to the pioneer communities. To Socialists and others who have absorbed Marxist
prejudices against any labor which does not result in the
material transformation of a commodity, this activity may
seem less productive than farming, mining or manufactur-
ing. Yet without it, life on the frontier would have been
even more drab and monotonous than in fact it was. Without it, the growth of American industry would have been
much less rapid since the internal market would have been
largely untapped.

Rabbi Isaac M. Wise, the late leader of Reformed Juda-

e economic advance of his
Reminiscences:

y may be divided into the fol-
eddler—he is as yet altogether
trunk-carrier, who stammers
opes for better times; 3. the
e hundred to one hundred and
, and indulges the thought that
man some day. In addition to
acy, which may be divided into
three classes: 1. __ 1-baron, who peddles through the
country with a one- or two-horse team; 2. the jewelry-count,
who carries a stock of watches and jewelry in a small trunk,
and is considered a rich man even now; 3. the store-prince,
who has a shop, and sells goods in it. . . . At first one is the
slave of the basket or the pack; then the lackey of the horse,
in order to become finally the servant of the shop."[1]

For some of these German Jews, the American dream
never came true and the golden land seemed a mirage.
Economic failure was the exception, however, rather than
the rule. In December 1890, the Census Bureau published
a report by John S. Billings, which summarized the social
status of 10,000 Jewish families, most of which had come
to the United States between 1850 and 1880 and were of
German origin.[2]

The success of these 10,000 families had been spectacular. Some forty per cent had at least one servant and ten
per cent had three or more. About half of the family heads
were in business—for the most part retail or wholesale trade
—and another tenth were salesmen. Twenty per cent were
accountants, clerks, bookkeepers or other white-collar workers. Five per cent were bankers; two per cent were professionals; another two per cent were farmers and ranchers.

One out of eight was a manual worker, but even these were, for the most part, in highly skilled occupations such as jewelry and watchmaking, tailoring and the printing trades. Only one out of every hundred Jews was still a peddler and about one in two hundred was an unskilled laborer or domestic servant.[3]

Political Attitudes

To the extent that they were politically committed, the majority of American Jewry remained faithful to the party of Lincoln between the Civil War and the Rooseveltian New Deal. The nomination of Ulysses S. Grant for the Presidency on the Republican ticket in 1872 briefly threatened this entente. Both Jews and non-Jews remembered Grant's intemperate order barring Jews from his military zone. Letters to the newspapers denounced the Republican standard-bearer as anti-Semitic. The furor died down when Grant denied the charge and nominated Jews to be governors of Washington Territory and the District of Columbia.

Far more important to American Jewry was the vigorous action taken by Republican Presidents of the nineteenth century against anti-Semitic demonstrations and pogroms, often organized by governmental action, in Russia and Eastern Europe. William Evarts, minister to Rumania under President Rutherford B. Hayes, went so far as to inform the government to which he was accredited that the United States Government was prepared to accept a measure of responsibility for the protection of foreign Jews against these outrages.

Jews took leading positions in local, city and state Republican organizations and San Francisco was for years dominated by Abe Ruef, one of the few American Jews who have succeeded at the career of political boss. A few Jews were elected mayors and congressmen on the Republican ticket.

Meanwhile, the tidal wave of Russian immigration had started, following pogroms and other outrages in 1881. There had been about 200,000 Jews in the United States at the close of the Civil War. Twenty-five years later, the figure had more than trebled. The majority of American Jewry was now Slavic. For a variety of reasons, perhaps the most important of which were that they had been ground down economically and compressed into a small part of the Russian Empire, these Jews were primarily manual workers and artisans. Moreover, they were impoverished.

Knowing no English, unfamiliar with the Western world, they crowded into self-made ghettos in New York and other eastern-seaboard cities. Here, they could speak Yiddish, retain their Russian Jewish customs and live, for a few years at least, in tight-knit Jewish enclaves.

As New York City gradually became the greatest Jewish metropolis in the world, the Jews played an increasingly large role in its politics. The city was, of course, Democratic and the dominant force within the Democratic Party was Tammany Hall.

The Jewish political leaders in New York State were of German stock despite the fact that most of their co-religionists were of Russian origin. Moreover, they were preponderantly anti-Tammany, a contrast with the era of Jackson and Van Buren, in which politically minded New York Jews had given solid support to the radical Tammany wing of Gotham democracy.

Examples of this New York Jewish political leadership were Henry Morgenthau and the three Straus brothers, Oscar, Isador and Nathan, who were Georgia-born, but had come to the big city and made mercantile fortunes.[4] Morgenthau, the father of Franklin D. Roosevelt's Secretary

of the Treasury, was a staunch supporter of Samuel J.
Tilden, the governor of New York, who ran for President
on the Democratic ticket in 1876, won a majority of the
popular vote, but was defeated in the electoral college
through congressional skulduggery. Remaining a strong
Democrat, Morgenthau fought Tammany. Isador and
Nathan Straus called themselves Cleveland Democrats,
refused to accept Tammany support and declined nomina-
tions for mayor of New York.[5]

By the turn of the century, American Jews were con-
forming to one of the standard political behavior patterns
of immigrant groups in the United States. Having succeeded
magnificently in their new homeland and now firmly en-
sconced in the ranks of the middle and upper classes, they
had abandoned their earlier support of radical movements
such as those of Jackson and Van Buren. In their majority,
they backed the Republican Party, the political expression
of business enterprise and of the virtues associated with
individualism. This support suggested that they considered
themselves absorbed into the ranks of the great American
majority. The Republican Party, after all, was more Protestant than Catholic, more mid-Western than Eastern, more
North European than representative of the newer immigrant stocks, more middle class than proletarian. Where
Jews were pillars of the Democratic Party, they tended, like
Morgenthau and the Straus brothers, to support the moderate and responsible policies of leaders of integrity such
as Tilden. They shunned, and at times combatted, both
the corrupt Democratic machines of the metropolises and
the wild, plebeian, ranting, conspiracy-ridden, populist,
Fundamentalist, funny-money brand of Democracy that
hung on the coattails of such leaders as William Jennings
Bryan.

At a time when American Jewish political behavior

seemed virtually stabilized in a mold of responsible conservatism and dedication to honest government, the waves
of destitute, oppressed and partially radicalized Russian
Jews were creating a quiet revolution within American
Jewry. By 1895, New York City had twelve Yiddish newspapers, most of which represented new doctrines of radicalism. *Die Naye Zeit* was anarchist; the *Arbeiter Zeitung*
was the organ of the revolutionary doctrines of Daniel De
Leon; finally, there was the Socialist organ *Der Forverts*
which was to become the dominant factor in the American
Jewish press.[6]

"Genteel" Anti-Semitism

Social anti-Semitism was virtually unknown in the United
States until the 1870's and 1880's. American Jewry had
always constituted an economic, intellectual and, to a lesser
extent, political elite. Thus, before the Civil War, the president of the outstanding Philadelphia men's club was, not
only a Jew, but the head of his synagogue. Moses Lazarus,
father of Emma Lazarus, the poetess,[7] was a founder of the
distinguished Knickerbocker Club. The Union League had
a Jew among its founders; Jewish weddings were carried in
society magazines; Jews were admitted into the most pa-
trician clubs.[8] This secure position was based, not only on
the Jews' visible role as part of the elite, but on the fact that
intermarriage was common. Hence, the Jewish and non-
Jewish elites were inextricably intermeshed, a fact which
made the religious and cultural differences between the two
groups comparatively unimportant. Under these conditions,
any social barriers raised against Jews would inevitably also
affect upper-class non-Jews.

These conditions were changed by the massive immigration of Slavic Jewry, which, in the course of a few decades, significantly altered the cultural, social and economic status of American Jews. To the extent that there had been political anti-Semitism in the United States prior to this influx, it had been directed against the Jews as capitalists, bankers and conspirators of the "gold monopoly." The new wave changed Jewry into a preponderantly urban group of un-assimilated peddlers, artisans and sweatshop workers, living in tenements and frequently imbued with revolutionary doctrines.

While this transition was barely beginning, anti-Semitism was made a national issue in 1877 when Joseph Seligman and his family were turned away from the Grand Union Hotel in Saratoga. Since the Seligmans were at the apex of the German Jewish aristocracy, this act shocked, not only American Jewry, but thoughtful non-Jews as well. Henry Ward Beecher "preached one of his famous sermons on this occasion"[9] and Bret Harte wrote a poem of protest which was widely reprinted.[10]

By the 1880's, New York City private schools began to exclude Jewish students and advertisements of summer camps and hotels, which stipulated that Jews would not be admitted, became common. In 1893, the Union League Club adopted a policy of closing its doors to Jews. This policy of ostracism from the best society was to continue for at least half a century. Since World War II, "genteel" anti-Semitism, like the far more virulent political anti-Semitism of discontent, has been on the decline in the United States.

Reprehensible and unjust as it was, upper-class anti-Semitism had little in common with modern political anti-Semitism. Its presence could reinforce the latter, but could never substitute for it. Social anti-Semitism empha-sized, in fact over-emphasized, the differences between the

Jewish and non-Jewish upper classes; hence, it was essentially a static movement, one of snobbishness. Modern political anti-Semitism, by contrast, sees the Jews as the central and dominant force in an international conspiracy designed to lead mankind to its doom. This sort of ideology presupposes a conspiratorial concept of history and a view of history in Manichean terms, as a fight to the death between the forces of absolute good and those of absolute evil. Regardless of whether the international Jew, the capitalist class or the white race was doomed to play the central role in these deranged and hallucinatory concepts of history, the movements created around them were inevitably revolutionary in character. In fact, the *raison d'être* of these devil theories is to justify orgies of destruction, in which classes, races, peoples and institutions are ruthlessly annihilated. Such movements cannot be upper class or conservative because their mainspring is the desire to destroy and this is inevitably in conflict with the conservative posture.

Populism and Anti-Semitism

In his challenging analysis of the Populist movement, Professor Richard Hofstadter propounded the view that it foreshadowed modern political anti-Semitism of the Nazi type.[11] Hofstadter points out that it propagated a conspiratorial theory of history in which all major social evils were attributed to the malevolent exercise of power by an international "gold trust." It revealed an obsession with the role of money in human affairs which has been characteristic of subsequent anti-Semitic ideologies. It had a very strong sadistic and eschatological component. The intellectual leaders of Populism, above all Ignatius Donnelly, wrote political novels in which the "gold trust" and the "people," each represented by huge conspiratorial organizations of a paramilitary sort, struggled for world power and destroyed each other in orgies of cruelty and blood. Finally, Populism exalted the purity of heart, fundamental wisdom, goodness and capacity for sacrifice of the common people. Distrustful of all intellectuals, of all sophisticated groups in society, Populism sought to transfer political power from elected officials, whom it regarded generally as corrupt men who had sold out to the gold interests, to the people directly. Its concept of democracy was the elemental one of Rousseau in which the people's will is supreme. It tended to regard the rights of dissenting minorities and of individuals as of little importance and to consider due process of law a spider's web of sophistries by which corrupt lawyers enabled their rich clients to escape the punishment they deserved.

The Populist wave consisted of a sequence of third-party political movements, all of which appealed to the discontent of Western and Southern farmers, between the end of the Civil War and the beginning of World War I. While these movements failed to coalesce into a durable political institution, they polled impressive vote totals and represented the views of a significant portion of the electorate. The Greenback Party, organized right after the depression of 1873 on a platform of issuance of fiat paper money to be secured by federal government bonds, merged with various working-class organizations to become the Greenback Labor Party. In 1878, it polled more than a million votes, or over 10% of the total, and elected fourteen Congressmen.

The last of these movements, the People's Party of the United States of America, was launched in 1891. Its main plank was unlimited coinage of silver at a silver-gold price ratio of sixteen to one. In essence, this was the same proposal as that made by the Greenbackers two decades earlier. It was a plan to increase the quantity of money in circulation. This was vital to the farmers as they found it virtually impossible to service their mortgage and other debts in bad times when crop prices were low.

The Populist program also included such planks as government ownership of railroads and telephone systems and a graduated income tax. In the 1892 elections, the People's Party polled over a million popular and 22 electoral votes. It elected three governors, several congressmen and a large number of lesser officials. Four years later, the Populists endorsed Democratic presidential candidate William Jennings Bryan, who ran on a platform of free silver. In succeeding elections, the third party movement gradually disintegrated.

These movements were not, however, mere demands for moderate and, in some cases, long-overdue reforms. They were denunciatory of all American governmental institutions, as corrupted agencies of the enemy. The Greenbackers called the Senate a club composed "largely of aristocratic millionaires who . . . generally purchased their elections in order to protect the great monopolies which they represent." The Union Labor Party observed in 1888 that both major parties were "hopelessly and shamelessly corrupt" and "unworthy of the suffrages of those who do not live upon public plunder." The People's Party considered, as Charles A. Beard aptly summarized it, "that America was ruled by a plutocracy, that impoverished labor was laid low under the tyranny of a hireling army, that homes were covered with mortgages, that the press was the tool of wealth, that corruption dominated the ballot box, that the fruits of the toil of millions are boldly stolen to build up colossal fortunes for a few unprecedented in the

history of mankind; and the possessors of these in turn
despise the republic and endanger liberty."[12]

Unlike the Marxists, the Populists did not envisage a
struggle for power between proletarians and capitalists. The
battle was between the productive classes and the parasites,
the people and the interests, the masses and the money
power. The Populist platform of 1892 declared that public
opinion was muzzled, the press bribed, business prostrated,
land monopolized, labor denied the right to organize and
"a hireling standing army, unrecognized by our laws, is
established to shoot them down. . . ."[13] Unless the people
were aroused to reverse these trends, what lay ahead was
"the destruction of civilization, or the establishment of an
absolute depotism."[14]

The Greenback and Populist monetary proposals were
similar in essence to the monetary and central banking
policies pursued by the United States from the era of
Franklin D. Roosevelt to the present except for the fact
that they were more timid and much more rigid.

The Populists, however, went far beyond advocating
mildly inflationary monetary measures. They misrepresented
the conservatism of the U.S. Treasury as a sinister and
deliberate conspiracy of the money trust against society.
The fact that epidemics of bank failure accompanied economic depressions did little to persuade them that the
bankers had not willfully engineered the latter.

To be sure, the Populists could never have created a mass
movement around the assertion, whether true or false, that
the American economy was being sold short by old-fogey
economics. The farmers facing foreclosure and the workers
out of jobs wanted to believe that their plight was due to
the machinations of evil forces. The symbolic representation of this evil became the money power. Occasionally,

this money power was incarnated as the English financier—a man who seemed to the Populists to be foreign, haughty, aristocratic, supercilious, crafty, shrewd and adverse to manual labor. At other times, the incarnation was the Jewish banker, the international Jew or simply the Jew. He was even more alien than the English banker. In fact, he was not even a Christian. He made a better scapegoat than the English banker because he was weaker. He did not have an aristocratic tradition or an established social position behind him.

Professor Hofstadter's interpretation of Populism has been challenged by several scholars, including notably Norman Pollack of Yale. In an article with the unfortunate title, "The Myth of Populist Anti-Semitism," Pollack concludes that "Populism contained some anti-Semitism," but that its extent has been exaggerated and its target was the Jews as agents of "the money power" rather than the Jews as a race or people.[15] Pollack searched the papers of Populist leaders Henry Demarest Lloyd and Ignatius Donnelly, and those of Populist sympathizer William Jennings Bryan, and also scanned Populist newspapers for evidence of anti-Semitism. He found that individual Jewish supporters of Populism were accepted and that some Populists welcomed Russian Jews in a proposed cooperative settlement. On the other hand, Pollack quotes such Populist organs as the Custer County (Nebraska) Beacon and the Saunder County (Nebraska) New Era as denouncing the decision of the 1896 Republican national convention to invite a rabbi to officiate as chaplain. "It was fitting," the Beacon for July 2, 1896 observed, "that this convention of gold worshipers should select a Jew to pray for them, for the fellows behind the scenes were Jews—the same class of fellows that persecuted the saints and crucified Christ."

The Monetary Mavericks

The connection between monetary mavericks, fascism and anti-Semitism has been strangely persistent. In many different times and places, men have invented some inflationary expedient which they believed would solve all society's economic ills and bring about a utopia. They then convinced themselves that the truths they had discovered were self-evident to any honest mind. When the ruling Establishment refused to see the light, the only possible conclusion was that that Establishment was working deliberately against the interests of the people. Thus, many of these reformers became fascists and other revolutionaries of a hate-saturated and destructive sort.

Ezra Pound, who broadcast for Mussolini to U.S. troops during World War II and was indicted for treason,[16] derived his anti-Semitism from half-baked monetary theories. In his diatribes, Pound generally coupled Jewry with usury. Major Douglas, a noted monetary eccentric, in the period between the two world wars developed a movement in Canada which soon became at least semi-fascist. The original 25 point program of the Nazi Party railed against "interest slavery." The most brilliant of all the monetary mavericks, Silvio Gesell (1862-1930), was a successful German businessman who turned to economic and monetary theorizing when in his late twenties. Although he took strong issue with the Marxists, he saw no more attractive revolutionary laboratory for monetary experimentation on the horizon and in 1919 joined the ephemeral Bavarian Soviet Republic as its Finance Minister. Before he could test any of his fiscal and monetary theories, the Republic was overthrown and Gesell was courtmartialed. He escaped a firing squad to die peacefully in Switzerland many years later, the leader of a monetary cult which had thousands of fervent disciples throughout the world.

Populism's Doomsday Books

The political novels of Populism's intellectual leaders were lurid dramas of world conflict to the death between the forces of light and the forces of darkness. In "Coin" Harvey's *A Tale of Two Nations*, the villains are Baron Rothe (obviously Rothschild) and his agent in America, Rogasner. These two proceed to bribe the Congress of the United States to demonetize silver, both to increase the profits of banker Rothe and to prevent the United States from outstripping England as a world power. In this naive and untalented novel, it is interesting to note that the Jewish villains are working as patriotic British subjects, not as principals in an international Jewish conspiracy. Mary E. Lease, another well-known Populist writer, branded President Grover Cleveland as "the agent of Jewish bankers and British gold."[17]

A much more significant Populist novel was *Caesar's Column* by Ignatius Donnelly. It depicts a brutalized society, in which the poor are degraded, exploited and dehumanized by an utterly ruthless ruling class which is depicted as Jewish. Donnelly presented the original theory that to survive "the awful trial" of Gentile persecution, the Jews had had to develop exceptional astuteness, physical toughness, the capacity to survive under inhuman conditions and the ability to take the long, calculating view. Superior in these areas, "the Jew was master in the contest with the Gentile" and became as ruthless toward the non-Jew as the latter had formerly been toward him.[18]

On the basis of this and other writings, Donnelly has

sometimes been characterized as an anti-Semite pure and simple, but this was not the case. In *Caesar's Column,* one of the three leaders of the avenging revolutionary army of the people is an idealistic Jew who has been expelled from his synagogue. In a subsequent novel, *The Golden Battle* (1892), the working people of the world rise up against and destroy their rulers. The leader of the revolution, Benazet, advocates national self-determination and helps the Jews build a national homeland in Palestine.

Donnelly always denied that he was anti-Semitic. "A plutocratic Jew," he wrote, "is no worse than a plutocratic Christian—in fact, he is half as bad. For the Jew, for nearly 2,000 years, had been proscribed, persecuted and hunted down, fenced into the corners of towns; hounded, pelted and stoned by ignorant populations when the Jews were preserving the knowledge of the one true God in the midst of an idolatrous world."[19]

Donnelly urged Jews to "get out of the gold bondage which is now destroying the human race." At the same time, he praised the contributions of Spinoza, Mendelssohn and Disraeli and hailed Karl Marx as "the Jewish reformer." His reaction to the Dreyfus case was one of shocked astonishment that "Christians, worshipping a Jew, the son of a Jewess, should entertain such terrible bigotry against the people of his race." He reminded anti-Semitic Populists that: "The Jews are not all plutocrats; a large majority of them are the poorest people in the world. The half-starved workers of the sweatshops of London, Berlin and New York are mostly Jews."[20]

Nevertheless, these sanguinary and apocalyptic novels seem to have been effective in injecting the Populist masses with anti-Jewish feelings.[21] At the 1896 convention of the People's Party in St. Louis, the Associated Press reporter was shocked at "the extraordinary hatred of the Jewish race" displayed by the delegates and visitors. "It is not possible to go to any hotel in the city," he added, "without hearing the most bitter denunciations of the Jews as a class and of the particular Jews who happen to have prospered in the world."[22]

This hatred was not directed primarily at actual Jews, who were not familiar figures to the Populists of the rural South and West. It was directed at "the Jew," conceived of as the embodiment and cause of unsatisfactory economic and social conditions. It would persevere in the propaganda of such bigoted and culturally primitive survivors of Populism as Senator Tom Watson, the intellectual author of the Leo Frank lynching which disgraced Atlanta in 1915. It would be resurrected in the anti-Semitic campaign of Henry Ford, who had absorbed many of the ideas and prejudices of Populism, notably hatred of banks and bankers. But it would not coalesce into a permanent anti-Semitic movement of the sort which prevailed in Germany and Austria for half a century prior to Hitler. Among the reasons for this was the fact that the social and economic evils which fueled the Populist fire gradually disappeared and the American mind soon became too well-informed and too realistic to fall for this sort of hallucinatory theory of history.

CHAPTER 7

The Fight Against Anti-Semitism: 1880-1914

THE MASSIVE IMMIGRATION from Eastern and Southern Europe into the United States between the 1880's and the outbreak of World War I was impelled by poverty and land-hunger and was attracted by American economic opportunity. The Jewish portion of that immigration, however, was primarily motivated by Czarist economic oppression and political persecution. Hence, it did not depend on whether the United States was enjoying prosperity or suffering from depression. It was more like a current than a tide. Nor was it magnetized into the new centers of burgeoning heavy industry, which attracted Slavs and Magyars, but rather concentrated in eastern seaboard cities which already had large Jewish populations. With packs on their backs, the German Jews had spread westward and southward from the Atlantic ports at which they debarked to become geographically distributed and represented in every state of the Union. But at the outbreak of World War I, when American Jewry was already overwhelmingly Slavic in origin, about half of the Jewish population of the United States was concentrated in New York City.

These Russian Jews had been compressed by Czarist edicts into an area known as the Pale of Settlement in the western portion of European Russia. Within the Pale, they were confined to specific towns and smaller settlements, hamstrung as to travel and occupation and subjected to a quota system that limited their access to higher education. Excluded from the Russian territories that were enjoying most vigorous economic growth, these Russian Jews were much poorer than the German Jews who had preceded them to the United States and much more heavily concentrated in light industries and such handicrafts as the needle trades.

Their sheer numbers radically transformed the whole structure of American Jewry. In 1880, when the mass exodus from Russian territories was about to start, Jews comprised 0.6% of the population of the United States. By 1917, the Jewish percentage was 3.5%—almost a sixfold increase. The newcomers were impoverished even by the low, sweatshop standards of the day. In 1900, the average immigrant arrived in the United States with $15 in his pocket; the average Jewish immigrant arrived with only $9.[1]

The Russian Jewish immigrant did not have enough capital to go into trade, even as a peddler. Instead he went into the sweatshops, worked inhumanly long hours for a pittance and lived in overcrowded and squalid tenements.

"For reasons which are not completely clear," writes Glazer, "Jewish immigrants earned rather more working at the sewing machine than did those of other national groups.

Apparently, the Jews were pioneers in the 'task system," the breaking down of the garment into a number of parts by a team of workers; but the contemporary observers of the time also believed that the Jews simply developed more dexterity and worked harder and longer hours. Whatever the reason, there is no question that Jews earned more than did non-Jews."[2]

John R. Commons, the historian of the American labor movement, noted in 1901 that proportionately fewer Jewish women than the women of other immigrant stocks worked in sweatshops, that the Jewish needle trades workers seldom brought up their sons in the business but instead had them "seek other callings," and that the Jews would characteristically "begin as helpers and advance to full-fledged mechanics," then "open contractors' shops" and proceed from there into the wholesale clothing business.[3]

In a study of Jewish social work, Herman D. Stein observed that "out of 1,000 who applied for help in 1894 from the United Hebrew Charities in New York City, only 67 required help in 1899, and only 23 in 1904."[4]

The thirst for education was unquenchable. A survey of 77 institutions of higher education by the Immigration Commission in 1908 disclosed that 8.5% of the students were first- or second-generation Jews and that Jewish students constituted 18% of those studying pharmacy and 13% of the students of law. The Jews comprised about 2% of the United States population at that time. While I am inclined to believe that this sample is not entirely representative and that the data it yields for Jewish participation in higher education may be inflated, the fact that the Jews were much more heavily represented in the colleges and universities than in the general population seems indisputable.[5]

Thus, the first generation of Russian Jews devoted their

energies to providing their children with higher education and to moving out of the class of semi-skilled laborer into that of skilled worker, contractor and independent business-man. Professor Commons rightly predicted that, within a generation, the Jews would no longer constitute the work-ing class of the New York needle trades, but would be displaced by the Italians.

The second generation of Russian Jews moved into small business and into those professions and semi-professional skills which did not require more education than they could afford. They concentrated on training as lawyers and phar-macists. The third generation would reach professions such as medicine and dentistry, which required protracted and expensive postgraduate training.

"The difference between the Jewish and other immigrants could be seen in many other characteristics," Glazer wrote. "In 1890, there were no Russian Jewish almshouse paupers in New York, and the proportion of Jews in penitentiaries was much below their proportion in the population. Jewish families were larger than other families,[6] and the Jewish death rate was considerably lower. The death rate for Jew-ish children under five was less than half of that for the city as a whole. Further, the Jews enjoyed school, and did well at it: 'In the lower schools,' an observer for the Industrial Commission wrote in 1900, 'the Jewish children are the delight of their teachers for cleverness at their books, obedience and general good conduct.' "[7]

Patterns of Social Discrimination

Throughout American history—though to a far lesser extent than in the history of other nations composed of a variety of stocks—there have been patterns of bias and discriminatory action against minorities and newcomers. This is not specifically a Jewish problem.

In the Jewish case, however, the impact of discrimination was aggravated by three factors. Of these, probably the element of least importance was the fact that the Jews were non-Christians in an overwhelmingly Christian society. The role that religion has traditionally played in anti-Semitism has led to a fixation on this subject. The decisive factor, as far as the United States is concerned, is that discrimination and prejudice have always been at a minimum in the South and West where religion plays a more important role than in the urban Northeast.

A second factor was the often brash and ostentatious manners of the Jewish *nouveaux riches*, whether German or Slavic in origin. This condition was sometimes recognized in the Jewish as well as the Gentile press at the turn of the century and we find the *San Francisco Hebrew*, for example, assuring its readers that this offensiveness of manner would vanish in time.[8]

Third, and probably most important, was the unprecedentedly rapid upward mobility of American Jewry, a phenomenon which characterized the Jews of Russian origin almost as much as it did their German-born predecessors. While the Jews were by no means the only immigrant group which moved persistently upward, their advance was more spectacular, and hence to the older upper class more disturbing, than that of the Irish, Germans, Scandinavians and other successful non-Anglo-Saxon groups.

The view that anti-Semitism in America began with the upper classes and was spread by them among the guileless and well-meaning masses was not confined to radical publicists such as Carey McWilliams. It was propagated by academically respectable people such as Professor Oscar

Handlin of Harvard, who generalized about the motivations and conduct of the American upper class in the following vein:

"The famous exclusion of Joseph Seligman from a fashionable Saratoga resort hotel . . . foreshadowed an evolving pattern that became a particular feature of fashionable resort life. . . . It was after all at the beaches and watering places that the putative aristocracy was most anxious to withdraw to itself so that appropriate group feelings would be cultivated and so that the proper friendships among young people would grow into the proper marriages. . . . More was involved in this development than the offended feelings of a few vain or ambitious families. High society set the standard for the country. . . ."[9]

The facts of the matter were slightly different. As Higham points out, when Joseph Seligman was refused accommodations because of his race by the Grand Union Hotel in 1877, Saratoga was already being abandoned by society in favor of such resorts as Newport. "Instead of a fortress of the best society, Saratoga was becoming a flashy resort of the *nouveaux riches*, where wealthy sportsmen mingled with prominent politicians, Wall Street tycoons, Western copper kings, ladies of easy virtue, as well as a good many Jews."[10] The Grand Union Hotel was no longer at the top of this socially meretricious ant heap and its ostentatious exclusion of the Seligman family can best be understood as an effort to regain some of its lost snob appeal. After the Seligman episode, Jews built rival hotels in Saratoga; the older establishments retaliated with blatantly anti-Semitic advertisements[11] and Saratoga in due course lost all pretense to being a center of fashion or good society.

In the Catskills in the late 1880's, the resorts were divided between those which accepted no Jews and those which were almost exclusively Jewish. A contemporary observer added that "prejudice was most pronounced among patrons of cheap boarding houses, where the charges ranged from $5.00 to $10.00 per week."[12]

The exclusion policy became more widespread and more ramified until America's entry into World War I. During the war years, it abated somewhat, due either to the shortage of labor or to the feeling of solidarity and good fellowship which men are always able to establish when they share an enemy. After Germany's defeat, social anti-Semitism resumed its prewar dimensions. During most or all of this period, Masonic lodges excluded Jews; they were not admitted into most of the better prep schools; social clubs and college fraternities were closed to them; entire recreational areas were off limits. The mechanics of exclusion often involved a generally futile counteroffensive by rich Jews. Thus, when one of the best hotels in Lakewood, a new and fashionable New Jersey winter resort, turned away Nathan Straus, he built a hotel on adjoining property which was twice as large and for Jews only. The result was that Lakewood rapidly became transformed into an all-Jewish vacation ground.

When a Jewish organization tried to persuade a Minnesota hotel keeper that he should not practice discrimination, the latter replied that he would just as soon have Jewish as Gentile guests. However, if he chose Jews, they would cease to patronize his place once the Jewish concentration reached a certain level.[13]

Higham found that the regional pattern of social discrimination was at its maximum in the large cities east of the Mississippi and north of the Mason and Dixon Line. The smaller towns, where the Jews were longer established and better integrated into the life of the community, were less hostile. Social anti-Semitism was less prominent in the West and "it touched the South least of all."[14]

Jewish Exclusiveness

The separation of Jews and non-Jews was not always at the instigation of the latter. There has always been a strong tendency among American Jews, one that continues today, to build walls around themselves out of fear that their children will marry Gentiles and be lost to the Jewish community. A study of intermarriage between Jews and non-Jews by Erich Rosenthal revealed the extent to which this attitude still prevailed in the 1950's.

Thus, in a Southern town of 125,000 inhabitants with a comparatively small Jewish population, Jewish parents permitted their sons to date non-Jewish girls, but did not permit Gentile boys to date their daughters. Since the Jewish boys had a higher-than-average educational and economic status, they were considered desirable dates. There were not enough of them for both the Jewish and non-Jewish girls and hence the former would often be sent to colleges with a high percentage of Jewish men, for the purpose of marriage.[15]

Another study, cited by Rosenthal, concluded that "if adult wishes were suddenly to become the sole deciding factor, adult Jews would live closer together than they actually do, with even fewer opportunities for neighborhood contact with non-Jews."[16] The reason for this desire for self-imposed ghettos was fear of intermarriage, which amounted to 13.1% of all marriages involving Jewish spouses in Washington, D.C., in 1956 and from 36.3% to 53.6% of such marriages in Iowa between 1953 and 1959.

Only 17.5% of the children of such marriages were identified by their parents as Jewish.[17]

A rabbi, not an isolated voice, complained that towns
exist where all the leaders of the Jewish organizations are
married to non-Jewish women. Despite the fact that these
wives worked diligently and effectively at Jewish community
problems, the rabbi found this state of affairs deplorable
because:

"When a Jewish boy falls in love with a non-Jewess, the
parents beseech the rabbi to speak to their son, to convince
him not to take *this step that will bring disaster and grief
upon them*. The first thing that the lad does, of course, is to
point to the president of the congregation, the president of
the Jewish Community Council, all of whom have non-
Jewish wives, all active and respected in the community."[18]

Jewish Action Organizations

The American Jewish Committee had been organized in
1906 to assist the victims of Czarist pogroms in Kishinev
and elsewhere and to serve as an agency to combat persecution of Jews abroad. In 1913, the long-established B'nai
B'rith (Sons of the Covenant) launched the Anti-Defamation League which was to concern itself primarily with the
mushrooming of anti-Semitism in literature, the press and
the movies and with the tendency to exclude Jews from
vast areas of American life.

One of the first major achievements of the American
Jewish Committee was to get the New York State legislature to pass a law which made it a misdemeanor for any
public accommodation to advertise a policy of excluding
anyone because of race, creed or color. This measure, which

fell short of more modern equal accommodation bills because it punished, not the act itself, but merely the advertising of an intent to commit it, became law on the eve of World War I. Similar legislation was passed by other states under the pressure of the Anti-Defamation League.

The next major step was to eliminate the "Jew Comedy" from the nascent American motion picture industry. "Whenever a producer wishes to depict a betrayer of public trust, a hard-boiled, usurious money-lender, a crooked gambler, a grafter, a depraved fire-bug, a white-slaver or other villains of one kind or another, the actor is directed to represent himself as a Jew," the Anti-Defamation League complained.[19] The ADL attempted to persuade the industry-sponsored National Board of Censorship to eliminate films that depicted American Jews as Shylocks or Fagins. The Board, however, was preoccupied with barring films that it considered lascivious or obscene and took no action. Jews had a substantial ownership of the theatres in which these early silent films were displayed. When one of these theatres boycotted *Rebecca's Wedding Day* in Chicago in 1916, Hollywood got the message and agreed to cease producing anti-Semitic films.

Typical of the widespread prejudice against Jews and other foreigners at the time was a World War I Army manual which declared that "foreign-born, and especially Jews, are more apt to malinger than the native born." The Anti-Defamation League protested to President Wilson who expressed shock and had the edition recalled and destroyed.

A much more serious problem was presented by great literature with a marked anti-Semitic orientation. Shakespeare's *The Merchant of Venice* with its malign depiction of the Jewish usurer, Shylock, was one of the plays that had to be "intensively studied" as preparation for college entrance examinations. In 1914, the Central Conference of American Rabbis successfully put pressure on the College Board to have it removed. Half a century later, when there were protests against the telecasting of *The Merchant of Venice*, the ADL stated that "a work of great artistic quality . . . cannot be subject to censorship." Nevertheless, New York's Shakespeare-in-the-Park troupe was subjected to heavy Jewish organizational pressure in the early 1960's to cancel a performance of *The Merchant of Venice*. The actors held their ground, "but the price of the pressure was an absurdly twisted production, featuring a triumphant Shylock, the like of which Shakespeare would never have recognized."[20]

The Leo Frank Case

In the comparative quiet of the immediate pre-World War I years, the Leo M. Frank case exploded like a bomb with a slow fuse. Leo M. Frank was a young Cornell graduate in engineering, of German Jewish origin, who had settled in Atlanta as manager of the National Pencil Company factory and was married to a local Jewish girl. When still in his twenties, Frank had been elected president of the Atlanta B'nai B'rith, the honor resulting from the fact that he was an intellectual, a college graduate, of German origin and a man who had travelled in Europe, in contradistinction to the bulk of Southern Jewry who "were a single proprietary and self-employed class of retail merchants, peddlers, traveling salesmen, brokers, agents and manufacturers."[21]

On May 26, 1913, Mary Phagan, a buxom, fourteen-year-old worker in Frank's pencil factory, who had gone there to collect pay that was owed her, was murdered in the cellar. When the police discovered the body, they noted that she had not been raped. Two barely literate pencilled notes were found beside her body, which accused a "long tall negro black" of having pushed her down and of having had sexual relations with her.

The police reasoned that the notes must be forgeries since Mary could not have written them while she was being murdered. They may have assumed that the forger of the notes, and hence the presumptive murderer, was a Northern white man because he used the word "negro" rather than "nigger."

Frank had been alone in his office during the afternoon when the murder was committed. He had the misfortune to be "far from prepossessing in appearance," being very short and thin with "prominent eyeballs, accentuated by thick eyeglasses." Testimony was introduced, most of it undoubtedly perjured, that he was in the habit of making dates with the teen-age girls who worked for him and having a Negro stand guard so he would not be caught in flagrante, that he frequented a brothel and that he was a sexual pervert.[22]

The most amazing thing about the case, however, was not the somewhat flimsy web of circumstantial evidence, but the fact that a jury convicted Frank of murder on the evidence of Jim Conley, a Negro and ex-convict. L. F. Woodruff, a reporter for the Georgian, wrote about this phenomenon with wonder and amazement, characterizing Conley as "a Negro of the type that the South has been trying since reconstruction to destroy, the meagerly educated, shiftless, gin-guzzling, half-anthropoid black that any nation could well be rid of."[23]

Golden's theory is that a Georgia jury condemned Frank

"because he was a Jew, a Yankee, a college graduate and a 'capitalist.' " An additional and very important ingredient in the witches' brew was the presence of Thomas E. Watson, a gifted and malevolent agrarian agitator and Baptist lawyer who had polled a million votes in 1896 as the vice presidential candidate of the People's Party. This embittered demagogue traded for more than a generation on the economic misery and discontent of the rural South, stirring up latent distrust of Catholics and Jews as aliens and enemies of "Christian America."

Watson edited a weekly hate periodical called the *Jeffersonian*. In it, he assailed the new factories that were gradually lifting the Georgia poor whites toward a more civilized standard of life. He managed to strike a modern note in his anti-Semitism in that he stressed a theme that Hitler and Streicher would expatiate upon—the alleged lasciviousness and sexual potency of Jews.

"Leo Frank was a typical young Jewish man of business, who lives for pleasure and *runs after gentile girls*," he wrote. "Every student of sociology knows that the black man's lust after the white woman is not much *fiercer than the lust of the licentious Jew for the gentile*."[24]

Watson referred to the man on trial as a "lascivious Sodomite;" another Georgia newspaper touched up Frank's photograph to make him look sinister and captioned the product "monster."

When the Hearst paper in Atlanta shifted sides and printed stories favorable to the defense, Watson thundered that Hearst was a half-Jew and a tool of Nathan Straus. Both statements were falsehoods.

The Jews of Atlanta did not at first regard the Frank murder trial as one involving an issue of anti-Semitism. Five members of prominent Jewish families were on the grand jury which indicted Frank and most Atlanta Jews seem to have at first believed him guilty.

Anti-Semitism was not injected into the trial until the prosecution's cross-examination of defense witnesses. Even here, it was sometimes introduced obliquely and indirectly. The main implied charges against the Jews were that they fraternized with Negroes, thus breaking down the South's racial mores, and that they were rich exploiters of labor. The last point was made in the highfalutin style which Watson affected:

"Frank belongs to the Jewish aristocracy and it was determined by rich Jews that no aristocrat of their race should die for the death of a working girl! Yes, Mary Phagan was only a factory girl; there was no glamour of wealth or fashion about her. She had no millionaire uncle; she had no Athens kinsmen to raise fifty thousand dollars for her: no mighty connections. While the Sodomite who took her sweet life basks in the warmth of Today, the poor child's dainty flesh has fed the worms."[25]

The trial was an outrage. While it was in progress, "large and boisterious crowds were gathered in the streets and were engaged in noisy demonstration, plainly audible in the court room, which was also crowded, and those assembled within its walls, as well as those outside, applauded whenever the State's attorney scored a point."[26] One of Frank's lawyers was told, "If they don't hang that Jew, we'll hang you!"

Frank was convicted and sentenced to hang. Appeal after appeal was taken. Finally, the Supreme Court turned down the defendant. In a memorable dissent by Mr. Justice Holmes, with Mr. Justice Hughes concurring, the minority observed: "Mob law does not become due process of law by securing the assent of a terrorized jury. We are not speaking of mere disorder, or mere irregularities in procedure, but of a case where the processes of justice are actually subverted."

William Randolph Hearst took up the case and launched a nationwide crusade against Georgia justice. John M. Slaton, the courageous Governor of Georgia, commuted Frank's sentence to life imprisonment on June 21, 1915.

Two months later, a mob disarmed the guards at Milledgeville Prison Farm, seized and abducted Frank, took him in a car to a lonely spot and hanged him. The mob was apparently organized and inspired by an impromptu vigilante outfit which called itself the Knights of Mary Phagan and was a forerunner of the revived Ku Klux Klan of the 1920's.

The murderer of Mary Phagan was Jim Conley, the Negro convict whose testimony cost Leo Frank his life. He told at least three people that he had killed Mary Phagan: his lawyer, a fellow convict who swore to it a decade after the lynching, and Annie Maude Carter, a female convict whom Conley had met in prison and whom he wanted to marry. This woman informed the authorities that Conley had confessed the murder to her and she turned over to them a sheaf of letters he had written to her in 1914. These letters conclusively proved that Conley was a sex pervert and contained phrases and mistakes in spelling and grammar identical with those in the two notes found beside Mary Phagan's murdered body.

Thomas Watson always referred to the lynching of Leo Frank as an "execution." He wrote: "In putting the Sodomite murderer to death the Vigilance Committee has done what the Sheriff would have done if (Governor) Slaton had not been made of the same mould as Benedict Arnold. LET JEW LIBERTINES TAKE NOTICE! Georgia is not for sale to rich criminals!"[27]

After the lynching, Watson suffered from the delusion that Nathan Straus was planning to have him murdered. He lived sealed up in his mansion, only leaving it when he had to and never riding on a train. "He is inclined to the grandiose," wrote a contemporary observer, "and forces those who deal with him to treat him as if he were lord of a manor."

In his declining years, Watson became the leading anti-Semitic propagandist of the country. As his biographer wrote, ". . . if any mortal man may be credited (as no one man may rightly be) with releasing the forces of human malice and ignorance and prejudice, which the Klan merely mobilized, that man was Thomas E. Watson."[28]

When Watson finally died in 1922, Eugene Victor Debs, the spellbinder who led the American Socialist Party, wrote his widow: "He was a great man, a heroic soul who fought the power of evil his whole life long in the interest of the common people, and they loved him and honored him."[29]

CHAPTER 8

From World War to Depression

FROM LINCOLN'S INAUGURATION to World War I, American Jews in their majority remained loyal to the Republican Party. This political alliance was cemented by the friendly attitude displayed toward Jewry by a succession of Republican Presidents and by vigorous American protests against the anti-Semitic outrages and pogroms in Russia and the Balkans. A second factor favoring the alliance was the fact that the Democratic machines in the North were preponderantly in the hands of Irish politicians. Hostility and at time intense antipathy had characterized the relations between Jews and Irish from the first decades of massive immigration of these two stocks. This deep-seated antagonism would eventually be mitigated by the gubernatorial and presidential candidacies of Alfred E. Smith and would disappear during the Kennedy era.

Theodore Roosevelt, in particular, had the strong support of Jewish voters. His friendship for individual Jews and his willingness to espouse Jewish causes was well known. On two occasions, he predicted that a Jew would some day be elected President and he earned the distinction of being the first American Chief Executive to name a Jew to a Cabinet post—Secretary of Commerce and Labor Oscar Straus. Both Roosevelt and his hand-picked successor, William Howard Taft, took diplomatic action against the Czarist Government because of the latter's complicity in the Kishinev massacre of Russian Jews in 1903.

The leading Jews in the United States backed Roosevelt. Jacob H. Schiff stated that he could not conceive of a Jewish voter failing to cast his ballot for the President.[1] The bulk of American Jewry was by now of Slavic origin and far more heavily working class than in the Civil War era and the Gilded Age. Hence, there were strong radical and Socialist undercurrents in American Jewry striving for political expression. However, this Russian element was still, to a very large extent, new and unacclimated and hence it tended to accept the guidance of the solidly established leaders of German Jewry. This condition could not be expected to prevail indefinitely.

The first major Democratic inroad into the Jewish vote occurred in 1912 when Woodrow Wilson ran for the Presidency for the first time. The *Boston Jewish Advocate* believed he deserved the support of American Jewry because "he has made culture the shining purpose of his life."[2]

There were no issues in the 1912 campaign of direct concern to Jews as Jews. The Jewish leadership and the Jewish vote split four ways. Louis Marshall, the outstanding leader of American Jewry and perhaps the most distinguished constitutional lawyer of his day, supported William Howard Taft; Henry Morgenthau returned to politics to support Woodrow Wilson; Oscar Straus backed Theodore Roosevelt and ran with him on the Progressive slate for Governor of New York; a large proportion of the Jewish vote went to the Socialist Party candidate, Eugene Victor Debs.

Under Wilson, the philo-Semitic policies of Theodore Roosevelt were continued and amplified. Morgenthau was given the post of Minister to Turkey, a strategic spot from the Jewish standpoint since the Ottoman Empire misruled Palestine and oppressed a large population of Jews and other non-Moslem minority peoples. Bernard Baruch was placed in charge of the mobilization of American industry for war and Wilson broke precedent by naming Louis Dembitz Brandeis to a seat on the Supreme Court. In New York State, which contained over half the Jewish population of the United States and which was a special area of concentration for Jews of Russian and East European origin, nine of the sixteen Jews elected to the Assembly were Democrats against only five Republicans and two Socialists.

The return to peace and "normalcy" brought the majority of American Jewry back into the Republican fold. The *B'nai B'rith News* paid a tribute to President Warren G. Harding on his death and praised his taciturn successor, Calvin Coolidge, as "a sturdy protector of law and order."[3]

In 1920, eleven Jews were elected to Congress—ten Republicans and one Socialist; the two Jewish Democratic candidates went down to defeat. In 1924, however, Progressive candidate for the Presidency, Robert M. Lafollette, running with Socialist Party endorsement, had a bigger vote in the most heavily Jewish districts of New York City than either the Republican or the Democratic standard-bearer.[4] This was a symptom of the fact that the political hegemony of German Jewry was rapidly crumbling.

Ku Klux Klan and Socialist Party

One of the forces influencing the gradual shift of American Jewry away from the Republican Party was the rise of the Ku Klux Klan. The Klan originally had been an organization of white Southerners of all classes to counteract the efforts of carpetbaggers, scalawags and Negroes to impose minority rule upon the South. It was led by such men as Confederate General Nathan Bedford Forrest and, if it resorted to violent measures, it did so in a milieu of race struggle and social upheaval.

The second Ku Klux Klan, which was born in 1915, had no common lineage with the first and was a very different sort of organization. A fraternal order, stressing "100% Americanism and the supremacy of the Caucasian race," this new Klan was apparently more interested in terrorizing and victimizing those it considered immoral than the Negroes, Catholics and Jews against whom it inveighed. Its distinctive quality, according to one of its historians, was "moral authoritarianism" and it served primarily as "an instrument for restoring law and order and Victorian morality. . . ."[5]

During World War I, the Klan served chiefly as a vigilante organization. Its growth began with the return to peacetime conditions when nationwide adverse publicity exposed its illegal activities and the financial manipulations of its leaders. These exposés had the entirely unexpected and undesired effect of causing the hooded order to gain membership at a spectacular rate. Between 1920 and 1924, the Klan increased its membership to a widely quoted maximum figure of six million. While this is almost certainly far in excess of its true enrollment, the Klan nonetheless was the largest and most powerful secret organization in American history.

As Seymour Martin Lipset has pointed out in a perceptive review of the literature about the Klan in its three incarnations, we know very little about such fundamental matters as the classes to which it appealed, the motivations of its members and the reasons for its rise and precipitate decline. The Klan was particularly strong in Southwestern cities which had been through a period of swift growth, suggesting the strong possibility that it appealed differentially to people without firm roots.

While there is some testimony that it appealed to the middle class, the weight of evidence is massively on the other side. As Grand Wizard Hiram Evans wrote in 1926:

"We are a movement of plain people, very weak in the matter of culture, intellectual support, and trained leadership. . . . This is undoubtedly a weakness. It lays us open to the charge of being 'hicks' and 'rubes' and 'drivers of second-hand Fords.' We admit it."

Lipset points out that in Kansas elections, Klan candidates drew their greatest strength from working-class districts and adds: "More interesting is the fact that a study of the Midwest Klan indicates that 'an impressive number of Milwaukee's Socialists also crossed the portals' of the Klan. A successful Socialist candidate for the Wisconsin Supreme Court was an avowed member and supporter of the Klan; he replied to the Socialists who attacked him for this by citing the large number of Socialists in the Klan. Working-class and Socialist voters backed the Klan in spite of its open animosity to trade unions and liberal political causes."[6]

In the early 1930's when the Klan was on the wane, Socialist organizers, after talking to the registered Socialist voters of a district, would sometimes be asked to come back in a few days to address a closed meeting of reliable people, "all true Socialists and Klansmen." Experiences of this sort would come as a disagreeable surprise to New York Socialists who imagined that the Party membership was immune from bigotry and certainly had nothing to do with anti-Semitism, basing this latter conclusion on the fact that the New York City membership was preponderantly Jewish.

The issue of the Ku Klux Klan threatened to split the Democratic Party. At its 1924 convention in New York City, William Gibbs McAdoo, the son-in-law of Woodrow Wilson, seemed the most powerful contender for the presidential nomination. In need of the votes of agrarian radical and Fundamentalist delegates, he assumed a stance of neutrality on the Klan issue and pandered to Klan populism by denouncing "sinister, unscrupulous, invisible government which has its seat in the citadel of privilege and finance in New York City."

Alfred E. Smith, an Irish Catholic from the working class, a product of parochial schools, a man who had served two terms as Governor of New York State and made an exemplary record, predictably demanded, to the cheers of galleries packed with Tammany followers, that the convention repudiate the Klan by name. The motion was defeated by one vote after William Jennings Bryan eloquently opposed it. McAdoo failed to win the nomination; a compromise candidate between the Smith and McAdoo factions, John W. Davis, seized the prize and went down to defeat by Calvin Coolidge.

In 1928, however, Smith did win the nomination. His presidential campaign became a rallying ground for anti-

Klan forces and as such captured the imagination and support of Jewish voters. Another factor in Smith's favor with American Jewry was his close personal and political association with Belle Moskowitz, who was both a nationally known leader of Jewish organizations and vice chairman of the Democratic National Committee. Jewish voters approved Smith's stress on social security and labor legislation, his support of civil liberties and his demand that public health services be enlarged.

With Al Smith its standard bearer, the Democratic Party now seemed to many Jews to be the rallying ground against the Klan and other movements of intolerance. In heavily Jewish districts of New York and Chicago, where Davis had polled only about a third of the total vote, Smith won 66% to 75% of the ballots.[7]

The permanence of this shift was signaled by the fact that two years later six of the eight Jews sent to Congress were Democrats.

In the 1932 elections, Franklin D. Roosevelt opposed the Republican incumbent, Herbert Hoover, in the fourth year of world depression. From the standpoint of specifically Jewish interests, there seemed to be no particular reason for preferring one candidate over the other. Both men had a record of friendship toward Jews. Domestic anti-Semitism was not a major force nor was it deemed a matter which lay within the powers of the federal government as defined by the Constitution.[8] Nazism was not yet a matter which aroused American Jews; in fact, Hitler would not be named Chancellor of the German Reich until two months after the election. To the extent that foreign affairs concerned Jewish voters, the apparent difference between the two candidates was that Hoover had a consistent and outstanding record of international cooperation, whereas Roosevelt seemed much more of an isolationist.[9] The Jews had, of course, suffered severe economic hardship during the depression, but they had suffered less than the other stocks of recent immigrants who had been economically less successful.

Yet the Jewish support for Roosevelt in 1932 was so overwhelming that it seemed almost unanimous. Fuchs, who has carefully analyzed the balloting in heavily Jewish electoral districts, points out that FDR received 84.7% of the vote in the 20 most Jewish precincts of Ward 24 of Chicago (which was over 90% Jewish). In the same precincts, 96% of the voters supported Henry Horner, the Democratic candidate for Governor, who was a Jew. In New York City, presidential candidate Roosevelt and gubernatorial candidate Herbert Lehman (Jewish) carried 92% of the two-party vote (that is to say, excluding the Jewish vote for the Socialist and Communist candidates) in the 17th Assembly District. In Boston, wards which had voted 78% Republican in 1928 went overwhelmingly Democratic four short years later.[10]

The Jews were not the only minority group which rallied behind the Roosevelt banner. As the protégé of Alfred E. Smith and the leader of the liberal wing of the Democratic Party, Roosevelt had overwhelming backing among Catholics, among stocks which had recently immigrated to the United States and among labor. The salient difference between the early Jewish support of Roosevelt and the backing given him by these other political blocs was that the Jewish identification was not based primarily on group self-interest. Jews, even those of a secular bent, saw in Roosevelt's programs the embodiment of ideals of brotherhood and charity which were deeply embedded in the ethical teachings of Judaism. The intensity of Jewish religious and ethical education made these concepts a vital part of the everyday lives and aspirations of ordinary Jews. This serves to explain the fact that Jewish support of Roosevelt did not lessen as one moved from the low-income to the high-income groups. It also serves in part to explain the intensity of this support and its consistency during the four campaigns in which Roosevelt sought and won the Presidency.

Henry Ford and Anti-Semitism

During this period, Henry Ford, production genius and political illiterate, spread the seeds of anti-Semitism more effectively than any other American. As Keith Sward, his most perceptive biographer, points out, Ford was a product of Populism, its callow radicalism, its conspiratorial conception of history and its Fundamentalist prejudices.

"Jew-baiting loomed large in the culture that had molded Ford," he wrote. "When the great anti-monopoly crusades swept out of the West from 1880 to the end of the century, *Puck* and the *Police Gazette* were caricaturing the Jew week after week. These journals, scattered over the hinterland, were given to lampooning the Jew as the villain of modern capitalism. They depicted Wall Street in lurid cartoons as a gigantic Jewish pawnshop. The same argument infiltrated the political thinking of the grain belt. When Ford was fifteen, in 1878, the Central Greenback Club of Detroit issued a philippic that laid the American railroad scandals and the hard times that followed the Civil War to the 'Rothschilds across the water.' The racialism of the back-country had taken some of its temper from organized religion. It was 'the Jews' whom the Protestants of the Bible Belt held accountable for the Crucifixion. More than that, Ford's native soil was Ku Klux Klan country."[11]

A first manifestation of Henry Ford's anti-Semitism was

his statement to Rosika Schwimmer, a Jewess who was enlisting Ford's cooperation in sending a "peace ship" to Europe in 1915 to persuade both sides to call off the war, that the Jews were responsible for that conflict. This observation was probably not taken very seriously at the time either by Mme. Schwimmer or anyone else, since Ford also blamed the conflict on liquor. Moreover, in his house organ, the *Dearborn Independent*, Ford fulminated against capitalist warmongers like any Populist or Socialist agitator.

Inveighing against "Wall Street Tories" and "armor-plate patriots," Ford denounced the "imperalists" who were selling arms to both sides to exploit the "common people."[12] He told newspaperman John Reed, later to win fame as eyewitness to the Bolshevik Revolution and author of *Ten Days That Shook the World*, that flags were "silly rallying points" for "crooked politicians" and profiteers and he promised, once the war was finally over, to haul down the American flag from his factory and raise instead a "Flag of All Nations" which he would have designed. Soldiers, he added, were either "lazy or crazy." In the event of American entry into the war, he promised to burn down his factory rather than fill arms orders. He appealed to the people to stop the war by direct action and offered to dedicate his "life and fortune" to peace.[13]

Ford went to Europe with Rosika Schwimmer and a retinue of insignificant and eccentric people in what Arthur Vandenburg (then a Michigan editor) described as a "loon ship." Since Ford's anti-Semitism was not directed against individual Jews, but was theoretical (that is to say, the most dangerous kind!), he invited such notables as Charles P. Steinmetz, Julius Rosenwald and Morris Hillquit to accompany him. These three and many distinguished non-Jews politely declined. Arriving in Europe, Ford was persuaded not to make more of an ass of himself by attempting to talk the governments of Europe into laying down their arms and he went home.

When the United States finally entered the war, Ford declared that it was "the best thing that ever happened" and urged the nation to back Uncle Sam "with a shotgun loaded to the muzzle with buckshot." Despite his previous threats to burn down his factory and his excoriation of war profiteers, he made another fortune on war contracts.

It would be easy to paint Ford as a scoundrel and a hypocrite except for the testimony of such observers as William C. Bullitt (then a newspaperman) that he was the "tenderest of the tender, the vaguest of the vague, a comic, charming child." (Ford at the time was 52.)

Like his great friend, Thomas Alva Edison, Ford was a free thinker, a Puritan in sexual matters, fanatically against alcohol, interested only in practical and tangible things, incapable of reading a balance sheet, and a monetary nut. Edison in his youth had been a disciple of "Coin" Harvey, "Sockless Jerry" Simpson and the other Greenback and Populist tub-thumpers of the day. In 1922, Edison advocated "pumpkin money," an idea lifted from Populist political platforms.[14]

Moreover, Ford theorized about civilization and the future of the world from a bottomless pit of almost total ignorance. During a 1916 libel suit, this exchange occurred:

Q. Do you know what "commenced" means?
A. Not very much acquainted with technical terms.
Q. Do you know of any great traitors?
A. No.
Q. Who was Benedict Arnold?
A. He was a writer, I guess.

Q. Mr. Ford, I have some hesitation, but I think in justice to yourself I shall ask this question: I think the impression has been created by your failure to read some of these things that have been presented to you, that you could not read. Do you want to leave it that way?

A. Yes, you can leave it that way. I am not a fast reader and I have the hay fever and I would make a botch of it.[15]

On May 22, 1920 Ford began an attack on Jewry with a front page editorial in the *Dearborn Independent* entitled "The International Jew: the World's Problem." The Jews were accused of "fouling the earth and plotting to dominate it" and of maintaining a clandestine "international super-capitalist government." The Jewish question was the "prime" issue for all mankind. This launched a campaign which was to continue for 91 consecutive issues.

Ford was so oblivious of the Jewish reaction to this campaign of hate that, when his old friend, Rabbi Leo M. Franklin, refused to accept the custom-built Ford that the auto magnate regularly gave him each year, he phoned the rabbi and asked: "What's wrong, Dr. Franklin? Has anything come between us?"[16]

There were two moving forces behind the anti-Semitic campaign. One was W. J. Cameron, a rural preacher turned journalist. Cameron was Ford's pen. He grumbled about being obliged to write the "cursed Jewish articles" and sneered at Ford behind the latter's back, but, faced with the choice between poisoning the American mind and sacrificing his salary, he chose the former.

Ernest Liebold lived up to his surname by collecting forged documents for Ford. A Czarist refugee named Boris

Brasol sold Liebold a notorious forgery known as the *Protocols of the Learned Elders of Zion* which purported to be the revelation of a secret plot by the Jews to gain control of the entire world and, if discovered, to blow up all the capitals of Europe. The document had first appeared in 1905 under the sponsorship of Serge Nilus, a Czarist official, as a means of arousing hatred against the Jews. Nilus had borrowed and plagiarized from a satire on Napoleon III which had appeared in France in 1864 and had nothing to do with the Jews.[17] Ford's men touched up the Nilus forgery to make it seem to refer to contemporary conditions in Europe and America.

The articles in the *Dearborn Independent* harped on the Protocols as their central theme. They blamed the Jews for being "lewd" and "erotic" and accused them of introducing chorus girls to the Broadway theatre to soften up the fiber of Gentile men. It was the Jews who plied America with liquor and corrupted the American mind with jazz. As a great expert on Benedict Arnold, Ford proclaimed that that traitor had been a Jewish agent.

Psychologically most interesting was Ford's charge that American Jews had dodged the draft in World War I. The facts of the matter were that Jews had then constituted 3.3% of the population, but had furnished 5.7% of the total American forces and 5.7% of the total American death roll. Over 20% of the Jewish soldiers were volunteers and more than 10,000 were officers. The dangerous branches of infantry and signal-aviation corps accounted for 26.6% and 6.5% of the American total, but 48% and 15% of the American Jewish total. If it was utterly false that the Jews had shirked their military duties, it was quite true that Ford himself had maligned American soldiers, urged them not to fight for their country and used every bit of influence at his command to enable his draft-age son, Edsel, to avoid military service.[18]

Over a hundred eminent Americans, among them former Presidents Woodrow Wilson and William Howard Taft, Jane Addams and William Jennings Bryan, had sent a public protest to Ford about his anti-Semitic articles, without effect. The presence of Bryan's name on this distinguished roster of non-Jews was interesting because he was frequently referred to as "the greatest Klansman of them all." To be sure, Bryan shared the Klan view that the Negro should be segregated. However, he was not anti-Jewish in any sense of the word and in fact served on the American Committee on the Rights of Religious Minorities, often spoke out in defense of Catholics and Jews, refused to support Ford's presidential aspirations because of the latter's anti-Semitism, denounced the *Protocols of the Learned Elders of Zion* as a forgery and called it a libel on "one of the greatest races in history."[19] (This, in short, was another case in which the contemporary liberal Jewish identification of anti-Negro with anti-Semitic attitudes had no basis whatsoever in reality.)

The campaign of hatred continued unabated for seven years. It attacked Americans for "flabby tolerance" of the Jews, praised the Ku Klux Klan for its anti-Semitism, demanded that Gentiles develop the "gristle to attack" and predicted the "exodus" of Jews from America.[20]

Ford's vituperative articles had spread around the world and been translated into a dozen languages. In late 1922, a *New York Times* correspondent went to Hitler's private office. The wall behind the future Fuehrer's desk was covered with a large picture of Henry Ford and "in the antechamber there is a large table covered with books, nearly all of which are a translation of a book . . . published by Henry Ford."

In America, the vast network of Ford dealers was pressured into selling subscriptions to the *Dearborn Independent* on pain of losing their franchises. In a letter to President Calvin Coolidge, the distinguished attorney and Jewish leader, Louis Marshall, commented as follows:

"The articles published abound in monumental falsehoods and malicious inventions, couched in virulent terms and designed to arouse suspicion, hatred and prejudice against those of the Jewish faith. There is no libel, no product of superstition or base concoction, that has ever been aimed at the Jews, that has not been rehashed in the columns of this sheet. . . .

"The Ford Motor Company thus seeks to coerce its agents, by means of carefully phrased threats, into becoming distributors of propaganda calculated to poison the public mind against the Jews, indifferent to the consequences, and designed not only to arouse the spirit of intolerance, but to inflict lasting injury upon the entire country, by sowing the evil seeds of racial and religious animosity.

"I am confident that it is within your power to abate this iniquity."[21]

Then in 1927, Ford made the mistake of leveling damaging charges against Aaron Sapiro, a Jewish attorney and organizer of cooperatives. Sapiro sued for a million dollars and a subpoena was finally, with great difficulty, served upon Ford.

Faced with a lawsuit in which he would be compelled to testify and be virtually certain to be torn apart in cross examination and also concerned over the fact that the Ford Motor Company was losing out to its competitors, Ford sent emissaries to Marshall for a settlement of the dispute. With the unmanly cowardice and country bumpkin slyness that he so often displayed in a crisis, Ford shifted the entire blame onto Cameron and Liebold, falsely alleging that they had acted without his knowledge or consent. The formal statement said that Ford had not participated personally in "the publication of the articles and has no personal knowledge of what was said in them." He apologized to American Jews for the "gross forgeries" published in his paper, claimed that he was "an honorable man" and as such duty bound "to make amends for the wrong done to Jews as fellowmen and brothers by asking their forgiveness for the harm that I have unintentionally committed . . . and by giving them the unqualified assurance that henceforth they may look to me for friendship and good will." Ford sent a separate apology to the Anti-Defamation League and gave his assurance that the *Independent* would never again print anti-Semitic articles.

Despite this promise, the Ford Motor Company in the 1920's offered employment to German Nazi agents and in the 1930's no less a Nazi than Fritz Kuhn, Fuehrer of the German American Bund, was on the Ford payroll.

After Hitler seized power, Ford's books, *The International Jew* and the *Protocols*, were translated and disseminated on a worldwide basis by a Nazi propaganda bureau over Ford's signature. Efforts by Congressman Dickstein and Louis Untermeyer to get Ford to repudiate the publications and stop the use of his name were evaded.

In 1938, Henry Ford received and accepted from Adolf Hitler the Award of the Grand Cross of the German Eagle, the highest award that the German Reich could bestow. When the America First Committee was launched, Henry Ford became one of its members. He predicted that Britain would lose the war.

Then came Pearl Harbor and another chameleon-like change. Ford informed the Anti-Defamation League that anti-Jewish propaganda must "cease for all time" and that it serves only to "divide our American community and to weaken our national unity." W. J. Cameron echoed his master on the Ford Sunday Evening Hour. Anti-Semitism, he declared, "is scurrilous stuff, a vestige of tribal barbarism, the negation of humanity, intelligence and Christianity." In the end, the "deadly acid" consumed the anti-Semite himself.[22] These were words from one who knew.

CHAPTER 9

Socialism, Communism and the Far Left

THE TIDE OF RUSSIAN JEWISH IMMIGRATION into the United States began in 1881 and soon thereafter Jewish participation in the American labor and Socialist movements became significant. The United Hebrew Trades was organized in 1888, for the most part by young Jewish intellectuals. They also joined the Socialist Labor Party which previously had been an almost totally German organization.[1] When Morris Hillquit began his career as a Socialist leader, the Party had one English weekly and soon thereafter founded an "American section" in New York City. "In our zeal for the cause," Hillquit reminisced, "we did not even appreciate the exquisite humor of a political party of the United States establishing a solitary 'American section' in the metropolis of the country."[2]

The Socialist Labor Party was dominated by Daniel De Leon, who was widely reputed to be a Sephardic Jew, but described himself as a "respectable Venezuelan Catholic."[3] De Leon originated the concept of Soviets and was, in Lenin's opinion, the only American who made an original and valuable contribution to Marxism. In his effort to capture the trade union movement and turn it into a vehicle of proletarian revolution, De Leon set up a new organization, the Socialist Trades and Labor Alliance. An ideological purist who never hesitated to split organizations over doctrinaire issues, he encountered the opposition of the Jewish labor leaders. The latter sided with the American Federation of Labor (AFL), and contributed to his isolation and decisive defeat.

Toward the close of the century, the Jewish groups involved in the labor and Socialist movements were, for the most part, moderates. The outstanding individual leader of Jewish extraction was the London-born cigar worker, Samuel Gompers, who headed the American Federation of Labor. More than any other man, Gompers was responsible for creating the American labor movement and fixing it in the non-Socialist mold it has maintained ever since. At one time a follower of Marx, he had become disgusted at the way Marx's Socialist followers sacrificed the immediate, bread-and-butter interests of the working people for political, revolutionary goals.

The "golden age" of the American Socialist Party was the 1902-1912 decade. Nationally, the organization was a fusion of variegated elements. There were hard-core revolutionary Marxists of the De Leon stripe, the remnants of Populist agrarian discontent, social reformers, Yiddish and other special language groups organized for the most part in trade unions that were more concerned with wages and working conditions than revolution, the wild anarcho-syndicalist and *lumpenproletarian* element of the IWW, Bohemians, a scattering of millionaires, do-good social workers and intellectuals, food fadists, militant atheists and eccentrics of every variety.

By 1912, there were 125,826 members of the Socialist Party—an all-time peak. Over a thousand Socialists held elective public office, including 56 mayors, 160 councilmen and 145 aldermen. Victor Berger of Wisconsin represented the party in Congress.[4]

The key influence for Socialism among American Jews was *The Forward*, which spoke to the East European Jewish workers and small tradesmen in their Yiddish tongue and at one time had a circulation of a quarter of a million. *The Forward* "bound together the Jewish community and made it socialist."[5]

Labor and Socialist strength among the Jews of New York and the other great Atlantic seaboard cities did not develop until more than a generation after the beginning of the Jewish exodus from Russia. The first great strike of Jewish workers was that of the waistmakers in 1909. The Amalgamated Clothing Workers of America, destined to become one of the two most powerful of the preponderantly Jewish labor organizations, elected Sidney Hillman its first president in 1914. The other key Jewish union in the clothing industry, the International Ladies' Garment Workers, began to win contracts from industry only during the second decade of the present century. A Jewish organization which was perhaps equally important at that time was the Workmen's Circle, a fraternal and insurance society, which was launched in 1905 and became a powerful force among Jewish labor a decade later.

The main reason for the lag of about a generation before

the Jewish immigration of Slavic origin turned toward Socialism was the power of Judaism. As long as religious traditions remained substantially intact, the Socialist doctrine lacked mass appeal. To many Jews, however, Judaism seemed irrelevant to the new American environment and their search for a substitute led them to the secular religious surrogates of Socialism and later Communism.

Socialists, Jews and World War I

In 1912, when the American Socialist Party was at its maximum strength, its membership and voter appeal were concentrated in rural and mining areas in the West and Southwest. In the next eight years, the Party shifted its geographic and ethnic base to the urban, industrialized East, where it developed differential attraction for foreign-born, and particularly Jewish, workers. During the first two decades of the twentieth century, New York never contributed more than 10% of the total Socialist vote; but by 1920, it accounted for 20% of Debs's nationwide total of 900,000 ballots.[6]

When the United States entered the First World War, Morris Hillquit and two other Socialist leaders prepared a declaration of unequivocal opposition which was promptly endorsed by the St. Louis convention of the Party. The war was characterized as a "mad orgy of death and destruction . . . caused by the conflict of capitalist interests." Wilson's declaration of war against Germany was branded a crime against the American people instigated by "predatory capitalists" and war profiteers. As a result of this stance, the Socialist Party was branded an agent of Imperial Germany, repudiated by the AFL and deserted by three-fifths of its members.

The heaviest defections were among the native-born and the more patriotic and moderate elements. Practically all the intellectuals of national reputation and stature defected. The Party press was denied mailing privileges and Socialist militants were prosecuted under the Espionage Act.

The Socialist denunciation of World War I as a capitalist plot against the working class of the world was consistent with Marxism and with the Populist view that the organs of American government were tools of the money power for the exploitation of the people. Underestimation of the value of political freedom and republican institutions would characterize the Party in World War I and in the early stages of World War II. In the first conflict, the Socialist Party preached subversion of the American war effort and in Oklahoma about two thousand irate farmers, many of them Socialists, took arms to paralyze recruiting. These night riders burned railroad bridges and committed widespread acts of sabotage. The so-called Green Corn Rebellion was crushed in a few months and 86 of its activists were sent to the penitentiary.

In addition to opposition to the draft, there was outright pro-German sentiment. For example, Victor Berger, one of the three top leaders of the Socialist Party and a Wisconsin politician, claimed that he had always hated the Kaiser, but "when I see the world taking arms against him, I feel that I must seize a rifle and take my place in the ranks and fight for him."[7]

The strong anti-war stance of the Socialist Party eventually brought in new elements and by 1919 membership was back to 110,000. But the composition of the party had changed drastically. The foreign-language sections, which had embraced less than 12% of the prewar Socialist membership now constituted a 53% majority. Of these, the

Slavic federations, embracing a powerful cohesive bloc of one-fifth of the Party membership, would later constitute the nucleus of the Communist Party. These Slavic federations were preponderantly Jewish.

The sudden growth of Jewish interest in militant Socialism was a consequence of the two Russian Revolutions of 1917. The first of these destroyed Czardom, a hated organ of centuries-long oppression, and substituted democratic institutions. The second, the Bolshevik Revolution, fired the imagination of many in a war-weary world and seemed to them to promise a new social order that would bring justice, brotherhood and peace.

Shortly after the first, democratic (Kerensky) Russian Revolution of March 1917, meetings were held in New York City to launch a left-wing movement to capture control of the Socialist Party and drive it toward sabotage and other illegal anti-war activities. The designated leaders of this left wing were two Russian exiles temporarily stranded in the United States—Leon Trotsky and Alexandra Kollontay. The Russian Revolution moved toward the left, however, and Trotsky and Kollontay plunged into its vortex, leaving the organization of the American Socialist left wing to less illustrious revolutionaries.

Of the three major leaders of the Socialist Party during World War I, Morris Hillquit, who was a Jew, was the most intellectual, moderate and constructive in his approach. Eugene Victor Debs, the Party's standard-bearer, was a man of extraordinary eloquence and purity of heart, but naive, credulous, badly informed, deficient in judgment and muddled in mentality. The third leader, Victor Berger, was an extremely able organizer and more of a social reformer than a revolutionary. Roche, a pro-Socialist source, makes the extraordinary statement that Berger was "one of the least lovable figures in the movement" and a man who had "built up a reputation as an anti-Semite by his unrestrained attacks on the New York Jewish wing of the party. . . ."[8] Actually, although he concealed the fact for reasons of political expediency, Berger was a Jew. Marx Lewis, who was his secretary when Berger served as a Congressman, considers Roche's charge groundless and informs me that Berger was an early supporter of a Jewish national homeland in Palestine.[9]

Jews and the American Communist Party

At its 1919 convention, the Socialist Party was split asunder by its left wing, which boasted the sympathy or adherence of some 70,000 card-carrying Socialist members. These left-wingers were organized, for the most part, in the Slavic language federations. When the showdown came, they either joined one of the two rival revolutionary organizations—the Communist Party and the Communist Labor Party—or else, disillusioned by factional bickering, dropped out of the left-wing movement.

As for the Socialist Party, it had ceased to be a significant national force. It surfaced in 1921 with a paper membership of 10,000 and was kept alive for many years thereafter chiefly by the prestige and charisma of its national leader, Norman Thomas, who polled 915,000 votes in 1932.

When the 1919 convention was over, a maximum of 40,000 Socialists had signed up as members of the two Red parties. Of these, perhaps 27,000 were in the Communist Party, of whom only 1,900 were officially characterized as English-speaking. Over three-fourths of the membership was organized in Slavic, Baltic and Jewish language federations. The rival group, the Communist Labor Party, probably had about 10,000 members and was also overwhelmingly Slavic. According to Benjamin Gitlow, a defected founder and leader of American Communism, the total membership of the two parties was closer to 25,000 than to 40,000.[10] The alien nature of American Communism was revealed by the complaint of its leader, Charles Ruthenberg, that in 1920 it didn't have five speakers able to present its case in the English language.

The "Palmer raids" by the Department of Justice reduced the membership of the Communist Party by more than 50 per cent between 1919 and 1920. The English-speaking membership declined by two-thirds and the East European membership increased from 75% to 82% of the total.

During the ensuing twenty years, the Communist Party of the United States remained a preponderantly foreign organization, but the extent to which it was a Jewish movement remained a matter of dispute. In his second volume on the history of the Party, Draper claimed that, during the 1920's, only about 15% of the Communist Party members were Jews.[11] It is difficult to take this statement seriously. For one thing, the *Freiheit*, a Yiddish language paper, boasted the largest circulation of any Communist daily: it had 22,000 readers as against the *Daily Worker's* 17,000 in 1925. For another, accounts by people who were Communists at the time agree in describing the movement as preponderantly Jewish.

The most thorough treatment of this matter is in Nathan Glazer's *The Social Basis of American Communism*. He evidently concludes, though he does not explicitly so state, that a majority of the Communist Party membership in the thirties and forties may have been Jewish. The evidence that he musters on this point is worth summarizing:

Although Communist leaders were normally taciturn about the extent to which Party membership was Jewish, Jack Stachel complained in *The Communist* for April 1929 that in Los Angeles "practically 90 per cent of the membership is Jewish." In 1945, John Williamson, another national leader of the American Communist Party, observed that, while a seventh of the Party membership was concentrated in Brooklyn, it was not in the working-class districts, but in Brownsville, Williamsburg, Coney Island and Bensonhurst, which he characterized as "primarily Jewish American communities." In 1951, the same complaint about Brooklyn was reiterated. A 1938 breakdown of Communist educational directors on a district level reported that 17 out of 34 were Jewish and only nine "American." The extent to which American Communism remained an organization of the foreign-born was revealed by a boast in *The Communist* for July 1936 that 45% of Party section organizers were now native-born as against none native-born in 1934.[12]

These estimates can be compared to data made public by then Attorney General Tom C. Clark on the national origins of 4,984 of "the more militant members of the Communist Party" in 1947. This showed that 44.0% were Russian-born, had at least one Russian parent or had a spouse of Russian stock. Only 8.6% were American-born of American parentage and not wed to spouses of foreign stock.[13] From this, I arrived at an estimate that about 40% of the Communist Party militants in 1947 were Jewish.[14]

The Jewish recruits to American Communism were, for the most part, solidly middle class and professional. They were concentrated in such professional organizations as the Teachers' Union which, according to the former Communist leader, Bella Dodd, had 4,000 members, of whom 1,000 were Communist Party members.[15] Based on scrutiny of surnames, Glazer concluded that all of the "Rank and

File" (Communist) teachers placed on trial by the Teachers' Union in 1932 were Jewish.[16] Jewish social workers provided another fertile field for Party recruitment. To a quantitatively less significant extent, government employees, lawyers, dentists and doctors were attracted to the movement, particularly during the years of the Popular Front (1935-39) and the World War II alliance with the Soviet Union.

If Jews were prominent in both the leadership and the membership of the American Communist Party, it did not therefore follow that a significantly large proportion of American Jewry was Communist. The membership of the Communist Party seldom exceeded 50,000 and was below 25,000 most of the time. By contrast, there were over 5,000,000 Jews in the United States.

Moreover, Jews played a leading and invaluable role in the organization of anti-Communist forces and in the education of the American people on the evils of Communism and the Soviet system. Among the more outstanding of these Jewish anti-Communist editors and writers were David Lawrence, Eugene Lyons, George Sokolsky, Victor Riesel, Bertram D. Wolfe, Isaac Don Levine, Ralph de Toledano and Victor Lasky. Most of these men exposed the Communist conspiracy at a time when it was neither fashionable nor profitable to do so. They risked their incomes and their careers and, in some cases, invited physical danger as well. In such varied fields as trade unions, politics, education and the arts, one could compile similar lists of Jewish anti-Communists without any difficulty.

Reactions to Red Anti-Semitism

In 1929, massacres of Jews by Palestine Arabs were described by the *Freiheit*, New York's Communist Party

Yiddish organ, as a "pogrom." The Party promptly repri-
manded the *Freiheit* for having failed to realize that these
murders were a "class war . . . against British imperialism
and their Zionist agents." The *Freiheit* proceeded to report
the Palestine struggle in a Nazi fashion. "Indeed," com-
ments Glazer, "the cartoons it ran of hook-nosed and
bloated Jews sadistically attacking Arabs could have appeared in any German anti-Semitic newspaper."[17]

This was a turning point. From then on, all the major
Jewish organizations became anti-Communist. This applied
to the central religious bodies, to the Anti-Defamation
League of B'nai B'rith, to the American Jewish Committee,
to the American Jewish Congress, to Hadassah and to the
Jewish community organizations.

The first great test of conscience for American Jewish
Communists was the Soviet *volte face* in 1939. During the
period of the Nazi-Soviet Pact, the Communist Party
caused anguish among its Jewish members by abandoning
its boycott of Nazi goods. The week after the Pact was
signed, the *Daily Worker* described it as "a triumph in the
fight against anti-Semitism."[18] In his pamphlet, *The Jewish
People and the War*, Earl Browder argued that it made no
difference to the Jews whether the Nazis or the Allies won![19]

The *Freiheit* claimed that the Soviet invasion of Poland
had been "good for the Jews" because, while two million
Polish Jews fell under the yoke of Hitler, the remaining
million had the privilege of being liberated by the Red
Army. Typical of the Jewish reaction to this casuistry was
the statement of the Zionist *Yiddisher Kempfer* that Stalin
had caused the war by freeing Hitler from the need of fighting on two fronts. It added: "We reject with loathing the
saving of a million Jews when it is bought at such a price."[20]

Leading Yiddish writers and a few Jewish intellectuals

left the Party. Despite an admitted 15% decline in Communist membership, most Jewish Reds remained in its ranks.[21] They proved that they were Marxists-Leninists first and Jews second, if at all.

The American Communist Party and its Jewish membership in particular were deeply shaken by Khrushchev's secret 1956 report on Stalin's crimes. American Communist Jews were finally forced to admit to themselves that the leading Jewish intellectuals of the Soviet Union had been exterminated under Stalin, that Jewish cultural institutions had been wiped out and that Russian Jewry had faced the danger of total deportation to Siberia.

Studying the scanty material available on Communist defections after this shattering blow, Nathan Glazer came to the conclusion that a disproportionate number of second-generation Jews (born in the United States, but of foreign-born parents) either joined the rebel Communist faction under John Gates or left the Party in disgust. The older, Yiddish-speaking Communists stayed.[22] One reason for this fidelity was that they had nowhere else to go. As for the defection of some of the second-generation Jews in 1956 and immediately thereafter, it is worth recalling that the anti-Semitic policies of Stalin may not have been the main reason. Two factors of perhaps equal importance were the official exposure of the Stalin regime as one of naked terrorism and the brutal suppression of the Hungarian popular uprising by Soviet armor in November 1956.

Jewry and Communism—the Dilemma

Ideologically committed to the notion that the strength of the movement depended upon the proletariat and not the middle class, the Communist Party made little effort to attract Jewish members. Its organizational publications were filled with breast-beating about the high proportion of middle-class elements: sometimes these were specifically identified as Jewish middle-class elements. Nor did the Party seek to adjust or conceal its policies as a means of attracting or appeasing Jews. With one brief exception, its attitude toward Zionism and the new state of Israel was one of unwavering hostility. It consistently supported Arab claims against Jewish claims, a line which inevitably implied the destruction of the state of Israel, and consequently the loss of hundreds of thousands of Jewish lives by military action.

Nevertheless, the Party continued to attract American Jews. It is true that it attracted only a minority of these Jews, but it was a proportionately much larger minority than the minority of Irish or Italians or Scandinavians who felt the appeal of Communism.

There are many possible contributory causes and explanations. The Communist Party in the United States is, and always has been, primarily a middle-class movement with especial strength in the large cities and among the intellectuals and the professionals. Ironically, whatever strength and influence it has managed to exert has been due to this fact. The ideology of Marxism-Leninism teaches that the proletariat is the invincible engine destined to revolutionize society, that the middle class is vacillating and vanishing and that the intellectuals are politically contemptible. The facts of life are that manual workers can exercise very little influence on political events, whereas the middle class, and above all the professionals and the intellectuals, are an extremely powerful force.

One reason for the strong Jewish component in American Communism, then, is the simple fact that the Jews of the

United States are concentrated in the great cities, very strongly concentrated in the professions and even more massively represented in the intellectual community.

Another reason is the widespread and drastic breakdown of Judaism during the past two generations. This has left a void and American Jews have searched for substitutes. Given their memories of the ghetto and of past epidemics of persecution, Jews have been prone to emphasize the ideal of brotherhood and to search for secular religions that promise a universal utopia.

For many reasons, Jews have tended to cling to the belief that Socialist or Communist movements would create a world in which all men would live in peace and anti-Semitism would vanish. As historic evidence controverting this expectation accumulated, American Jews reluctantly began to abandon the secular collectivist faith, but the illusion that equality and fraternity are the promise of the left dies slowly and dies hard.

CHAPTER 10

Fascist and Pro-Nazi Movements

FASCIST AND ANTI-SEMITIC MOVEMENTS acquired a power and importance in the United States during the twelve years of the Roosevelt era that they had never had previously. During the great depression, revolutionary movements of all sorts sprouted in the soil of despair. These included the Socialist and Communist organizations and their various splinter groups, fascist and anti-Semitic societies of every shape and variety, mass movements based on instant economic panaceas that would transform cane cutters into kings, mad money schemes, spiritualist revivals, movements based on visions, technocratic plans for the reorganization of society and plain rackets that fattened their unscrupulous leaders on the contributions of the ignorant, the deluded and the credulous.

During the worst years of the great depression, these mushrooming organizations were noisy, but insignificant. When the New Deal failed to eliminate unemployment or to bring about any real and durable economic revival, disillusionment once again became widespread. Out of this arose an incipient coalition of demagogic mass movements, resembling both fascism and Populism and seemingly strong enough to threaten the power structure of the New Deal.

This threat was averted by the assassination of the man who seemed destined to take over national leadership of this new political force—Huey Long of Louisiana. With Long dead, the fascist, anti-Semitic and Nazi coloration of the movement became more intense. The issue of more drastic governmental measures to bring about economic recovery now merged into, and in short order was submerged by, the issue of America's stance in the gathering international conflict.

The final manifestation of the American fascist movement was the coalition of groups that banded together to prevent the United States from throwing her power on the side of the Western democracies in World War II. This was a bewildering amalgam of pacifists, old-fashioned isolationists, professional Jew-baiters, Socialists, fascists, Anglophobes, Nazis and outright German agents. Pearl Harbor destroyed it as a mass movement. The one leader of any national stature who had chosen to identify himself with this rabble, Colonel Charles A. Lindbergh, abandoned it and dedicated his energies to the American war effort. The decent elements dispersed, leaving the outright fanatics, the subversives—the hard core of sedition. These were either dealt with by the courts or else allowed to continue their propaganda activities among the little sects of the political underworld.

Father Coughlin and Huey Long

Father Charles E. Coughlin, the silver-tongued Detroit radio priest, was not the most powerful figure in the American proto-fascist movement. That distinction belonged to Senator Huey Long of Louisiana (the Kingfish). Coughlin's distinction was the much less enviable one of being the most powerful spokesman American anti-Semites have ever had, with the possible exceptions of Thomas Watson and Henry Ford.

Huey Long had nothing against Jews; as a matter of fact, he had many Jewish friends. He had no use for the Nazis and realized that Jews outnumbered Germans in Louisiana by about two dozen to one. His ideology was more Socialist than Populist. He came from Winn Parish, where Socialist spellbinders had talked class war and the iniquities of capitalist exploitation and where IWW militants and lumber company henchmen had shot out their differences.[1]

Nevertheless, if Long had lived, he would almost certainly have launched a third party in 1936 with himself as presidential candidate.[2] There is good reason to believe that that party would would have moved inevitably in a fascist direction. Certainly Lawrence Dennis, the saturnine and brilliant intellectual leader of what he believed to be "the coming American fascism," thought this. He considered Huey Long "the nearest approach to a national fascist leader" America had yet seen and hailed Long and Coughlin as men who were not "as yet fascists or friends of fascism," but who were making fascism "the alternative to chaos and national disintegration." He thought Long "smarter than Hitler," but still in need of a brain-trust.[3]

Moreover, Long's national director was Gerald L. K. Smith, a former hard-shell preacher, a spellbinder and a man who had previously promised would-be American Nazi Fuehrer, William Dudley Pelley, that he would organize storm troops for him. Smith would spend the next thirty years in a vain effort to organize politically effective fascist and anti-Semitic movements and in the process would gradually sink deeper into the murk of the political underworld.

On September 8, 1935, a bullet in the Kingfish's belly put an end to these nightmarish perspectives. The spotlight passed to Father Charles E. Coughlin, a Detroit priest in his middle forties, whose weekly radio program reached about ten million listeners and brought him half a million a year in contributions and as many as a million letters weekly. Coughlin's staff of 150 did its best to answer the letters.

Nine years before, Father Coughlin had launched the "Golden Hour of the Little Flower" and it had almost instantly become a popular religious program. Soon he turned to the political scene with vigorous denunciations of Communism. At the same time, he asserted that the conservative was the "wolf in sheep's clothing" who was the most dangerous of all Communists because he was determined to perpetuate the "policies of greed."[3-A]

There were other ingredients for this witches' brew of ideological confusions that was eventually to turn into something very similar to the fascist ideologies then rising toward power in Central Europe. Like the Populists, Coughlin was consistent in his preoccupation with monetary policy, his hatred of the international bankers and his advocacy of every sort of inflationary policy on the horizon, from the devaluation of the dollar and the free monetization of silver to the more far-out inflationary devices gaining popularity among the California leaders of the mass marches from depression into utopia.

At first, he was an enthusiastic backer of Roosevelt and the New Deal. The choice was between "Roosevelt and ruin;" the New Deal was "Christ's deal." The fact that some sort of entente was possible between the Roosevelt Administration and a priest who believed that capitalism was utterly doomed and that the world must return to the sort of regulated system of guilds, fixed prices and wages, and laws against usury that had prevailed in the Middle Ages merely illustrated the degree of ideological confusion on both sides.

This uneasy alliance continued in a faltering fashion until 1935. In the spring of that year, Brigadier General Hugh S. Johnson, the former Administrator of NRA, now a radio commentator and writer, let loose a blast in *Redbook* at the political alliance then hesitantly taking shape between Long and Coughlin.

"These two patriots may have been reading last summer's lurid story about an American Hitler riding into Washington at the head of troops," Johnson wrote. "That would be definite enough to Huey because he knows what part of the horse he can be, but we have a right to object most vigorously to the sanctification of such a centaur by having the head wear the collar of Rome and come intoning the stately measures of the church in pious benediction on such a monstrosity."

Referring to Coughlin's radio addresses "as blatant bunk from the very rostrum of religion," he called upon the

American people to reject the "magic financial hair tonic put up by partnership of a priest and a Punchinello, guaranteed to grow economic whiskers on a billiard ball overnight."[4]

Six months later Long was dead and Coughlin described his murder as "the most regrettable thing in modern history." As the 1936 presidential campaign approached, Coughlin was driven reluctantly toward the idea of a third party, which would be an anti-Roosevelt alliance of malcontents. Coughlin's Social Justice movement mobilized behind the presidential aspirations of Congressman William Lemke, standard-bearer of the so-called Union Party. The platform and campaign were almost pure Coughlin with their heavy stress on monetary reforms and inflationary devices, their denunciation of the "Communistic philosophy" of the New Deal and their even more bitter excoriation of the Republican Party for allegedly breeding Communists with its outworn policies of economic royalism.

The other ingredients in this new alliance were Dr. Francis E. Townsend, an honest California doctor, whose pension plan for the aged had become a nationwide crusade, and the sinister Gerald L. K. Smith. Smith would harangue vast audiences and rouse them to such a pitch that they would promise to hang anyone who interrupted him. As for Coughlin, he privately admitted that he was afraid of Smith.[4-A] When the votes were counted, the Lemke ticket went down to disastrous defeat, having polled fewer than a million votes, and the Union Party was dissolved.

Nineteen thirty-six was the turning point. Until then, the Coughlin movement and its National Union for Social Justice had been an alliance based upon economic discontent, advocating a large number of ill-considered measures designed to bring back prosperity and capitalizing on

Roosevelt's evident failure to restore anything approximating full employment. When the movement went down to crushing electoral defeat, when Coughlin discovered that Roosevelt was still a political magician who could pull landslide victories out of paltry economic achievement, he evidently decided that there was no point in proceeding along a road that led nowhere.

Father Coughlin, perhaps foolishly, crossed his Rubicon and in a radio address characterized the President of the United States as a "liar," a "scab" and a "betrayer." The Vatican took a hard look at the priest of the Shrine of the Little Flower and, through *l'Osservatore Romano*, criticized him for extremism.[4-B]

The crisis on the horizon was the expansion of Nazi Germany toward European, and later, world conquest. An aware minority of Americans anxiously watched the unfolding German tragedy and wondered when the impending struggle between Nazism and the Atlantic Powers would erupt and whether American involvement would not be necessary to Free World survival.

Another minority was also farsighted, but was determined to keep America isolated from the coming crisis. Pacifists and those who believed that American national interests could best be served by remaining aloof from Old World conflicts found themselves in reluctant association with those who consciously sought to bring about Nazi victory on a global scale. The logic of political conflict would drive dissenters, who had begun as honest pacifists or isolationists, toward political anti-Semitism and partisanship of Nazi aims.

The National Union of Social Justice was transformed into the Christian Front Movement. In 1937, Father Coughlin first stressed anti-Semitism as a major theme. In late 1938, he began quoting from the *Protocols of the Learned Elders of Zion* as proof of a supposed "Jew-Bolshevik plot" to conquer and then destroy the world. When his attention was called to the fact that the *Protocols* had been decisively exposed decades before as a forgery, Coughlin made the extraordinary statement that he was interested, not in their "authenticity," but in their "factuality."[5]

A General Jewish Council was organized to combat this campaign, consisting of the American Jewish Committee, the American Jewish Congress, the ADL and the Jewish Labor Committee. The Council did a superlative job of refutation, one of its main achievements being the printing in parallel columns of an article by Coughlin and a speech by Goebbels. The similarities were damning enough to convince millions of Americans that Coughlin had ceased to be an independent critic and had become a mouthpiece of Nazi propaganda.

The Hard Core and the Underworld

"When the MAD MOB gets in MOTION make sure that they dig all the blood-sucking banksters out from under their piles of rock and steel. Line them up against a wall and SHOOT them. . . . Now we are to give up our LIVES for the Delusions of Grandeur of a Merciless Monster, FRANKLIN DELANO ROOSEVELT, SOME NECK— for a ROPE."

This quotation, complete with capitalizations and block letters, represents the political thinking of George W. Christians, one of the hard-core leaders of the American fascist underground, a man convicted of sedition in 1942.

Thirty of these Nazis and alleged Nazi sympathizers were

put on trial for seditious conspiracy in 1944. For the most part, they were a scurvy lot, often with criminal records, who compensated for their own richly deserved sense of inferiority by living in worlds of fantasy. For example, there was a shifty-eyed little man of Greek-Polish origin and un-pronounceable nomenclature who had been confined in an asylum and dishonorably discharged from the Army. He called himself C. Leon de Aryan. Another defendant was the Duke of St. Saba, who was also known as Lieutenant General Count V. Cherep-Spiridovich. Actually, he was a small-time Indiana lawyer named Broenstrupp, who made a poor living on the side by soliciting money from aging and credulous women. Another was Silver Shirt Fuehrer William Dudley Pelley who claimed that he had died and gone to Heaven.

With the exception of Lawrence Dennis, a misfit in this menagerie, there no intellectuals among them. The fact that they were a mangy lot, short on education, brains and integrity, did not prevent them from being dangerous. There were outright organizations of terror such as the Iron Guard. Its leader, James Banahan, told undercover agent John Roy Carlson: "You'll be known as the Death Legion, and will specialize in terror. . . . Not faith, hope and charity, but faith, hope and terror. . . . In time of war, we are all sabo-teurs. We'll blow the hell out of this country."

A similar, but more effective, Irish American Nazi was Joseph Ellsworth McWilliams, Yorkville Fuehrer and head of the American Destiny Party. A former Communist, who had lived with and sponged on Jewish friends, McWilliams tried to apply Communist and Nazi methods of street war-fare to the United States. He boasted of recruiting "the meanest, the toughest, the most ornery bunch of German soldiers, Italian veterans and Irish IRA men in the country."

With a convicted pimp and a burglar as his henchmen, McWilliams beat up policemen in the streets of New York. Open violence against Jews was part of the basic plan to build a mass movement around hard-core nuclei of terrorists. These assaults were to polarize public opinion and strengthen the ranks of the Nazi terrorist brigades.[6] In retrospect, these movements of nihilism seem unimportant and more appropriate subjects for a book on crime than one on politics. At the time, however, there was some reason to believe they were gaining dangerous minority support. The fact that the Japanese attack on Pearl Harbor aborted this treasonable campaign does not mean that it never had any real potentialities for trouble.

Who Backed Father Coughlin?

In December 1938, the Gallup organization published a detailed analysis of the supporters of Father Coughlin. At the time, he was attacking "Jewish Bolshevism" and quoting from the *Protocols*.

Half of the Negroes polled backed Coughlin. Among Catholics, 42% approved, 25% disapproved and 33% voiced no opinion. In the Protestant sample, 19% were favorably inclined, 31% hostile and 50% were don't-knows. Oddly enough, despite the fact that Father Coughlin had been engaged in openly anti-Semitic propaganda since July, 10% of the Jewish sample was for him.

Within the Protestant community, Coughlin had strongest backing (29%) among the Lutherans, a heavily German denomination. Opposition to him was much stronger among the Episcopalians and Congregationalists, both high-income, high-education groups, than among Baptists and Methodists.

Among Protestants with above-average incomes, almost four times as many opposed Father Coughlin as favored him. Among people of average income, this proportion dropped to two-to-one against. The ratio dropped steadily with the poor about equally divided between pro and con.

The Coughlinites were more likely to vote Republican than Democratic, but this may not have indicated a general conservative trend. It was more probably an expression of hatred of Roosevelt and opposition to his pro-British foreign policy. The minority of the well-to-do who backed Coughlin were strongly (74%) anti-FDR, whereas only 25% of the Coughlinites on relief opposed Roosevelt.[7]

Thus, the Coughlinites were primarily urban Catholic workers, many of whom were on relief. Lipset points out that this class composition contrasts somewhat with Austro-German anti-Semitic movements, which were based primarily on the middle class and its white-collar and professional sectors. Coughlin also had considerable support from the farmers, which was not surprising considering the fact that his monetary panaceas and hatred of the Jews and international bankers were closely parallel to Populist propaganda. The Gallup survey did not go into the educational status of Coughlin supporters, but there are sound reasons for believing that, on the average, the educational level was very low.

Lindbergh and America First

Charles Augustus Lindbergh, the idolized aviator of the late 1920's, was the son of a cold, morose Minnesota congressman, who wrote books against "invisible government" and the money trust, believed labor was the only source of value and that the rest of society was parasitic, and favored various inflationary panaceas. Lindbergh, Sr., had been influenced by the writings of "Coin" Harvey and Ignatius Donnelly and his mind had been "churned into an almost frenzied confusion" by the works of Henry George, Edward Bellamy and Karl Marx.[8]

The Lone Eagle cooperated with Alexis Carrel in medical research during the thirties and a father-son relationship soon developed between the two men. An eccentric genius, Carrel was an elitist who stressed that men are definitely not created equal. When asked whether the Nazis did not have a "natural laboratory" for creating "supermen" through attaining racial purity, Carrel answered: "It is difficult to say if a pure race is an advantage. It may be that crossing civilizations, as we do in America, produces the finest minds. We do not really know the genesis of great men. Perhaps it would be effective if we could kill off the worst of these purer races and keep the best, as we do in the breeding of dogs."[9]

Lindbergh made his first trip to Germany in 1936, where he associated with high Nazi officials, was photographed with Goering in the latter's house and attended Olympic Games which other Americans boycotted. He had been asked by the American Military Attaché in Berlin to find out all he could about the Luftwaffe. Lindbergh was given unprecedented access to German airplane factories, air bases and other facilities. After a world survey of airpower, he gave what was described as a "terrifying report" on German strength to the American Ambassador in London, Joseph Kennedy, and to British Deputy Air Director John Slessor.

Returning to the United States, Lindbergh became deeply concerned with keeping the United States out of the European War. He believed that it was time to "turn from our quarrels and to build our white ramparts again . . . to guard our heritage from Mongol and Persian and Moor." In a radio address, he declared: "These wars in Europe are not wars in which our civilization is defending itself against some Asiatic intruder. . . . This is not a question of banding together to defend the white race against foreign invasion."

In 1940, Anne Morrow Lindbergh published a thin volume called *The Wave of the Future*, which immediately became a best seller. She claimed that "the leaders of Germany, Italy and Russia have discovered how to use new social and economic forces. . . . They have felt the wave of the future and they have leaped upon it." She thought that "the evils we deplore in these systems are not in themselves the future; they are scum on the wave of the future."[10] What the Lindberghs apparently admired in the Nazi and Soviet systems was their authoritarianism, their centrally planned economies and their supposed "virility" and "dynamism."

Eloquent speeches and articles, written in some instances with the aid of Lawrence Dennis, catapulted Lindbergh into prominence as the one leader of national stature in the movement against American involvement in the war. The main organization representing this position was the America First Committee. At the insistence of General Robert E. Wood, Lessing J. Rosenwald, a Jew, had agreed to serve on its executive committee. Simultaneously, Henry Ford was named to the same board. The purpose had been to show that the movement was not anti-Jewish and that it united all groups opposed to American belligerency. Rosenwald, however, could not stomach Ford and resigned.

In a speech delivered a few short months before Pearl Harbor, Lindbergh unknowingly crossed the boundary between what the molders of public opinion consider legitimate opinion and what they deem bigotry. "No person with a sense of the dignity of mankind," he declared, "can condone the persecution the Jewish race suffered in Germany." He then proceeded to warn American Jews that, instead of working for war, they should be opposing it in every way, "for they will be among the first to feel its consequences. Tolerance is a virtue that depends upon peace and strength. History shows that it cannot survive war and devastation."

This may have been bad prophecy, but it seems, in the calmer light of later years, to have been plainly a prediction and not a threat. Yet it was generally denounced. The Hearst press called it an "intemperate and intolerant address." Thomas E. Dewey found it "inexcusable." Alfred E. Smith condemned it as an appeal to "anti-Semitism." In the opinion of Wendell L. Willkie, it was "the most un-American talk made in my time by any person of national reputation." Norman Thomas refused to give any more speeches at America First rallies, but the mail received by America First backed Lindbergh seventeen to three.

In retrospect, it seems clear that Lindbergh was never an anti-Semite.[11] He may have been morally insensitive to the oppression of the Jews and to other Nazi crimes, but that is a different matter. He was a believer in elites, who somehow accepted the mistaken notion that the Nazis represented an elitist political philosophy. His destruction of his own great reputation was made more complete by his unfortunate association with Lawrence Dennis and by the intellectual heritage of hopeless confusion which he received from his father.

Footnote on Senator McCarthy

Neither the late Senator Joseph R. McCarthy nor that amorphous political movement known as "McCarthyism" belongs in a chapter on anti-Semitism. This statement, however, will be increasingly less obvious as the years pass. Particularly since McCarthy's death, the writers of the Liberal Establishment have vilified his activities against Communism in government and elsewhere and invested them with the odor of fire and brimstone. Posthumously, as depicted by his increasingly vociferous enemies, the man emerges as a would-be leader of the forces of fascism and anti-Semitism.

An appraisal of McCarthy and "McCarthyism" obviously lies outside the scope of this book. For present purposes, all I shall do is clarify a few facts about the relationship of Jews to McCarthy and of McCarthy to Jews and about the composition of the McCarthy supporters and their relationship to anti-Semitism.

The battle against McCarthy was a favorite cause of the American liberal movement. It was not a specifically Jewish cause, but the Jews joined in it and were highly conspicuous in it. In 1954, the Conference of American Rabbis, with 600 reform rabbis present, condemned Senator McCarthy *unanimously*, requested that he be stripped of his committee chairmanship and also expressed disapproval of the term "Fifth Amendment Communist."[12]

The ADL's Forster and Epstein wrote about the wrongs allegedly done innocent men and the ADL in the fall of 1952 listened to then Senator Herbert Lehman give his hackneyed speech about how the "McCarthyites" "turn neighbor against neighbor, religion against religion, and whole bodies of our citizens against their government and the institutions of government. . . ." (If the "McCarthyites" had been given opportunity for rebuttal, they would probably have observed that, if your neighbor is subversive, it is your duty to turn against him; if your church is preaching bad doctrine, you had better do something about it, and if your government is going against what you consider the national interest, it is your obligation and duty as an American citizen to criticize it.)

Seymour Lipset, whose respect for facts and intellectual competence is refreshing, is the best source on the composition of the McCarthy movement.[13] Analysis of public opinion polls reveals that the pro-McCarthy element was very similar to the pro-Coughlin element. McCarthy support varied inversely with education, was much more intense among Catholics than Protestants or Jews, was particularly strong among Americans of Irish, German and Italian extraction, was marked among farmers, was greatest among unskilled and semi-skilled labor and was least among such high-status occupations as the professions and business management. Unlike Coughlin, McCarthy had very powerful support among small businessmen. Moreover, Senator McCarthy never proposed any radical programs and his supporters tended to be conservatives in economic and social matters. His movement arose in a period of prosperity, not depression.

There has been a good deal of sociological analysis of the fact that McCarthy at times expressed intense hostility toward upper-class Americans who served the Communist conspiracy. Thus, on February 20, 1950, the *Congressional Record* published McCarthy's observation that: "It is not the less fortunate, or members of minority groups who have been selling this nation out, but rather those who have had all the benefits the wealthiest nation on earth has had to offer—the finest homes, the finest college educations, and the finest jobs in the government that we can give. This is glaringly true in the State Department. There the bright young men who are born with silver spoons in their mouths are the ones who have been the worst."

It was entirely true that State Department and Foreign Service officers were drawn disproportionately from the socially elite colleges and universities and the higher the position the more markedly was this the case.[14] Nor is it surprising that a man such as McCarthy, who had had to struggle against hard odds to reach his position in life, should resent lack of patriotism among those to whom America had given everything. Sociologists have tried to make much of the hypothesis that "McCarthyism" was primarily a movement against the Anglo-Saxon Protestant elite. This factor may have been present. Fundamentally, however, McCarthyism was precisely what it appeared to be on the surface. It was a movement for the vigorous and stern suppression of Communism. For over twenty years, public opinion polls had consistently registered the desire on the part of large majorities of the American people for much more drastic measures against the Reds than a liberal administration was willing to introduce or than the Supreme Court was prepared to sustain.

Finally, we come to the attitude of McCarthy and his supporters toward the Jews. Even the most prejudiced liberal enemies of McCarthy have been forced to recognize that not only had he no hostility toward Jews whatsoever, but that many of his most important and closest advisers were Jewish. This applied to the columnist, George Sokolsky, who was also his close friend; to his top legal counsel, Roy Cohn, and his staff consultant, G. David Schine. On Far Eastern affairs, the late Alfred Kohlberg was one of McCarthy's chief advisers.

A 1954 opinion poll by the International Research Associates attempted to measure the extent of anti-Semitism among McCarthy supporters. The key question, concerning attitudes toward a Jewish candidate for

Congress, was asked of non-Jews only. To everyone's amazement, the poll revealed that, while 38% of the anti-McCarthy people would be "more likely to vote against a Jew," only 12% of the pro-McCarthy element expressed this prejudice. Some 30% of the pro-McCarthy respondents said the issue was immaterial, as against only 16% of the anti-McCarthy respondents. This large and statistically significant difference, one that revealed much more hostility to Jews among the anti-McCarthy than the pro-McCarthy group, has been confirmed by further analysis.[15]

Thus, the portrayal of the pro-McCarthy movement as anti-Semitic does violence to history and to the available evidence. That myth will no doubt continue to flourish, however, as long as the posthumous vilification of McCarthy is considered the litmus test of true liberalism.

CHAPTER 11

The Anti-Defamation League and the Right

SINCE 1963, the Anti-Defamation League of the B'nai B'rith has been engaged in a lavishly financed campaign against what its spokesmen call "the radical right." ADL-financed books and pamphlets seek to alert the nation to this supposed danger to its existence. Libraries, schools and service organizations are flooded with tendentious literature denouncing "the radical right" as un-American.

As the Anti-Defamation League understands it, the "extreme right" does not consist merely of the little hate groups and the Nazi and anti-Semitic rabble. It is much broader. On this point, let me quote Dore Schary, motion picture director and National Chairman of the Anti-Defamation League.

"It has been estimated," Mr. Schary writes (but without

revealing who made the estimate), "that some 20 per cent of the American electorate can be grouped as Extremists on the Right Wing. Therein dwell the Radical Rightists and the Extreme Conservatives. Therein also can be found those who would vote for a candidate who ran on an anti-Semitic or anti-Negro platform. Such a candidate would attract the racists, the bigots, the kooks and the yahoos to be found among the Extremists who are tempted into accepting the phony nostrums and panaceas of any or all fake medicine men who range the political scene in America."[1]

This vituperative paragraph is taken from the foreword of a major publication of the Anti-Defamation League. The grammar and incoherence of thought it displays are unhappily characteristic of Mr. Schary's prose. The significance of the quoted paragraph is that Schary groups conservatives, whom he calls "Extreme Conservatives," with "Radical Rightists" and neo-Nazis. The foreword in which Schary linked Extreme Conservatives with supporters of anti-Jewish candidates was dated June 29, 1964. A month later, the Republican National Convention nominated Barry Morris Goldwater, a half-Jew who spoke with pride of his Jewish ancestry, for the office of President of the United States. Senator Goldwater received the almost unanimous support of those very conservatives whom Schary had tried to link with anti-Semitism.

The Anti-Defamation League supposedly exists to refute slanders against the Jewish people and promote tolerance among the non-Jewish majority. It is difficult to believe that the best way of bringing this about is for the national chairman of the ADL to slander some twenty per cent of the American people as associates of "kooks," "bigots" and "yahoos." The shrillness of style, recklessness of statement and readiness to substitute abuse and invective for a reasoned approach characterize the ADL attack on American conservatives. If this organization is supposed to promote tolerance, it presents a very bad example to the public. When one examines the activities of the ADL at a lower echelon, the picture remains basically the same. The West Coast organ of the Anti-Defamation League, for instance, stated that its civil rights director intended to "blast at the right-wing philosophy at every opportunity" and to have "every member of the B'nai B'rith appoint themselves [sic] Paul Reveres. . . ."[2] Yet in terms of the ostensible objectives of the League, its officials have no business either blasting at right-wing philosophies or, for that matter, defending them.

The Christian Anti-Communism Crusade

The most important publication in the Anti-Defamation League's campaign against the so-called right wing is *Danger on the Right*, written by two top officials of the League and published under its copyright in 1964. Typical of the methods used by the ADL against those it considers right-wing extremists is the treatment accorded Dr. Fred R. Schwarz and his Anti-Communism Crusade in this book.

The son of an Austrian Jew, Dr. Schwarz served as a college lecturer in mathematics in his native Australia, then went through medical school and became a successful physician and psychiatrist. A devout Christian, he became convinced in 1950 that the West was dangerously complacent about the threat of Communist expansion. He decided to launch an organization which would continuously sound the alarm about this menace. Since the United States was the leader of the Free World, he also decided to base his organization, called the Christian Anti-Communism Crusade, on American soil. The new organization held "freedom rallies" in major American cities (one of them filled the Hollywood Bowl), and set up schools throughout the country to educate community leaders to the danger of Communism. This last operation seemed not unrelated to Thomas Jefferson's observation that eternal vigilance is the price of liberty.

Unable to dismiss Dr. Schwarz as an anti-Semite or a "yahoo," Arnold Forster and Benjamin R. Epstein, the authors of *Danger on the Right*, rely heavily on the sneer. He is "the good doctor;" his speeches are "lurid;" throughout he is attacked as a fear peddler, and there is the nasty insinuation that he is in the anti-Communist cause for the money it brings him. This last innuendo was refuted by Dr. Schwarz in a press statement which showed that the salary and expenses he took from the Crusade were less than what he had earned as a doctor. Typical of Forster's and Epstein's reporting is the following:

"At another meeting, Schwarz's Reds were evidently short of rope and had to rely on revolvers. After working his listeners to the edges of their seats with horrendous tales, with the pauses and the studied emphasis of the trained performer, the Doctor said: 'When they come for you . . . on a dark night, in a dank cellar, and they take a wide-bore revolver with a soft nose bullet, and they place it at the nape of your neck. . . .'

". . . it seems wholly incredible that Americans in this day can be frightened by this kind of arrant nonsense, yet thousands and thousands of Americans have been influenced by the Extremists of the Radical Right and are pouring millions of dollars a year into the laps of these self-appointed America-savers."[3]

In characterizing Dr. Schwarz's accurate description of the execution methods of the Soviet secret police as "arrant nonsense," Epstein and Forster merely reveal their own naiveté. They apparently assume that Communist seizures of power are no longer followed by the wholesale liquidation of "class enemies" and suspected counterrevolutionaries. The comparatively recent experiences of Cuba, Zanzibar and China demonstrate the opposite.

It may seem to the authors of *Danger on the Right* that Dr. Schwarz is excessively emotional about the execution of anti-Communist Americans. This is a matter of taste and style. The ADL was emotional about the extermination of European Jewry.

In addition to the sneering tone which Epstein and Forster habitually adopt toward those who seek to arouse Americans to the Communist threat, the quoted passage contains the disreputable implication that Dr. Schwarz is in it for the money. This *ad hominem* innuendo reveals more about the character of the authors than it does about their subject. Despite the fact that Epstein and Forster are salaried employees of the ADL, nobody suggests that they write books for mercenary reasons.

There is also the suggestion, so comforting to the vanity of liberal readers, that Dr. Schwarz's followers are imbeciles. Yet a Stanford University study, cited by Forster and Epstein, revealed that more than half of them were business and professional people; a majority were college graduates, and more than half made over $10,000 a year.

Some of the money collected in tuition fees for Dr. Schwarz's 5,000 schools and at the rallies and "freedom forums" was devoted to reaching the largely illiterate masses of Latin America. The comic book technique was used. The stress was on Communist forced labor and Communist mistreatment and killing of priests. This material was beamed on Mexico, which suffered from intense Communist propaganda activity, and on British Guiana, which seemed on the verge of a Communist takeover. The Epstein-Forster comment is characteristic:

"Horror comics for Mexican children—a strange 'educational' enterprise for an organization which is, according to its articles of incorporation, 'irrevocably dedicated to religious, charitable, or scientific purposes.' "[4]

The comic books obviously were not primarily for children; they were for illiterate and scarcely literate adults. Nor is there anything incongruous in efforts by a religious organization to combat the destruction of religion and the murder of priests. Dr. Schwarz's Latin American efforts contributed to thwarting Cheddi Jagan, the Red leader of British Guiana, from turning that country into a Communist state. At the time, England had washed her hands of the matter on the theory that it was an American problem. When the late Lord Douglas Hamilton tried to arouse Washington to the danger, he found that the Kennedy Administration was unconcerned.[5] Dr. Schwarz was one of the few people who tried to prevent another Latin American country from falling into the Soviet orbit. For this he deserves something better than the sneers of Epstein and Forster.

When Schwarz attempted to organize an anti-Communist rally in Madison Square Garden, the Anti-Defamation League and some "liberal" Protestant church groups did everything in their power to make it a failure. Dr. Schwarz was shocked to learn that his organization was being branded as anti-Semitic and that the ADL was a probable source of that charge. He wrote the ADL that, if there was any anti-Semitism in his organization, he would like to cooperate in eradicating it. The Anti-Defamation League simply ignored the letter. When it was taken to task for doing so by *National Review,* a spokesman for the organization indicated that they were not going to be maneuvered into endorsing Schwarz!

Thus, it appears that the Anti-Defamation League has reached a point at which it will not cooperate with conservative and anti-Communist organizations in combating anti-Semitism within their ranks. This raises the question of whether it is primarily concerned with fulfilling the purpose for which it was organized—defending American Jews against slander—or with furthering the peculiar ideologies of its leaders.

John Birch Society and Christian Front

The real bête noire of the ADL is, not the Christian Anti-Communism Crusade or any of the dozens of loosely organized right-wing groups, but the John Birch Society. In contrast to other anti-Communist groups, the Birch organization has a comprehensive, all-embracing ideology, is highly disciplined and has a dedicated and politically active membership.

Whether the Birch Society is a force for good or evil, whether it is effective or ineffective as an anti-Communist agency are questions which lie outside the scope of this book. The only issue we are concerned with here is whether it is either actually or potentially anti-Semitic. That, by the way, would also seem to be the only issue with which the Anti-Defamation League should concern itself. American Jews may be individually for or against the John Birch Society, but this is hardly an ADL problem.

The sequel to *Danger on the Right* was *Report on the*

John Birch Society 1966. The authors of this brief book are our old friends Epstein and Forster; the sponsor was the Anti-Defamation League; the text began with the usual Dore Schary foreword couched in that gentleman's graceful prose. In attempting to explain why the ADL is committed to an all-out attack on the John Birch Society, Schary observed:

"The new extremism, which soon came to be known as the Radical Right, was, in fact, a reappearance of an older manifestation. In the middle thirties, it appeared as the Coughlin movement, flowered into the reactionary America First movement, and ended suddenly when the Japanese attacked Pearl Harbor. In the early fifties, it reorganized itself, its guise somewhat changed, and became known as 'McCarthyism.' After nearly five years of controversy, the American people forced it into oblivion, unfortunately only temporarily.

"Slowly it re-emerged as the Radical Right. For nearly four years, the ADL watched it, issued periodic reports and, at the end of 1963, decided the situation was serious enough to warrant full exposure. . . .

"Many Americans believed that the stern rebuke the national electorate administered to Barry Goldwater . . . in the 1964 presidential campaign spelled the death knell once more of Right Wing extremism in our country. Unfortunately, they were wrong. In truth, the 1964 campaign period served as the Radical Right's great opportunity to organize its following more effectively and to unify itself more solidly."[6]

The implication is that we are dealing with a movement which has preserved its continuity over a generation. There is the further implication that this movement is anti-Jewish. Schary's attempt to link the supporters of Goldwater with the violently anti-Semitic Coughlin movement of the thirties can have no other significance. However, both of Mr. Schary's assertions are falsehoods.

Let us consider first whether there is a fundamental continuity of movement, purpose and personnel between the organizations headed by Father Coughlin in the 1930's and 1940's and by Robert Welch in the 1960's. As I have already pointed out, the Coughlin movement was strongest among the poor and weakest among the rich. Almost four times as many Protestants with above-average incomes opposed the radio priest as supported him, whereas Protestants on relief were equally divided between pro and con. The Coughlin movement arose during a profound depression, demanded radical monetary measures and excoriated the bankers and the financial system. Thus, it was fairly characteristic of social revolutionary movements, whether Fascist, Populist, Socialist or Communist.

The characteristics of the John Birch Society are very different. The movement was born and grew during a period of unparalleled prosperity. It staunchly supports free enterprise and is politically conservative. It advocates hard money and deplores deficit spending. Far from favoring a stronger government to impose radical social and economic measures, it desperately fears the modern state as an engine of serfdom and Socialism.

Its class appeal was carefully analyzed in a Gallup Poll of Birch supporters taken in California in January 1962. This revealed what any open-minded observer would have expected—support of the Society was heavily concentrated in the upper-income and more highly educated groups. Pro-Birch people were 35% more heavily represented in the upper-income group than the population as a whole. People with three years of college or more were 80% more likely to favor the Society than the California average, whereas those with only grade school education were 60% less likely to favor it.

The Birch supporters were preponderantly Republican. They were more likely to be men than women. Birch strength was slightly greater among Protestants than among Catholics. It was least among Jews, but the belief that California Jewry was solidly opposed was contrary to the facts. Actually, there was only 17% less Birch support among Jews than the statistical expectation.

The Birch support was greatest in the peak productive period—the 30-49 age group. It was average among men and women in their twenties and least in the age group over 50. Thus, the stereotype of the Bircher as "a little old lady in tennis shoes" was wrong as to age, sex and probably footwear as well. In terms of occupation, the Society was strongest among farmers, retired people, professionals and businessmen and weakest among skilled and unskilled workers.[7]

Thus, in California in 1962, the John Birch Society was in many fundamental respects the very antithesis of the Coughlinite Christian Front. It was conservative, not radical. It demanded hard money where Coughlin had urged inflation. It supported a free-enterprise economy and the Jeffersonian ideal of a weak, decentralized government. It was a product of prosperity, not depression. It appealed more to Protestants than to Catholics, more to the rich than to the poor, more to the educated than to the ignorant.

A 1962 questionnaire study conducted in the San Francisco Bay area yielded some evidence that Birch supporters tended to be more ethnocentric and more hostile to Negroes than average, but the sample used was too small for statistical reliability. Hostility toward Jews was somewhat above average, but Lipset described the difference as "relatively minor."[8]

History as Conspiracy

The John Birch Society nevertheless has some of the characteristics of American Populism. These include simplification of issues, a fear of foreign entanglements and a distrust of that which is foreign, an inclination to endow the traditional American majority with the virtues of rugged courage, honesty and good intentions and a belief that this constructive element is being betrayed by corrupting alien forces. Fear of these corrupting forces is characteristic both of the John Birch Society and of the various anti-Semitic groups. However, the anti-Semites see these forces as manifestations of a world Jewish conspiracy whereas the Birch supporters see them as manifestations of an international Communist conspiracy. This is the difference and it is a crucial one.

The Birch view of the world has frequently been criticized as a distorted conspiratorial view of history. A "conspiracy," according to the *Oxford English Dictionary*, is a "combination of persons for an evil or unlawful purpose." Unfortunately, a great deal of modern history is precisely that, the most flagrant examples being the Nazi and Communist movements.

The John Birch Society does not merely present a conspiratorial theory of history. It goes far beyond that and presents us with a view of the world in which there are only two real forces: those of good and those of evil. These are in absolute conflict, a conflict which can end only with the destruction of one or the other of the two great adversaries. This conflict completely fills the stage of history and all phenomena are explained in reference to it and as a part of it. This is probably the reason for the willing acceptance by some Birch supporters of the view that fluoridation of water supplies is a Communist plot to poison and stupefy the American people.

If the conflict is all-embracing, it does not follow that everyone is aware of it. On the one side, as the Birchers see it, are the Communists with their vast hosts of liberal and social-democratic allies, a power in aggregate so enormous that Welch reached the odd conclusion that the United States was already 60% to 80% Red-dominated. On the other side are the band of dedicated men and women enrolled in the John Birch Society to fight these forces while there is still time. At present on the sidelines are the great mass of honest, decent Americans who live humdrum lives in ignorance of the danger threatening their country, but who can be aroused and mobilized.

In the Zoroastrian system, all creation divides itself into that which is Ahura's and that which is Ahriman's and these two forces wage eternal battle. In the Manichaean system it is Light against Darkness, God against Satan. In Communism, the world dualism is between Proletariat and Bourgeoisie; in Nazism, between Aryan and Jew. In each instance, we have a closed system, which reduces all social phenomena to their role in an all-embracing conflict between Good and Evil which cannot be compromised, but must be fought to the death.

"Welch is himself not an anti-Semite, and anti-Semitism is not a part of his Society's program and never has been," Epstein and Forster wrote in 1964.[9] In fact, Robert Welch has consistently urged Jews to join the Society and has welcomed them into its ranks. Among the Jewish intellectuals who had once been members of the John Birch organization are William S. Schlamm, Julius Epstein and Morrie Ryskind. The late Alfred Kohlberg was active in the Birch Society. The American Jewish League Against Communism has endorsed the John Birch Society. The Society has strongly opposed Nasser's plans for the destruction of Israel and has consistently objected to American aid to the Egyptian dictator. Welch has also pointed out that the Birchers have been attacked as "Jews and Jew-kissers" by such notorious anti-Semites as Elizabeth Dilling.[10]

One of the first books on the radical right of the 1960's had only two references to Jews and anti-Semitism: one referred to the fascist movements of the thirties, the other dealt with Rockwell's group and other neo-Nazi gangs.[11] When the *Los Angeles Times* investigated the charge that the John Birch Society had anti-Semitic tendencies, it concluded that there was "absolutely nothing in any of the society's available literature or in the utterances of any of its members to bear this out. The Anti-Defamation League of the B'nai B'rith has found no such evidence. . . ."[12]

Robert Welch has pointed out, moreover, that while there are many people of Jewish origin who are Communists, they are not Jews, but renegades from Judaism, and that Karl Marx was probably "the most vicious anti-Semite of all times." He warned Jews that irresponsible charges of anti-Semitism against right-wing patriots who were innocent of the charge might drive some of the latter into actual anti-Semitism. This would divide decent Americans and thus help Communism. Even if "smeared unmercifully," he said, he would continue to tell his thousands of Jewish friends: "I wish you would pay more attention to how you are being used to help a cause in which you do not believe. But I shall remain your friend, no matter what happens, and I hope you will still remain friends of mine."[13]

From its inception, the John Birch Society has been plagued by the problem of anti-Semitic infiltration. To a certain extent, this sort of thing is unavoidable. Nazis and anti-Semites attempt to penetrate the action organizations of the Right just as Communists attempt to penetrate the action organizations of the Left. The only difference is that the Communists are considerably more successful and get a much more friendly reception. A right-wing organization should be judged, not by whether this sort of penetration is attempted, but by whether it is tolerated.

Anti-Semitism and the John Birch Society

Merwin K. Hart, who has been characterized by the ADL as a notorious anti-Semite, was leader of Chapter 26 of the Birch Society in New York until his death in 1962. There have been others who used their position in the Society to disseminate the *Protocols of the Learned Elders of Zion* and to spread neo-Nazi and anti-Jewish propaganda. A widely publicized case was the employment for more than a year of Westbrook Pegler as a columnist for *American Opinion*, the official periodical of the John Birch Society. Pegler wrote gutter attacks on such prominent Jews as then Senator Herbert H. Lehman, describing him as a man without honor or conscience and the "prophet of a set of pushcart sophists."[14] Pegler declared himself to be a racist and had the effrontery to attack Eugene Lyons, an outstanding anti-Communist and senior editor of the *Reader's Digest*, because Lyons was foreign-born (and probably also because Lyons is a Jew). J. B. Matthews and another member of the staff of *American Opinion* resigned in protest.

Pegler continued to publish below-the-belt attacks, not

only against Jews, but against anybody or any group that aroused his hatred. He expressed regret that President Roosevelt had not been assassinated in 1933, compared his widow unfavorably with a brothel keeper and claimed that it was the duty of all intelligent Americans to "proclaim and practice bigotry."

Welch publicly expressed his misgivings about Pegler's writings, but was restrained from further action by a misconception of freedom of the press and perhaps by a feeling that Pegler was old and pathetic. When Pegler's articles became increasingly rabid, Welch got rid of him. The delay in this necessary therapeutic measure reflected the Birch Society's depressed and rather hostile view of the world, a view that made Pegler's writings seem to bear some resemblance to reality.

The most significant charge in the ADL's 1966 report on the John Birch Society was that *American Opinion* had published articles by Eric Butler, described as a notorious anti-Semite and the author of *The International Jew*. Butler was in fact identified as the "regular Far Eastern correspondent" of the Birch organ.

John Rousselot, a former Republican congressman and former Director of Public Relations for the John Birch Society, admitted that the Society "has been concerned with the problem of anti-Semitic infiltrators," but added: "We have dealt very decisively with the problem." As far as can be ascertained, the Society expels members who use it to spread anti-Semitic, Nazi or Ku Klux Klan propaganda.

His single-minded concentration on Communism to the exclusion of all else led Welch into a bizarre and quite untenable theory of the origins of anti-Semitism. In several 1965 addresses, which were taped and sold for $50 as a set of records entitled *One Dozen Trumpets*, he explained:

"The Protocols of the Learned Elders of Zion, which has been used so extensively and disastrously to create trouble, was written either by Lenin or for Lenin deliberately to serve their purposes. . . . Just as in Germany . . . they [the Communists] created the whole Nazi Party and they drugged Hitler and the Nazi Party—which was not part of the original Hitler plan at all—into persecution of the Jews. There's no doubt that was planned and put into effect in Germany by Stalin 'cause it served their purposes there."[15]

The fact that Welch misunderstands the origins of European anti-Semitism and the further fact that his organization is often obtuse about recognizing anti-Semitic propaganda does not mean that the Society is either anti-Semitic itself or in danger of becoming so. As long as it remains a conservative movement of well-educated, upper- and middle-class Americans, any tendency toward anti-Semitism seems most improbable. Jew-baiting is not an upper-class occupation. In fact, the fascist Mosley movement in England during the period between the two world wars lost its upper-class support when and only when it took an open anti-Jewish line.[16]

Between 1963 and the end of 1965, the John Birch Society had a phenomenal growth. Membership almost doubled to approximate 100,000 and cash income more than quadrupled.[17] Messrs. Epstein and Forster suggest the possibility that this new membership may be more fanatical and hence potentially more bigoted than the old.

There is little reason to take this judgment seriously. The Society has placed greater stress on respectability and Rousselot and others have tried to tone down, muffle or explain away some of its more extreme utterances. Its leaders have expressed their determination to cope with the problem of anti-Semitism and their desire to attract more

Jews into the organization. A split in the leadership of the Society in the summer of 1966 resulted in the resignation of Professor Revilo P. Oliver of the Classics Department of the University of Illinois. Dr. Oliver's book reviews in *American Opinion* had made many readers conclude that he was anti-Semitic.

The Anti-Defamation League attack on the John Birch Society is unnecessary and uncalled for, since it thus makes Jewry seem to be the spearhead of a combined assault on an anti-Communist movement. This is grist to the mill of the professional anti-Semite. The attack, moreover, has been couched in such a manner as to antagonize rather than persuade. If the John Birch Society and other anti-Communist organizations have often been far from astute in detecting anti-Semites within their ranks, a constructive solution would be for the Anti-Defamation League to extend them quiet assistance. Instead, leaders of the ADL seemingly do everything in their power to create an atmosphere of intense hostility, even going to such absurd lengths as refusing to shake hands with Rousselot in public.

CHAPTER 12

Jewish Voting Behavior: 1932-1967

JEWISH ELECTORAL SUPPORT of Franklin D. Roosevelt rose steadily during the four campaigns in which he won the Presidency and by 1944 was almost unanimous. Thus, an analysis of voting behavior in seven primarily Jewish wards in Chicago revealed FDR majorities of from 70.9% to 95.9%. The differences in these percentages were not correlated with income.[1]

These mounting Roosevelt majorities among Jewish voters could be explained in terms of the international crisis. In the 1940 election, the Republican candidate, Wendell L. Willkie, leaned toward a much more genuinely neutral American foreign policy than that which the Administration was pursuing. The campaign occurred at a time when the Nazis had conquered France and, with their eastern

front secured by a non-aggression pact with Stalin, seemed
on the verge of invading and subjugating England. Failing
decisive American intervention, it seemed highly probable
that Hitler would finish his conquest of Europe and proceed
toward mastery of the world, exterminating world Jewry in
the process. The massive Jewish support of Roosevelt was
entirely understandable in this context and the even greater
support given him by heavily Jewish districts in 1944 was
a tribute to his having turned the tides of battle and helped
bring the Axis to its knees.

This rising Jewish enthusiasm for Roosevelt was not
shared by the other minorities which had given him such
powerful backing in 1932. By 1944, Roosevelt's support
among voters of German, Italian and Irish stock had been
seriously weakened. Sentimental and other ties toward
original homelands which were suffering from American
ground invasion or air assault helped explain the first two
defections. In the Irish case, traditional hostility toward
Britain, together with the pro-fascist virus so effectively
implanted by Father Coughlin and other Irish agitators of
lesser stature, contributed to the shift toward the Republican opposition.

With Roosevelt dead and Nazism shattered, the issue of
whether the New Deal alliance of discontented minorities
could be preserved seemed unsettled. As fas as the Jewish
part of this alliance was concerned, the decisive issue was
whether the primary attracting force had been the international one of the survival of world Jewry or the domestic
programs of redistributing wealth, expanding social services,
binding business enterprise with the cords of proliferating
governmental controls and extending the power of the
Executive Branch indefinitely and in all directions.

Harry Truman was unable to capture Jewish support to

the same degree as his predecessor. For one thing, his character and personality were not such that either Jewish voters or liberal intellectuals in general could wholeheartedly admire. His plain language, his habit of making snap decisions and his inability to invest his high office with the dignity it deserved made a painful impression.[2] He lacked the eloquence, the pseudo-intellectual polish, the theatrical mannerisms and the histrionic ability which had helped make Roosevelt the darling of the Jewish electorate.

This comparative lack of enthusiasm for the new President was not due to any repudiation of Truman's liberal-to-radical domestic program. It was based much more on the fact that Truman, under grave provocation, had refused to continue the Rooseveltian policy of seeking a permanent alliance with Soviet Russia at all costs. Truman had quickly discovered that Stalin was violating his agreement at Yalta to uphold democratic procedures in the Balko-Danubian area and was threatening the stability of the Middle East with subversion and Communist-led insurrection and civil war. Accordingly, the American Chief Executive proclaimed the Truman Doctrine and committed U.S. power to the defense of the independence of Greece and Turkey.

Proof that this was a real issue was the strong Jewish support of Henry Agard Wallace, the presidential candidate of the Progressive Party. The *raison d'être* of this third-party movement was to obtain continuing American support of the Soviet Union and American acquiescence in continuing Soviet aggression. Its domestic program was essentially a rehash of Communist-inspired, popular-front type social demands which, if enacted, would have hogtied the American economy. The Wallace movement, as President Truman observed many years later, gave the Communists a front by means of which they were able to infiltrate

American national politics and spread disunity and confusion. A mystic and zealot, Wallace was apparently innocent of the way in which the Communists were manipulating his movement.[3] Years after this sorry political fiasco, Wallace would reminisce to the press in bitterness and sorrow about the way he had been used as a cat's paw by the subversive element.

Based on an analysis of heavily Jewish wards in key cities, Fuchs found that Wallace won from 12% to 27% of the vote, whereas nationally he had attracted only about 2%.[4] Many of the Jewish supporters of the Progressive Party were no doubt unaware of the fact that it was an instrumentality of the Communist Party, but they could not have been unaware of the fact that Truman had referred contemptuously to "Henry Wallace and his Communists" and that the *raison d'être* of the new movement was to get the United States to appease Soviet Russia.

Truman probably got from 60% to 75% of the Jewish vote, Wallace from 15% to 20% and Dewey, the Republican standard-bearer, from 10% to 20%. This ardent support of Wallace by a significant minority of American Jews was not characteristic of the behavior of any other ethnic or national group of high educational, social or economic status in the United States population. Thus, an analysis partly financed by the Ford Foundation revealed that the only other areas in which Wallace was strong were: Negroes (overwhelmingly so), the foreign born, union members and the college-bred.[5]

Stevenson and Kennedy

The emergence of Adlai E. Stevenson on the national political horizon in 1952 gave American Jews another idol.

In the 1952 elections, about three-quarters of American Jewry supported Stevenson. The actual percentages, as calculated by three public opinion polling organizations, ranged from 73% (Survey Research Center of the University of Michigan) to 77% (American Institute of Public Opinion). This was considerably greater than the support which Stevenson was able to muster from any other special group. Neither Negroes nor trade union members nor any other national or ethnic minority gave him comparable backing.[6]

An intensive study of Ward 14 in Boston, which Fuchs believed to be typical of the Jewish voting pattern nationally, revealed some interesting facets. Among both Jews and Gentiles, the more highly educated gave more support to Eisenhower than did the less educated. The pro-Democratic percentage among Jews ranged from 68.3% among college graduates to 71.5% for elementary school graduates.[7] Among non-Jews, Stevenson support was twice as great among the poor as among the rich. With Jews, however, Stevenson had more support among the economic upper-class than the lower-class groups.

A very significant finding was that, as Jews lost their Jewishness, they tended to become more liberal-to-radical. What seemed to be occurring here was a transfer of identity from the Jewish community to the larger unity of nation or world. This was expressed as an almost religious dedication to every scheme for the expansion of social welfare. Within the Jewish communities of Europe, the virtues of charity and benevolence had been stressed by rabbinical authority and social welfare measures had provided temporary aid to worthy poor people. Among American Jews, there was a strong tendency to apply these standards of conduct to the larger and much more heterogeneous unit of the nation.

However, the social welfare programs often served primarily to keep substandard groups in permanent idleness, destroying their incentive to work. Jewish supporters of the policy of continually increasing and indiscriminate federal largesse to the underdog were apparently blind to the difference between Jewish community and melting-pot nation.

Fuchs found a means of measuring what he called "ethnoreligious involvement" with Judaism and the Jewish community. Those who scored highest in this respect were only 46.2% pro-Democratic, whereas those who scored lowest were 80.1% pro-Democratic. This finding was corroborated by the discovery that Jews of German and Austrian origin (many of them refugees from Nazism), who were presumably much more assimilated into the Gentile world, were significantly more favorably inclined to Stevenson than Jews of Slavic origin.[8]

Several other reasons have been assigned for Jewish adulation of Adlai. The former Illinois governor had handled some security matters during World War II in a wishy-washy manner and had incurred the scathing criticism and contempt of Senator McCarthy. The extent of hostility toward McCarthy among Jews was amazing. Thus, a Gallup Poll of June 1954 found strong disapproval of the senator among 65% of the Jews interviewed as compared with 31% of the Protestants, 38% of the Democrats and 45% of the college graduates.[9] While there was, as I have already shown, no evidence that either McCarthy or his supporters were anti-Semitic, a very large number of Jews uncritically accepted the liberal caricature of the Wisconsin senator as an incipient Hitler.

The Jewish rejection of Eisenhower in favor of Stevenson was extraordinary from both a personal and a political standpoint. The Republican standard-bearer had emerged as a towering figure in the struggle against Nazism and was unconditionally committed both to the Free World and to the philosophy of individual freedom. His experience as a military man had taught him to make decisions and to carry them out.

Eisenhower's Democratic opponent had never done anything of consequence in world affairs, had little in the way of experience to recommend him and was more distinguished for self-depreciatory epigrams and lofty moral sentiments than for actual leadership. As events would show in a glaring fashion, Stevenson's natural tendency was to favor passivity or inaction. In the crises that the West would face, his voice would be heard on the side of appeasement of the Soviets. At a time when strength of leadership was needed, American Jewry was buying weakness.

Despite some misgivings about his Catholicism, his Irish origin and the alleged anti-Semitic tendencies of his father, John F. Kennedy got the overwhelming endorsement of Jewish voters. Thus, the California Poll showed 91% of Jewish voters, but only 73% of Catholics and 38% of Protestants, supporting him.[10] "No other group, whether classified by religion or by race, age, occupation, residence or birth, was so solidly Democratic. Negroes were next, with 82.9%, and Catholics third, with 77.9%. Groups 60 to 70 per cent for Kennedy were unskilled labor, craftsmen and foremen, foreign-born persons, and renters."[11]

An analysis of heavily Jewish precincts in and near Chicago showed that the Jews had begun to react politically with a more intelligent regard to their own economic interests than in previous elections. In four lower-middle-class precincts in Chicago itself, no less than 85.8% of the vote went Democratic in 1960. In three groups of middle-class precincts, however, the Democratic vote ranged between

63.8% and 77.8%, while in one upper-class precinct, only 51.8% of the vote was for Kennedy.[12]

Despite the fact that Barry Goldwater was half Jewish and "proud of my heritage," American Jewry voted overwhelmingly against him. A Gallup Poll in September 1964 showed that Johnson's most solid support came from non-whites (94%), but the Jews (with 91% backing him) were a very close second. So massive was the Jewish prejudice against him that Goldwater and his campaign organization made practically no attempt to win over Jewish votes. Some Jewish secular and religious leaders attacked Goldwater with a violence and disregard for truth that were shocking. Thus, Rabbi Joachim Prinz gave a political harangue from his Newark pulpit at Temple B'nai Abraham in which he alleged that "a Jewish vote for Goldwater is a vote for Jewish suicide."[13] Prinz was not an obscure rabbi, but a man who had been president of the American Jewish Congress, where he had incidentally distinguished himself by intemperate accusations.

The truth about Goldwater and the bigots was expressed by the Republican candidate in his New York City speech of October 26th, where he said: "The Nazi and the fascist types—the bigots—they're not going to vote for me—because my grandfather was a Polish Jew."

When the returns were in, most of the minority groups were found to have been heavily for Johnson. Within this element, the Negroes and Jews were remarkable for their virtual unanimity. The Voter Profile Analysis service showed that Negro precincts in six Northern and Southern states turned in majorities of 93% to 99% for Johnson. The Jewish precincts ranged from 89% to 95%. By comparison, Irish were in the 66%-to-88% range, Italians about the same and Slavs 72% to 88% behind the Democratic candidate.[14]

The salient difference between Negro and Jewish support for Johnson was that the former was based on the expectation of specific material benefits for the colored minority as a group whereas the Jewish political stance was motivated by much broader national considerations. Anti-Semitic propaganda to the contrary, Jews are not much swayed by the fact that a candidate may be Jewish. If he is also conservative, they will almost invariably vote against him. Thus, in 1961, Jewish election districts in Brooklyn backed Robert F. Wagner, a Catholic, two to one against Arthur Levitt, who was Jewish, for the Democratic nomination for Mayor of New York. In the election, Jewish votes helped bring in Wagner and defeat the Republican candidate, Louis J. Lefkowitz. This tendency has been visible in Jewish political behavior in New York City ever since 1903 when Jewish voters abandoned Cyrus Sulzberger and backed John S. Ahearn, an Irishman.[15] The lesson for politicians—particularly conservative ones—is that very little mileage can be gained by putting up Jewish candidates.

Another case of the Jewish voters cutting off their own noses was the vote in 1964 on various state and city "public accommodations" ordinances. These measures restricted or totally abolished the right of house and apartment owners to refuse to sell or rent on the basis of race. The purpose was to enable Negroes to move into previously white residential areas. Since residential discrimination against Jews had become pretty much of a dead letter, the Jewish interest was identical with that of the other whites. Experience had shown that an influx of Negroes often caused panic selling, the deterioration of once attractive neighborhoods and substantial loss of property investment.

In Detroit, some Jewish districts voted ten-to-one against a homeowners' rights ordinance designed to permit landlords to sell or rent at their discretion. In Los Angeles,

Jewish districts voted two-to-one against Proposition 14, a very similar measure, which was approved by California voters as a whole by a two-thirds majority. What is even more significant is that Los Angeles lower-middle-class Jewish precincts, which were already experiencing the Negro presence, also voted against Proposition 14, though by less decisive majorities.

A similar issue was the 1964 fight of Alabama Governor George C. Wallace to win direct primary contests in various states for the Democratic nomination for President of the United States. In some Maryland precincts that were heavily Jewish, the vote against Wallace was better than ten to one. In all of the three states in which he campaigned—Indiana, Maryland and Wisconsin—Wallace found the Jewish vote massively against him. On this issue, the Jews were on the other side of the fence from such other traditional Democratic supporters as the voters of Italian, Irish and Slavic extraction, not to mention the Southern whites of Anglo-Saxon stock. These other groups supported Wallace largely because they wanted to prevent the mixing of Negroes and whites en masse in public schools and residential areas. Here again, where an issue of principle was involved, the Jews voted against their own material interests.

Vietnam Appeasers

As the American war effort in Vietnam began to move forward from stalemate, some of the less restrained Jewish organizations took steps to harass the Administration. In November 1965, Rabbi Jacob Weinstein, head of the rabbinical arm of American Reform Judaism, alleged that a "consensus curtain" was descending on the United States and that critics of American Vietnam policy were becoming

the victims of "public hysteria." Before the same meeting—
the 48th General Assembly of the Union of American
Hebrew Congregations—Rabbi Maurice N. Eisendrath,
president of the Union, echoed Weinstein's complaint and
warned of "neo-McCarthyism." Seemingly echoing Indo-
nesian ex-dictator Sukarno, he said that American Vietnam
policy bore "all the stigmata of the white man's imperialism." Then in an orgy of mangled English prose, Eisendrath
added: "We are the victims of a cultural creep of this
strange and painful anomaly—a government brilliantly
progressive in its domestic policy and blunderingly archaic
in its foreign policy."[16]

The use of the clichés that Communist propaganda
habitually selects did not apparently disturb the 3,000
delegates to this affair. Surely, the two rabbis could not
have been unaware of the fact that the protests against
American Vietnam policy had on occasion involved such
clearly illegal activities as burning draft cards and trying to
stop the movement of troop trains. They must have known
that many of these "honest dissenters" from American
foreign policy had come out openly for Viet Cong victory,
had displayed the Viet Cong flag at their rallies and had
appealed to students to give blood to wounded enemy
soldiers so they could return to the lines and kill more
Americans.

Rabbi Eisendrath was quick to characterize the defense
of freedom against an aggressive totalitarian system in
Vietnam as "white man's imperialism" and "archaic." Presumably, this religious leader had not been equally oblivious
to the moral issue when the United States faced the challenge of Nazism.

Scarcely ten days later, the American Jewish Congress,
the most intemperate of the major Jewish organizations,

demanded that draft boards should not revoke deferments "as a means of silencing political dissent."[17] When Lieutenant General Lewis B. Hershey, Director of Selective Service, was unmoved by this plea, the American Jewish Congress demanded that he be removed from office.[18]

The American Jewish Congress did have a point. The law did not authorize drafting men as a punitive measure. Moreover, placing beatniks of soggy loyalty in uniform without segregating them from patriotic American soldiers might tend to lower military morale and place the armed services in disrepute.[19] On the other hand, deferment was supposed to keep out of uniform those more useful to the nation as civilians. The little group of Communists, fellow travelers, cowards and obstructionists was of no use to their country in either capacity.[20] In World War II, the United States had attempted to solve a similar problem by drafting pro-Nazis and placing them in special pick-and-shovel battalions, which were in fact penal units. Here they were segregated from honorable soldiers.

In February 1966, a Conference on Judaism and Peace was held under the auspices of the Synagogue Council of America, representing the three branches of Judaism. At this gathering, Rabbi Arthur J. Lelyveld, who was described as the Chairman of the Justice and Peace Commission of the Central Conference of American Rabbis (Reform), asserted that the United States had blocked free elections in Vietnam because the unpopular government it backed "could not possibly win that election."[21] Rabbi Lelyveld had no qualifications for predicting the outcome of Vietnamese elections and the erroneousness of his judgment would be shown in the September 1967 presidential balloting, but this was not the first time the pulpit had provided a convenient refuge for ignorance and dogmatism.

A few days later, the American Jewish Congress appealed to President Johnson to stop bombing the enemy in North Vietnam and to invite the Viet Cong to join in peace negotiations. The Congress claimed that it did not deny "the validity of the American concern for freedom in all parts of the world"—a generous concession indeed—but it added that "the overriding moral imperative of the moment is the need to return peace and freedom to the torn and agonized land of Vietnam."[22] The leaders of the American Jewish Congress failed to explain how negotiations with the Viet Cong were going to restore "freedom" to the Vietnamese.

In view of the fact that the Jews had suffered so appallingly at the hands of Nazi totalitarianism, it seemed doubly tragic that they should be led by men who were either callous or morally obtuse toward Communist totalitarianism in Southeast Asia. It was, of course, true that the successive military regimes in South Vietnam were by no means democracies, but the vital point was that they constituted a framework within which free institutions might flourish whereas a Viet Cong victory implied the extermination of such institutions, the liquidation of those who opposed totalitarianism and the long night of the police state. The blindness of Jewish and other religious leaders to this fundamental issue was not due to any incapacity to understand the significance of human freedom nor was it due to any contempt for the Vietnamese people. The fundamental distortion related to a psychic need to prettify and embellish authoritarian systems of the left, a propensity to view them as the result of idealistic efforts to better the lot of the common man and a chronic blindness to the basic similarities between Nazism and Soviet Communism.

CHAPTER 13

Economic, Social and Intellectual Elites

THE RATE OF AMERICAN ECONOMIC GROWTH since World War II has been so fantastically swift that one often thinks of American opulence as a comparatively new phenomenon. Yet there has never been a time in the history of the United States as a nation when Americans were not more prosperous and in enjoyment of better material standards of living for the masses than any other people on earth.

Even at its birth, the American Republic offered the common man wealth and opportunity which in Europe were undreamed of. By contrast, living standards in England had declined drastically during the Industrial Revolution.[1] Colin Clark, one of the world's foremost authorities on the subject, calculated that the annual real income of the average Englishman in 1800 was equivalent to $121 of

1925-34 purchasing power.[2] The real income of the average American in the same year was equivalent to approximately $255 in dollars of like value.[3] Although one-fifth of them were slaves, Americans lived more than twice as well as Englishmen. Indicative of the comparative opulence of America in its infancy as a nation are the frequent complaints by indentured servants and hired white farmhands at the frequency with which they were served fresh salmon.

During almost the entire span of American history, the exception being part or all of the 1881-1920 period when massive immigration of impecunious Russian Jews was occurring, American Jews enjoyed higher living standards than the United States average. For the period before World War I, evidence has already been given which supports this statement.

As for income, Bernard Lazerwitz reported in 1961 that 54% of non-New York Jews, but only 18% of Catholics and 18% of Protestants had annual incomes in excess of $7,500.[4] Herman P. Miller showed that in 1953-55 about one out of every five Jewish families, as compared with about one out of twenty Protestant and Catholic families, made over $10,000.[5] Both studies showed that Jews were correspondingly under-represented in the population below or close to the poverty line; that is, those earning less than $3,000 (Lazerwitz) or less than $4,000 (Miller). In a carefully researched article, William Attwood, National Affairs Editor for *Look*, reported two astonishing estimates: although Jews comprised only 3.5% of the population, "they receive 10 per cent of the total personal income; of America's 9,000 millionaires, about 20 per cent are Jewish."[6]

The advance of Jews of Russian and East European origin from indigence to opulence in three generations is one of the more remarkable economic developments of the modern age. In 1880, when the immigration began on a large scale, per capita income in East Europe and Russia was from a third to a fourth that of the United States. As late as 1900, Jewish artisans in Lithuania and Russia were very fortunate if they were able to make as much as 250 rubles ($125) in the course of a year. A Census sample of adult Russian Jewish males in the United States showed that they were earning an average of $461 a year in the first decade of the twentieth century.[7]

The second generation of Russian Jews made a massive transition from manual labor to white-collar occupations and independent business. By 1900, almost 10% of the employed native-born children of Russian Jewish immigrants were clerks as against 2% of their fathers. Another 10% were salesmen as compared with 3% of their immigrant fathers. Some 20% of the first generation, but only 5% of the second, were tailors. The movement into the professions was not yet on a large scale, but the second generation was 50% better represented in that area than the first.[8]

By the early 1930's, this situation had radically changed. About an eighth of the entering classes in American medical schools were Jewish. Jews were massed in such professions as medicine, dentistry and law. In Trenton, there were ten times as many Jewish as Gentile doctors and six times as many Jewish lawyers. In San Francisco, eighteen of every thousand gainfully employed Jews were lawyers and judges and another sixteen were doctors.[9]

By 1930, Jews were three times as well represented in trade and twice as concentrated in the professions as the general population.[10] According to a 1937 estimate, about two-thirds of New York City lawyers were Jews, some 64%

of the dentists, 56% of the physicians, but only 29% of the engineers.

Prior to World War II, "Jews occupied a marginal position in the professions."[12] They were excluded from the best practices, societies, specialities, firms and hospitals. Thus, a survey made in Cincinnati in 1948 showed that, of 286 accountants employed in the fifteen largest firms in the city, only three were Jews. It was hard for Jewish physicians to qualify in such special fields as surgery, urology and orthopedics. In 1948, fewer than 40 surgeons were certified from among Brooklyn's 4,000 Jewish physicians whereas 130 surgeons derived from Brooklyn's 1,500 non-Jewish physicians.[13]

Jews were definitely under-represented in the national, state and local governments, probably because they found that working inside large bureaucratic organizations, where advancement was generally based on seniority, gave them inadequate opportunities to rise to the top. Avoidance of careers which emphasize security rather than opportunity, team work rather than individualism, and conformity rather than risk-taking has been characteristic of Jewish behavior in both Europe and America. However, with the onset of the depression, Jews swarmed into teaching and social work. These careers appealed to their interest in education and were consistent with the emphasis on charity and philanthropy in Judaism. Moreover, these were poorly paid areas which expanded rapidly in personnel under the administrations of Franklin D. Roosevelt and his successors.

Surveys of fourteen Jewish communities made between 1948 and 1953 revealed an astonishing homogeneity in employment pattern.[14] From 75% to 96% of the employed Jews in these cities worked in non-manual occupations, that is to say, as professionals, proprietors of businesses, officials and managers. By contrast, only 38% of the 1950 gainfully employed population of the United States was in these fields.[15]

Moreover, the Jews were concentrated in the higher-status areas of the non-manual income earners. Comparing the fourteen cities surveyed in 1948-53 with ten cities investigated in 1935-45, Glazer reported that the proportion of professionals had risen from about 11% to around 15% of the gainfully employed Jewish population. At the same time, the proportion of Jews working as salesmen and clerks fell drastically.

The proportion of Jewish lawyers and doctors did not rise significantly, if at all, between these two periods. What happened was that Jews flocked into such fields as architecture, journalism, engineering and teaching at the college level; they became a major element in the entire aesthetic elite, ranging from the plastic arts through music, literature, cinema, radio, television and the legitimate stage. In addition, their contributions to the social sciences grew at a geometric rate.[16]

There were two significant qualitative changes involved. The first was that the American Jew became a major component in the American creative minority as a whole—scientific, aesthetic, executive and bureaucratic. The areas of partial to almost total exclusion were such comparatively unimportant ones as the *Social Register* and the best country clubs and such vital ones as high executive posts in major corporate enterprise.

The second significant qualitative change was that the American Jew could no longer be considered primarily as an exemplar and champion of rugged individualism and free enterprise. He was no longer overwhelmingly concentrated in business enterprises which he owned and ran himself and in free professions where he was his own master and his own employer. These activities were still areas of heavy Jewish concentration, to be sure, but they were no longer the occupational hallmark of American Jewry.

What the Jew was doing was rapidly to spread out into those other activities of the American brain and power elite which he had previously avoided or which had heretofore been closed to him. While remaining economically part of the upper class and primarily a brain worker, he was becoming an organization man like the rest of the new elite. In government departments, as a military scientist or as a specialist in space travel, as statistician, market analyst, public opinion forecaster or in any one of dozens of similar positions and vocations, the Jew, like his non-Jewish colleague, would find himself part of a team, required to coordinate his work closely with that of similar teams in cognate areas, perhaps using intricate and enormously expensive laboratory and computer facilities and compelled increasingly to function in accordance with complex operational patterns. The area in which insight and hunch prevailed was shrinking, while that dominated by more or less routinized operational procedures was steadily expanding.

The pattern of Jewish representation in the executive, business, military, political and social elites, as revealed by name-frequency analysis, seems much more erratic than that found in the American intellectual elite as a whole. In politics, a 1950 roster of American politicians showed that Jews were under-represented: they furnished 42% of their quota of Republicans and 66% of their quota of Democrats. Among labor leaders, however, they were about 100% over-represented as of 1946, a not surprising fact considering the liberal-to-radical trend in Jewish political behavior.

The military career held little attraction for American Jews. In the early 1960's, Jews were represented up to 52% of statistical expectation as active officers and up to 86% as retired officers in the U.S. armed forces. This condition reflected a traditional Jewish aversion to the military career, dislike of war and distaste for routinized occupations in which advancement is largely by seniority. As the military calls more and more for imaginative scientists and men interested in pioneering in new fields, Jewish participation will probably increase.

The pattern in business enterprise is interesting and somewhat contradictory. Of the 75,000 entries in *Poor's Register of Directors and Executives, U.S. and Canada,* 1963, over 6%, or more than twice the expected representation, was Jewish. In the more selective *Who's Who in Commerce and Industry* for 1961 (23,000 entries), Jews were only 44% over-represented. When we turn to the top leadership of the greatest corporations in the United States, as listed by *Fortune* magazine in 1964, we find that Jews were under-represented by 18% in industry and by 25% to 62% in banks, public utilities, insurance companies and transportation. In merchandising, a traditional Jewish occupation, an analysis of 1,438 top officials and directors showed that Jews were over-represented by 304%.[17] These findings are generally confirmed, as far as insurance and banking are concerned, by detailed surveys made by the Anti-Defamation League.[18] The latter surveys point out that, not only is there a paucity of Jewish executives in American life insurance companies, but those who are so employed are concentrated in selling and are seldom placed in line jobs at company headquarters.

The extent of discrimination against Jews in American heavy industry is revealed by Lewis B. Ward's estimate that less than 1% of its executive personnel is Jewish despite the fact that 8% of all college graduates and 25% of graduates from the Ivy League colleges and universities are Jewish.[19] While these figures present a prima facie case for rampant discrimination against Jewish candidates, they should not be interpreted naively. That is to say, the executives now in heavy industry, to the extent that they are college-bred, are the products of American colleges and universities over a span of about 30 years. During most of this period, Jews were not as heavily represented among total graduates as in the case of the figures just cited. Moreover, abandonment of adversely discriminatory hiring practices would not immediately change the composition of corporate executives to any significant extent; it would merely change the composition of the newly hired ones.

In a study financed by funds made available by the American Jewish Committee, Lewis B. Ward attempted to analyze the underlying rationale of anti-Jewish discriminatory patterns in corporate employment. His method was intensive analysis of the views of 550 young men who had recently taken corporate jobs and 324 company employees who had recruited them.

The study analyzed (1) the actual characteristics of the corporations and the characteristics of corporations preferred by the recruits and (2) the actual characteristics of the recruits and the characteristics of recruits preferred by corporations.

New light was shed on this situation by Ward's challenging findings. Recruiters characterized 188 of 324 corporations involved as pursuing ethnically mixed hiring policies, 80 employing Protestants only, 42 employing only Catholics and fourteen open exclusively to Jews. The salient differences between the ethnically mixed corporations, on the one hand, and the Protestants-only and Catholics-only enterprises, on the other, were that the former were larger, had wider stock ownership, were much more inclined to take risks and were much less insistent that "trainees must avoid sympathy with unions." The ethnically open companies were better structured organizationally, more consistent in their supervision, offered more fringe benefits and put greater stress on public and community service. Only 74% of the executives of the Protestants-only companies were described as "well-educated," whereas 91% of the mixed and 93% of the Jews-only companies were in that category.

The same basic difference between organizationally tight, aggressive, adventurous, risk-taking and service-oriented companies, on the one hand, and organizationally slack, passive, risk-avoiding and conventional organizations, on the other, was reflected in the recruiters' preferences in candidates for employment.

The Protestants-only companies preferred trainees who were *"tolerant, cheerful, considerate,"* while ethnically mixed companies preferred those who were *"systematic, precise,* and *orderly."* In respect to unfavorable traits, the Protestants-only group showed a preference for passive characteristics. The ethnically mixed companies, Ward found, "prefer *opinionated, carefree, hard, argumentative* and *rebellious,* while Protestants-only prefer *pessimistic, distant, bashful, retiring* and *commonplace.* Furthermore, the Protestants-only group gives greater preference to *unambitious* as against *reckless,* and to *placid* as against *clumsy.* It gives less preference to *egotistical* as against *apathetic,* and to *willful* as against *slow."*[20]

The chief requirements for the Protestants-only companies, in short, were that their trainees be socially pleasing, able to fit into the human environment and not likely to rock the boat with new ideas.

All four groups of trainees (Protestants, Catholics, Jews and agnostics) were strongly hostile to this conventional, social, risk-avoiding, security-oriented type of business leadership. In describing the sort of corporation they would like to work for (generally in painful contrast to the sort of company they did work for), an overwhelming majority of all four groups wanted an organization which did not discourage taking risks. They wanted emphasis on profits, better trainee salaries and tended to prefer smaller businesses, probably because promotion might be more rapid there.

When Jewish trainees were compared with the other three groups, the similarities were more striking than the differences. However, there were differences and these reflected a fairly consistent pattern. In comparison with the other groups, Jewish trainees were more interested in risk-taking, in a straight profit orientation, and in better starting salaries. They showed more decided preferences for smaller size, less stability in the business, more flexible organizational structure and less fixity in company policies.

In terms of personal traits, the Jewish men have "less preference than do Catholics or Protestants for *tolerance* and *cheerfulness* as against being *systematic* and *precise*, respectively. On the other hand, Jews have less interest in being *stable* and *cautious* as against being *serious* and *attractive*. . . ." With two exceptions, "the Jews and agnostics show considerably greater willingness than Protestants and Catholics to admit to active, though undesirable, qualities as against undesirable qualities that are passive." The Jews and agnostics see themselves as "more *opinionated, egotistical, stingy* and *rebellious* than do Protestants and Catholics, when these qualities are paired with *pessimistic, apathetic, shallow* and *commonplace* respectively." In a previous study, Ward showed that executives were more tolerant of subordinates whose undesirable qualities were passive than of those whose undesirable qualities were active.[21]

While the Jewish sample is small, it seems large enough to reveal a consistent pattern of differences in temperament and character. The traits stressed by the Jewish and agnostic candidates are more in line with the requirements of the ethnically open corporations, which tend to be bold, innovating, quick to welcome new ideas, research-and-development-oriented and ever on the lookout for new opportunities. These traits are, however, reprobated by the smaller, more stodgy companies which tend to prefer the conventional, to avoid change and hazard, to prefer a congenial to a competent leadership team. The swift pace of scientific and technological advance and the accelerated rate at which it impinges on business enterprise suggest that the future belongs to the first type of company and that the second type will slowly be relegated to a more modest role.

The increased stress on research and development, the desperate need for young executives with imagination and daring, the fact that most large corporations are committed, in theory at least, against ethnic discrimination and the effective work done by the Jewish organizations in this area in recent years—all these factors suggest that the discrimination problem will become of dwindling importance.

It is an extraordinary thing that, in the face of widespread corporate discrimination against their employment at executive levels, American Jews have achieved a proportionately greater role in U.S. business leadership *as a whole* than any other national group. And despite this discrimination, they have managed to obtain for themselves better incomes and higher living standards than any comparable group.

American Jews not only enjoy a much higher economic and social status than the national average, they also constitute a proportionately larger component of the intellectual and creative elite. This is not merely an American, but an international phenomenon. While there are many reasons for this state of affairs, the most important one, in my opinion, is the biological advantage which the Jews enjoy because of two thousand years of selective breeding for brain power. The nature of this biogenetic process was indicated in an earlier chapter and elaborated in more detail in another book.[22]

The first salient difference between American Jews and American Gentiles in this area of creative intelligence is educational level. Whereas only about 30% of American youth plan on a college education, a 1963 survey published in the *American Jewish Year Book* showed that more than three-quarters of the Jews of college age were enrolled in some institution of higher education. A 1965 survey of the Jewish community of Wilkes Barre, Pennsylvania, revealed that more than 90% of Jewish high-school students in the ninth through the eleventh grades and *all* the Jewish high-school seniors planned to go to college.[23]

These differences in planned college attendance reflect differences in life goals and in intellectual ability. The traditional Jewish stress on learning and the Jewish belief that education must be a life-long process account for part of the much higher college-attendance ratio. The other factor involved is that many of the nation's youths who decide *against* college do so because they are convinced, rightly or wrongly, that they are not intelligent enough to graduate.[24]

The second point to be made is that Jews have greater upward occupational mobility than Gentiles. In the early 1920's, Lewis M. Terman launched a study of the gifted children in California public schools which proved to be a milestone in the measurement and analysis of human intelligence. The Terman study continued for several decades, following the careers of these exceptional students and analyzing the intelligence and psychic characteristics of their children. Terman found that 57.5% of the Jewish gifted children became professionals as against only 44% of the Gentile gifted. Yet only 15% of the Jewish fathers, as contrasted with 35% of the Gentile fathers, had been of professional status.[25] Terman found, incidentally, that there were twice as many Jews in the gifted group as would have been expected on the basis of Jewish representation in the California population and this despite the fact that some parents of gifted children successfully hid the fact that they were Jewish.

Studies of the Jewish communities of Camden, Detroit and Providence published in 1963 and 1964 revealed that about a fifth of the gainfully employed Jews were in professional and semi-professional occupations. However, among the youth, the concentration in these intellectually exacting occupations was much greater. In Camden, some 60% of Jewish men between 25 and 34 were in the professional and semi-professional category and the other two cities reported similar findings.[26] These surveys no doubt exaggerate the national breakdown of Jewish concentration in the professions since the Jewish communities of New York, Chicago and Philadelphia traditionally have had large populations of manual workers and shopkeepers. Even with this qualification, the Jewish concentration in the professions is probably greater than that of any other ethnic element in the American population.

Finally, Jews tend to be more successful in the professions than non-Jews to the extent that success is measured by monetary reward. Havemann and West in a classic report on the college-bred in America found that Jewish college graduates consistently earned more than non-Jewish graduates. Thus, in 1947-48, the year in which the survey of 9,064 graduates from 1,037 institutions of higher education was made, 27% of Jewish, but only 21% of Protestant and 15% of Catholic graduates, were earning more than $7,500 a year. Believing that these differences might be due to the presence of proportionately more Jews in the professions and to the greater concentration of the Jewish population in big cities, the authors eliminated these factors. They found that the difference still remained. In other words, Jewish professionals living in metropolitan areas consistently earned more than Protestant and Catholic professionals in the same or similar areas.[27]

Name-Frequency Analysis

Using a method which I call name-frequency analysis and which is fully described in an earlier book,[28] I made some estimates of the position of Jews, as well as of other national and language stocks, in the American intellectual, executive and power elites.

I found that Jews were 263% over-represented in the student bodies of colleges and universities and 365% over-represented in the student bodies of Ivy League and Seven Sister colleges and universities. In Phi Beta Kappa, the

outstanding national honors society with a total membership, living and dead, of about 180,000, Jews did about as
well as the American average during the period 1776-1922,
did 286% better in 1923-1961 and 339% better in 1962. In
Mensa, another organization composed of the intellectual
elite, Jews were 374% over-represented in the North American membership as of June 1965.[29] Jewish participation in
National Merit Scholarships, however, was only about
twice the statistical expectation.

In the *Directory of American Scholars* for 1957, Jewish
representation was about 70% better than the national
average. Judging by entries in the 9th and 10th editions of
American Men of Science, Jews contribute more than two
and one-half times their share of physical and biological
scientists and more than three and one-half times their
share of social and behavioral scientists.

In *Who's Who in America,* the Jewish representation
rose from an insignificant figure to 61% more than the
national average in 1964-65. In the professions, the Jewish
contribution is particularly impressive in those fields related
to medicine and those where self-employment is customary.
In descending order, Jews are over-represented 478% in
psychiatry, 308% in medical specialties,[30] 299% in dentistry, 283% in mathematics, 263% in law, 231% in medicine, 70% in architecture, 18% in the Foreign Service and
9% in engineering. Judging by patents granted between
1952 and 1963, the Jews are 110% over-represented in in-
vention, where they share top honors with the Dutch.

In eight rosters of contemporary literature and writing,
I found that the Jews led other groups by a rather impressive margin. Their representation was 108% more than the
statistical expectation. The Dutch with 47%, the Scots
with 40% and the Welsh with 38% over-representation

followed. In two rosters of living American artists, the Jews again led the other national-linguistic groups and were 89% over-represented. They were followed, after a considerable lag, by the Scots, English and Dutch.[31]

The Jewish contribution to music is even more outstanding. In 1933, Keith Sward found that of 145 American composers listed in two standard reference works, 14.5% were Jewish. Of those composers whose works had been performed by symphony orchestras, 23.8% were Jewish or partially Jewish. Almost half of the conductors of America's four outstanding orchestras in the early 1920's were Jews. Of the violin soloists who performed with orchestras, Sward found 34.6% were Jewish. Of those who made four or more appearances with orchestras, 70% were Jewish. Sward found that in twelve symphony orchestras, 51% of the first violins, 34% of the strings and 9% of the brasses and woodwinds were Jewish. He also reported a tendency for the percentage of Jews to rise with the excellence of the orchestra. Jews were even more heavily represented in American popular music. However, in three European orchestras in January 1933, the month in which Adolf Hitler became Chancellor of the German Reich, less than 5% of the musicians were Jews.[32]

The causes of this concentration are unknown and a matter of controversy. Max Weber, the eminent German sociologist, made the interesting observation that the Old Testament relies more heavily on acoustical than on visual imagery[33] and H. Rosenthal made the same point in comparing the ancient Jewish prophets with the holy men of other religions. Rosenthal also speculated that, since musical genius is often concentrated in partially deaf families, Jewish musicality might be related to some genetic hearing defect.[34] Sward studied the innate musical capabilities of

300 Jewish and 200 non-Jewish children to see whether there were inherent differences in musicality. He found that, where the intelligence levels were the same, there were no such differences. However, he thought, "the Jewish child may be a superior all-around organism by 'nature'."[35]

In *The Geography of Intellect*, Stefan Possony and I pointed out that, between 1901 and 1962, 16% of the Nobel laureates in science were Jews. We cited the 1844 prediction of Sir William Osler that: "Should another Moses arise and preach a Semitic exodus from Germany and should he prevail, they would leave the land impoverished. . . . There is not a profession which would not suffer the serious loss of many of its most brilliant ornaments, and none more than in our own [medicine]." We then pointed out that, in the pre-Hitler period, 1901-1933, eleven of the 36 Nobel scientists born in Germany and Austria were Jewish. In the post-Hitler period, 1934-1960, only 22 German- or Austrian-born scientists won the Nobel Prize and of these eight were Jewish.[36]

Turning to the United States, we find that 67 American scientists won this supreme honor between 1901 and 1965 inclusive, and of these 18, or 27% of the total, appear to be Jewish, judging by their surnames and other available evidence.[37] As Jews constitute only 3% of the U.S. population, they appear to be about nine times as productive of Nobel laureates in science as the average.

CHAPTER 14

Unders Czar and Commissars

THIS CHAPTER and the one that follows deal with the vicissitudes and struggles of Russian Jews under the Czarist and Bolshevik regimes and with the reaction of American Jewry to the plight of their co-religionists in Russia. To some readers, such an extended discussion of the minority problems of a foreign country may seem extraneous to the subject of this book. I believe, however, that this is not the case.

Most American Jews derive from Russia. Their traditions and ancestral roots are therefore bound up with the Russian experience. Czarist persecution of its Russian subjects imbued them with fierce hatred of that autocratic regime, which they brought with them to America and which helped propel them in a Socialist or Communist direction. Enthusiastic espousal of the Soviet cause by a small minority of American Jews and an unreasonably tolerant attitude toward Soviet conduct by many others derived in large part from their Russian background and their distorted interpretation of it. The Nazi propaganda identification of Jew and Bolshevik tended to make American Jews sympathetic toward the Soviet Union and blind to its intense anti-Semitism. This Russian background also partially explains American Jewish support of the policies of appeasement of the USSR pursued by Franklin Roosevelt and John Kennedy. Similarly, it sheds light on American Jewish hostility toward cold war strategy and internal security measures designed to counteract Communist subversion. Fortunately for both America and American Jewry, this baneful emotional and ideological link with Russia is being destroyed by events and by the passage of time.

The extent of Jewish participation in the successive revolutionary movements which convulsed and eventually overthrew Russian Czarism has for many decades been a violently controversial topic. Resorting to gross exaggeration, the Nazis and their fellow travelers sought to portray the Bolshevik state as dominated and controlled by Jews. This propaganda theme continued to be echoed even during the years when Stalin was exterminating Jewish Communist leaders and dejudaizing the Soviet bureaucracy. It was loudly proclaimed during the worst period of Soviet persecution of Jewry under Khrushchev. On the other hand, disclaimers of Jewish influence on the Bolshevik Revolution and the Soviet State have often been considerably more sweeping than the facts warranted.

Earlier Revolutionary Movements

Upheavals of peasant masses and social revolutionary movements in religious guise have been chronic in Russian history. The first modern revolutionary uprising in Russia was the Decembrist conspiracy of December 26, 1825. Chagrined by Czar Alexander the First's progressive abandonment of those liberal doctrines which he had proclaimed in his young manhood, a group of Guards officers, for the most part of aristocratic origin, conspired to transform Russia into a Westernized state. The more conservative Decembrists aspired to a constitutional monarchy. The intellectual leader of the movement, Colonel Paul Pestel was influenced by the French Revolution, favored sweeping social changes, land reform, a powerful centralized state and an ardently nationalistic ideology.

Upon Alexander's death, the nation was divided between the claims of Grand Duke Constantine to the throne and those of his younger brother, Nicholas. The firmness of the latter made Constantine step aside, but, when the Guards were called upon to swear allegiance to Nicholas, 3,000 troops led by Decembrist officers mutinied in St. Petersburg. They were put down by numerically superior force, their ringleaders executed and some 300 punished in other ways.

Of these Decembrists, only one, Grigorii Peretz, was of Jewish descent, and he was a convert to the Orthodox faith. In his most important work, *Russkaia Pravda* (Russian Truth), Colonel Paul Pestel demanded that the Jewish communities be deprived of all autonomy and that the Jews be completely absorbed into a unified Russian nation. His alternative solution was that they be sent to some underpopulated place in Asia Minor and encouraged to form an independent Jewish republic.[1]

The crushing of the Decembrists ushered in a long period of comparative civil peace. By the 1860's, however, the so-called nihilist movement began to become a powerful influence on the minds of radical students and intellectuals. Stressing total personal emancipation from conventions, it sought to reduce life to purely utilitarian standards, rejecting poetry, literature and everything that was not immediately useful, as well as religion, tradition and the authority of the family. By the 1870's, the nihilist movement had become preponderantly populist. It lost interest in personal defiance of established beliefs and institutions and stressed going to the peasants to transform them into a revolutionary force. Inspired by the doctrines of Herzen and Bakunin, these intellectuals idealized the Russian *muzhik* and envisaged a socialistic society based on peasant communes.

The intellectuals went to the peasants, but the latter were unimpressed and unmoved. After this failure, the movement of resistance turned to individual terrorism, reasoning that the dramatic act of assassinating prominent Czarist officials would inspire the common people to resist autocracy and would, at the same time, weaken and eventually disintegrate the highly centralized Russian state. The terrorist offensive of the small group known as *Narodnaya Volyia* (the People's Will) scored its greatest achievement when it hunted down and finally murdered Czar Alexander II in 1881. The political effect of this ill-considered crime was to remove a statesman who was successfully westernizing Russia, and to usher in an era of insensate repression and reaction.

The Jewish role in the revolutionary movements of Czarist Russia became significant during the populist era. This was a direct result of the proselytizing zeal of Russian Orthodoxy. As long as the Jewish religious authorities were permitted to remain responsible for education in the Jewish community, rebels were the exception. As a Minsk rabbi put the matter in a proclamation protesting the assault on the Governor of Vilna by Jewish revolutionary terrorists in 1902:

"How do we Jews who, according to all sense and reason, are always obligated to pray for the well-being of the sovereign power, without which we would long since have been swallowed alive—how do we Jews dare to climb to such high places and meddle in politics? O beware Jewish children! Look well at what you are doing! God only knows what you may bring upon our unfortunate nation, upon yourselves, and upon your families. Our people always were proud of one thing—that they never had any rebels among them; and now you desire to wipe out this virtue too."[2]

These revolutionary Jews were, as a rule, dejudaized to such an extent that they had lost all feeling of identification with their people. According to one account, a Jewish *narodnik*, or populist, took part in a pogrom in Kiev because he believed it would be directed against the lives and property of rich Jews exclusively and would thus be entirely acceptable from a revolutionary standpoint. When he discovered that the rioters turned their fury against poor Jews, but did nothing to rich Gentile merchants, he had a nervous breakdown.[3] Nevertheless, the Jewish strength in the *narodniki* movement during 1878-1880 was only a bit over 4%, corresponding to the ratio of Jewish to total Russian population.

As the revolutionary movement turned toward the urban workers and became more clearly Socialist, it won greater Jewish support. Thus, Mark Natanson, a Jew, was one of the founders of the Land and Liberty movement of 1876.

Jewish Opposition to Czarism

From the 1880's on, Jews were active in the leadership of all Russian revolutionary movements which opposed

Czarist oppression. This was a *volte-face* from the traditional Jewish injunction to be loyal to the ruling authorities and to abstain from Gentile politics.

There were three major reasons for the change. The most important was the policy of discrimination and oppression which Czarist Russia consistently pursued against its Jewish citizens. The measures applied consisted primarily of restricting Jewish residence to specified towns and villages in the Pale of Settlement, limiting Jewish access to higher education through the imposition of quotas,[4] and instigating pogroms, or massacres and pillagings of the Jewish communities. The objectives of this policy were concisely expressed in a statement which has sometimes been attributed to the reactionary and learned adviser to Czar Alexander III, Constantin Petrovich Pobedonostsev, to the effect that the only solution to the Jewish problem would be for one third of the Jews to emigrate, another third to become Christians and the remaining third to die.

An additional factor was the desire of the regime to Russify and convert its Jews. The motivation for this was partly religiosity, partly fear. When Napoleon invaded Russia in 1812, the Russian authorities expected that the Jews would aid the invading forces in return for Napoleon's outstanding contributions to the emancipation of the Jews of Western Europe. The Jews, however, remained loyal in accordance with the traditional policy laid down by rabbinical authority. The Russian authorities nevertheless continued with their efforts at amalgamation, conversion and assimilation. The authority of the Jewish *kahals*, or community organs of self-government, which had extended to administration, tax collection and justice, was systematically undermined. Jewish religious schooling was discouraged and, instead, Jewish youths were encouraged to attend secular schools. The latter were supposed to serve as agencies of assimilation and conversion to Christianity. Frequently, they became vestibules for entry into the career of professional revolutionary. Czarism, with its characteristic myopia, had undermined Jewish institutions that taught obedience to the state, without substituting an equivalent system of moral and intellectual authority.

The third reason for the prominence of Jews in the leadership of all the component facets of the revolutionary movement against Russian absolutism was superior Jewish intelligence and capacity. The reasons for this state of affairs have already been outlined. In backward Russia, the gulf between the capacity of the average Jew and that of the average non-Jew was no doubt much greater than in the West. For one thing, the Russian people were preponderantly *muzhiks*, or peasants, and all the contemporary accounts of Czarist Russia agree in emphasizing the immense mental sloth and backwardness of this element. For another, the Russian nobility, until at least the reign of Catherine the Great, was uncouth and unthinking by Western standards. The main historical cause of Russian intellectual backwardness may well have been the Mongol invasion which devastated the Russian cities and decimated their inhabitants during the thirteenth century. This involved the liquidation of most of the intellectuals and scholars, together with a large part of the merchant class and the nobility, thus impoverishing the Russian gene pool to an undetermined extent.[5]

The Russian mind was energized by Peter the Great, Catherine and some of her successors by means of forced westernization. This involved the immigration and naturalization of Germans and other Western Europeans, the introduction of Western thought and the reconstitution of

Russian society along French lines. From the time of Catherine the Great, Russia was ruled by Germans, who had no legitimate claim to the name Romanov.[6]

The Jewish Bund

A large majority of Russian Jewish Socialists was organized in the Bund, or the General Jewish Workers League, which had been launched by Arkady Kremer (1865-1935) at a Vilna conference in 1897. Unlike the Jewish leaders in the Bolshevik movement, the Bundists did not repudiate their Jewish heritage. Kremer defined the objectives of the new organization in his keynote address to the Vilna gathering as embracing both "the struggle for general Russian political demands" and "defending the specific interest of the Jewish workers, carrying on the struggle for their civic rights and, above all, combating the discriminatory anti-Jewish laws."[7]

In early 1905, the Bund had 23,000 members as against a combined Menshevik and Bolshevik membership of only 8,400. The importance of the Bund was such that about 40% of the Russian Socialist delegates recognized by the Paris Conference of the Second International were representatives of the Jewish organization.[8]

The Bund demanded "national-cultural autonomy" for Russian Jewry, involving complete Jewish control of Jewish education and other cultural activities by Jewish authorities elected through a universal, direct and secret vote. This attitude was opposed by both Lenin and Stalin, who denied that the Jews of Russia constituted a nation since they were not a territorial unit in the sense that the Georgians, Armenians and other minority nations were.

The other political movement which had mass support

among Russian Jews was Zionism. This was consistently opposed by the leaders of the Bolshevik Revolution, as it has been ever since by their successors, and was branded either as bourgeois nationalism or as imperialism.

Jewry and the Bolshevik Revolution

The mass of Russian Jews were not attracted to the Bolshevik Party prior to the October Revolution. However, individual Jews were extremely prominent in the leadership of the Party. Of these, the most outstanding was Leon Trotsky (Lev Davidovich Bronstein), who served as Commissar of War, created the Red Army and was coupled with Lenin as the junior member of the ruling duumvirate. Five of the 21 members of the Central Committee of the Communist Party at the time of the Bolshevik seizure of power were Jews, as was its Chairman, Jacob Sverdlov.

Jewish leadership in the newly hatched Communist International was also conspicuous. The first Secretary of the Comintern, Angelica Balabanova, was a Socialist of Polish Jewish origin who had worked with Benito Mussolini in the editorship of the Italian Socialist Party newspaper *Avanti.*[9] She became disgusted with Lenin's use of criminal methods and criminal elements and resigned her post. Her successor, Gregory Zinoviev (Apfelbaum) headed the Comintern for eight years. Among the leading agents of the Communist International was the brilliant journalist Karl Radek (Sobelsohn). The short-lived Hungarian Soviet Republic was led by Bela Kun (a variant of Cohen) and the organizer of the Workers' and Soldiers' Soviets of the even more ephemeral Bavarian Soviet Republic was Eugen Leviné.

In the Soviet Union itself, the triumvirate which succeeded Lenin consisted of Joseph Stalin (a non-Jewish Georgian), Gregory Zinoviev (Apfelbaum) and Lev Kamenev (Rosenfeld). Among the second-string leaders of the Soviet state were Gregory Sokolnikov (Brilliant), Solomon Lozovsky, who would head the Red International of Labor Unions, and Moses Uritsky, chief of the Petrograd *Cheka* and the number-two man in the Soviet secret police. Moreover, for the first twenty years of its existence, this *Cheka* (or OGPU or NKVD or MVD, as it was successively called) had a disproportionate number of Latvians and Jews in its top leadership.

As late as December 1937, 11% of a list of 407 *Chekists* decorated for meritorious service bore recognizably Jewish names. As Leonard Shapiro sardonically observed: ". . . anyone who had the misfortune to fall into the hands of the *Cheka* stood a very good chance of finding himself confronted with, and possibly shot by, a Jewish investigator."[10]

The composition of the Bolshevik rank and file was a very different matter. Jewish membership in the Communist Party declined from 5.2% in 1922 to 4.3% in 1927 and 3.8% in 1930. Among the *Komsomols* (Young Communist League members), the Jewish ratio also dropped, but more gradually. During the entire period, Jews were about 150% more numerous in Communist ranks than in the general population. Since the Jews were overwhelmingly urban and literate in a sea of peasant illiteracy, this was not surprising. Other national minorities also had a disproportionately large Communist Party membership and the Latvians, for example, were 1,100% over-represented in the Party.[11]

The other side of the coin is that Jews were also prominent in the more democratic revolutionary movements, which Bolshevism ruthlessly suppressed, and in attempts to destroy the Communist dictatorship. The *Cheka* leader Uritsky was shot to death in August 1918 by a distinguished

Jewish poet and army officer named Kannegiesser, who "was revolted by the fact that so many of the Bolsheviks were Jewish" and who could not forgive Uritsky for his legalized murders.[12] On the same day, August 30, 1918, a woman named Fanya Kaplan, a dedicated Socialist Revolutionary who had served eleven years at hard labor for a terrorist act under the Czarist regime and had almost gone blind in prison, fired two bullets into Lenin's lung, neck and shoulder. She believed that Lenin had betrayed the revolution when he dissolved the duly elected Constituent Assembly, thus giving the coup de grâce to nascent Russian democracy. While she failed in her objective of killing the Soviet dictator, her attempt may have hastened his stroke and his death some six years later.

In his efforts to build a monolithic, totalitarian Communist Party, Lenin had to battle for years against such Socialists as Julius Martov (Tsederbaum), who were repelled by his contempt for all democratic procedures. Among those who resisted Lenin's consolidation of the so-called dictatorship of the proletariat were the Menshevik leader, Raphael R. Abramovitch, and the left-wing Socialist Revolutionary, I. N. Steinberg. The latter served briefly as People's Commissar of Justice under Lenin, but fought the destruction of due process of law and the concentration of judicial power in the hands of the *Cheka*. Steinberg was imprisoned, but eventually allowed to go into exile.[13]

Another Jewish revolutionary leader, who proved to be an implacable enemy of Communism, was Boris Savinkov, the legendary head of the Terrorist Brigade of the Socialist Revolutionary Party. He served as Deputy Secretary of War in the democratic government of Kerensky which was overthrown by the Bolsheviks in November 1917. In July 1918, Savinkov led a revolt of army officers against the Communist dictatorship in Yaroslavl, 150 miles from

Moscow. Savinkov was defeated by a combined operation of the Red Army and Imperial German forces. Surrendering under a pledge that they would be treated as German prisoners of war, Savinkov and his followers were turned over to the Bolsheviks who promptly shot 428 of them.

The last great effort to checkmate the consolidation of the Bolshevik dictatorship was the mutiny of the Red fleet at Kronstadt in 1921. The demands of the fleet were immediate, secret elections; freedom of speech, assembly and the press for all labor, peasant and Socialist organizations; abolition of Communist control over the armed forces, and re-establishment of a free market in food products.

This uprising was put down with massive ruthlessness and brutality, not to mention deceit. The suppression was accompanied and followed by a reign of terror against all who urged a more lenient course. The Anarchists supported the Kronstadt demands for freedom and denounced the Communist dictatorship. Perhaps their most intellectually distinguished leader, Aaron Baron, was put in prison by the *Cheka*, whence he never emerged. His wife, Fanny, and the theoretician Lev Chorny were shot by the *Cheka* in Odessa. Emma Goldman, Alexander Berkman and Perkus were equally daring in their denunciation of the Soviet police state. They managed to avoid the Leninist lead cure for dissent only because of their American citizenship.[14] In short, the prominence of Jews in the leadership of the Bolshevik Party was no greater than their prominence in the leadership of other, less totalitarian parties.

Lenin's Jewish Policies

The view that Soviet persecution of the Jews was an aberration explicable by the paranoid condition of Stalin in his later years and by the peasant prejudices of Khrushchev is an illusion. Persecution was also characteristic of the Leninist era. It is true that these persecutions assumed more crude and more violent forms and hence aroused more widespread indignation in the West under the dictators who succeeded the founder of Bolshevism. Moreover, under Khrushchev, there was, as I shall show later, a decisive qualitative change. Previously, anti-Semitism had been formally condemned by the Council of People's Commissars (August 9, 1918) as "fatal to the interests of the workers' and peasants' revolution" and as an evil which all Soviet organs should tear out "by the roots." Once Khrushchev came to power, this condemnation of anti-Semitism was forgotten and the Soviet Chairman became the most vocal and tireless advocate of an official policy of discrimination against Russia's Jewry.

Nevertheless, the policy of discrimination had always been inherent in the nature of the Soviet system and had been manifest from its earliest days. The increase in the crudeness and irrationality of these persecutory measures reflected the fact that a revolutionary regime had aged into a comparatively static police state. Where intellectuals with a broad knowledge of Western culture had led Russia in this first phase of Soviet development, Russian politicians with insular mentalities, parochial prejudices and a conspicuous dearth of culture proved more appropriate for the task of consolidating the authoritarian state. With this deterioration in the mental and moral caliber of the Soviet leadership, persecution of the Jews became more overt.

In 1918, the Zionist movement was legal in Russia and had 1,200 chapters and about 300,000 members. In the following year, it was denounced by a policy-formulating conference of Jewish Communist groups as "counter-revolutionary," furthering "the influence of clericalism and nationalist attitudes" and serving "as an instrument of united imperialism which combats the proletarian revolution."[15] In 1920, Zionism was abruptly illegalized and, in the course of the next few years, all known Zionists were either sent to Siberia or shot.

As early as 1919, Jewish communal organizations were abolished and persecution reached such petty extremes as to supply a Jewish home for the aged exclusively with pork. The official Leninist-Stalinist line on the national question was that the Soviet Union should foster cultures which were "national in form, socialist in content." Practically speaking, this meant the coordination of all the existing institutions of the national minorities, the imposition of Bolshevik control over them and their utilization exclusively as vehicles of Communist indoctrination. In the Jewish case, however, the status of the Jews as a national minority was officially denied and Jewish civic and religious institutions were simply liquidated.

In this process, the Jewish Communist leaders played a major role. With few exceptions, they had turned their backs on their culture and abandoned any identification with their own people. They displayed the persecutory zeal which is so often characteristic of the turncoat.

An anecdote that casts a revealing light on the extent of this apostasy is what Bertram Wolfe calls "The Strange Case of Litvinov's Diary."[16] In the early 1950's, Gregory Bessedovsky, a defected Soviet diplomat who lived in Paris, offered what purported to be the secret diary of the deceased Soviet Commissar for Foreign Affairs, Maxim Litvinov, to a British publisher. The latter turned the Russian typescript over to the well-known British historian of the Soviet state, Edward Hallett Carr, for an evaluation. Carr reported that the typescript "has a prima facie claim to be regarded as authentic, and a serious historical document" and eventually wrote an introduction and notes to the English edition.

Harper and Brothers considered putting out an American edition, but were not satisfied with the evaluation of Professor Carr, whose histories have sometimes been critically reviewed as apologies for the Soviet regime. The firm went to the distinguished Russian scholar and former leader of the American Communist Party, Bertram D. Wolfe, for another evaluation. Wolfe concluded that the diaries were a clumsy fabrication which, beneath an apparently hostile attitude toward the Soviet state, served to justify Stalin's decisions as wise and statesmanlike.

What is pertinent to the subject of Soviet anti-Semitism is that the opening pages made Wolfe suspect that the "diaries" were the product of a forgery mill. In them, a rabbi named Schechtman approached Litvinov, as one Jew to another, to complain that the League of the Godless had had the rabbi of Kiev arrested for currency speculation. The anecdote presented Litvinov and Soltz, the fanatical chief of the Central Control Commission of the Communist Party of the Soviet Union, as Jews who were always ready, under any and all circumstances, to come to the aid of a fellow Jew. Later, the diary depicted the last Jewish member of Stalin's Politburo, Lazar M. Kaganovitch, in the same light.

Wolfe pointed out that actually, "both Litvinov and Soltz had rejected their Jewish heritage in their youth. Their Jewish origin tended to make them more rather than less hostile toward religious and anti-communist Jews. . . . I realized that I was dealing with something which I have frequently met in French boulevard 'revelations'; the 'international Jewish conspiracy,' the myth of a Jewish solidarity overriding all political and other differences."[17]

Pogroms during the Civil War

The Ukraine became a battleground for the revolutionary and counterrevolutionary armies and armed factions that turned much of Russia into a graveyard during the desperate years that followed the Bolshevik Revolution. Frightful pogroms were organized by the drunken and undisciplined armies of the White General Denikin and, above all, by the rabble army of Simeon Petlura, whom Salo Baron characterizes as a Socialist. The Jews were massacred by the Whites for supporting the Bolsheviks and at times they were massacred by the Red Army because they were part of the bourgeoisie. Practically the only force that protected them in the confused, incredibly bloodthirsty struggles of the Ukraine was the black-flag, or Anarchist, armed forces of Nestor Makhno, former schoolteacher and convict, boozer and military genius, a leader so hostile to the concept of state power that, wherever he went, he released all convicts and burned the prisons. Makhno printed money which contained the legend that nobody would be prosecuted for forging it.[18] The other force protecting the Jews was their own armed militia, which had served them in good stead under the Czars and which prevented pogroms from breaking out in Odessa throughout two terrible years of civil war. However, the Socialist leaders of Ukrainian Jewry managed to talk the Jews out of setting up these defense units elsewhere. Largely as a result, more than 30,000 were massacred and perhaps another 120,000 died of wounds and concomitant causes—the whole amounting to one-tenth of the Jewish population of the Ukraine.[19]

Between Two Wars

The large majority of Russian Jews consisted of small merchants and artisans. The former were regarded as capitalists and generally disfranchised. Except during the period of the New Economic Policy (a partial and temporary return to free market conditions under Lenin), they were expropriated and forced into other occupations. The artisans were not considered full-fledged proletarians, but rather vestiges of an obsolete form of industrial organization. Thus, the Jews as a whole were deemed to belong to, or to be closely related to, the enemy class. They were not regarded as proletarians and peasants, whose loyalty to the regime would spring, in theory at least, from their class position, but rather as vacillating elements. The Soviet solution to the problem of Jewry was: first, to proletarianize the Jews by driving them into factories; second, to destroy their culture and religion and hence make them an undistinguishable part of the Soviet "community" of nations; and third, to encourage their disappearance as a people by intermarriage and assimilation.

In order to capitalize on Zionist aspirations, the Soviet Union proclaimed its own special Jewish homeland in Biro-Bidzhan, an area in eastern Siberia which was subject to violent seasonal extremes of temperature. Lacking in transportation, communications or housing, it had the additional disadvantage, from the standpoint of Jewish settlers, of lying in the path of probable Japanese invasion were Russia to be attacked by Japan and Germany simultaneously. This scheme, while lauded abroad by liberal and Socialist adulators of the Soviet regime, was a colossal failure. At the eve of the Second World War, there were fewer than 20,000 Jews in Biro-Bidzhan and they constituted a decided minority of its population.

The great purges of the 1930's, affecting the leadership of the Communist Party, the Red Army, the Soviet civil bureaucracy and the NKVD, brought about a decisive change in the role of Jews in the direction of the world's first Communist state. Stalin eliminated the old Bolsheviks, the internationalists and those who had supported rival factions in the Communist Party of the Soviet Union, replacing them by younger men who had grown up within his apparatus and were considered to be unconditionally loyal to him. This necessarily involved the liquidation of virtually the entire Jewish component of the top leadership of the Party, the state, the Army and the secret police. These men were often replaced by elements who had risen within the Soviet hierarchy during the years in which it had been the state. Naturally, these replacements tended to be more Russian in origin and outlook than their predecessors.

When the purges finally subsided, the one Jew remaining on the Politburo was Lazar M. Kaganovich, Stalin's brother-in-law, who lived through the years of terror by throwing his subordinates to the wolves. The purges, writes Seton-Watson, were particularly intensive among "the small groups of persons living in cities far from their national territory, for instance, Greeks in Odessa, Armenians in Ukrainian towns, Tatars in cities of Central Russia. The incidence of the purge on Jews, much the most numerous of the scattered minorities, was exceptionally high."[20]

The Second World War

At a time when Jews had been largely eliminated from the top positions in the Soviet state, Nazi propaganda tirelessly reiterated the legend of Jewish domination, citing the leadership rosters of 1917 and 1918. Bolshevism was equated to *jüdisches Untermenschentum* (Jewish subhumanity). When the Nazi armies rolled across western Russia, the Jewish population, which was concentrated in those areas, remained largely unaware of what was in store. The reason for this was that the Soviet government, during the year of the non-aggression pact with Hitler, had suppressed the facts about German extermination of the Jews in occupied Poland. The Nazi armed forces were under orders to eliminate all Red Army officers, hard-core Communists and Jews. Almost three million Jews were trapped and killed in Russian territory during World War II and the statement, made in 1945 by the pro-Soviet writer, Corliss Lamont, that over a million Jews were evacuated from the threatened areas and given priority in transportation, is an utter falsehood.[21]

Anti-Semitism has always been deeply ingrained in the Russian peasantry and working class. Hence, it was at all times latent in the ranks of the Red Army. Naturally, Nazi propaganda attempted to fan this hostility into open desertion and mutiny. The Soviet authorities kept their own peoples in the dark concerning the extermination of the Jews, probably in the interests of refuting the Nazi identification of Communism with Jewry.

Early in the war, Henryk Erlich and Victor Alter, Polish Jewish Socialist leaders who had escaped the German juggernaut and found refuge in Soviet Russia, petitioned Stalin to set up a Jewish Anti-Fascist Committee, which could arouse the Free World to the extermination of the Jews of Eastern Europe by the Nazi special detachments known as *Einsatztruppen*. Stalin made a notation on their letter that they were to be shot forthwith. This was done, but Foreign Minister Molotov continued to assure Western observers, who were concerned with the fate of these two prominent political leaders, that they were in good health and would soon be released. In 1943, he finally admitted that they had been executed, falsely charging that they had propagandized among Red Army soldiers in favor of a speedy, negotiated peace with Nazi Germany![22]

The Broader Setting

This complex, and at times bizarre and baffling course of Soviet anti-Semitism seems almost totally irrational as indeed were many of the specific actions taken. Yet, the fundamental hostility of the Soviet regime toward its Jewish subjects had a rationale of its own. That hostility will, I believe, disappear if, and only if, the Soviet Communist system gradually evolves in the direction of economic and political freedom.

The fundamental difficulty is that Soviet Communism won power by organizing the have-not elements of the population against those classes and groups which were more highly privileged, better educated, more powerful, more productive, more intelligent and endowed with greater creativity than the average. The success of the class elite of Imperial Russia was attributed by the Bolsheviks, Mensheviks and other Marxists to ruthless exploitation. For the continuing plausibility of this propaganda, it was essential that the Soviet people believe in the inherent equality of all social, economic and ethnic groups. Unfortunately for the guardians of the Soviet state, there were certain groups which consistently outperformed the average, even under the Soviet system, whenever they were given opportunity to do so. The most important of these groups were the remnants of the upper and middle classes, the intellectuals and the Jews. Soviet propaganda excoriated these elements, attributing their achievements to misconduct and imputing to them sordid and even treasonable motives. The mania for biological equality reached such extremes that intelligence testing was abolished by a 1936 proclamation of the Central Committee of the Communist Party of the Soviet Union as "a device for perpetuating the existing class structure by mass tests which demonstrated the superiority of the dominant classes and 'superior races.' "[23] Even more, the Soviet Union purged and exterminated its best geneticists in the late 1930's and placed genetics under the control of Trofim Lysenko, an extreme environmentalist whose work is regarded by most Western geneticists as unsound. From that period on to Stalin's death, a Soviet geneticist risked imprisonment or death if he dared challenge the dogma that acquired characteristics could be inherited, a proposition the falsity of which Western science considers self-evident. The importance of Lysenko's perversion of genetics to Soviet ideology was that it implied that all human beings could be shaped at will by environmental forces into any form that the totalitarian state considered convenient.

The international revolutionary policies of Soviet Communism involve mobilizing the have-not nations and peoples for a worldwide struggle against the established order. Again, the premise of Soviet doctrine is that the poverty, illiteracy, hunger and intellectual stagnation of these have-not peoples is due, not to any inherent defects in their own make-up, but to oppression at the hands of "imperialist' nations.

Once the state of Israel began its rapid cultural, social, political and economic advance, Soviet propaganda attributed its successes, not to the dedication, energy and intelligence of its Jewish settlers, but to its supposed role as a lackey of imperialism. This is not primarily a case of blindness to the facts of life. Rather it is a recognition of the necessities imposed by revolutionary propaganda and doctrine. In order to inflame Israel's envious, have-not neighbors, it is vitally necessary to explain away Israel's success in terms other than the greater intelligence, energy and self-reliance of the Israeli people. Soviet propagandists have to avoid any intimation that an Arab conquest of Israel could not possibly solve the basic problems of the Arab world. They have to avoid any statement which might suggest that Israel without its Jewish population would again become what it had been for centuries—a primitive rural slum comparable to neighboring Middle Eastern areas.

In addition to all this, the Soviet political system functions best when it is able to deal with subjects who are prone to obey and accept unquestioningly, who are deficient in individualism, in the love of personal freedom and in the habit of skepticism. The existence of a highly gifted minority within its frontiers is in itself a threat to the monolithic unity, whether real or imaginary, of the Soviet world. Even worse, the Jews of Russia share common cultural traits with the Jews of the West. Hence, there is a potential bridge, a channel of communication and an opportunity for invidious comparison between Soviet and Western accomplishments. A further objection to the Jews is that in Judaism they have a religion and a philosophy of life which emphasizes moral and humane conduct and is hence largely at variance with the class ethics of Marxism-Leninism.

Even their thirst for education and self-improvement was held against the Jews by certain Soviet leaders who suffered from the lack of any real culture and who had ambiguous feelings about their own worth. The fact that the Jews clustered in cities opened them to the charge of "cosmopolitanism," a word which covered a badly defined terrain between sophistication and tolerance of non-Soviet concepts, on the one hand, and being security risks because of exposure to foreign influences, on the other. The tendency of Jews to work as businessmen, which in the Soviet scheme of things often meant as officials and accountants in state enterprises, opened them to the suspicion of being inherently non-proletarian and perhaps even secret advocates of free enterprise.

Finally, the Zionist hope for a Jewish National Homeland and the realization of that hope in 1948 added another strong ingredient to the witches' cauldron of suspicion, envy and hatred. The intensity of the pro-Israel sentiment of Soviet Jewry was revealed by the spontaneous, unauthorized and politically hazardous demonstrations with which Moscow Jews greeted Israeli diplomatic representatives to the USSR. These expressions of sentiment intensified the Kremlin's fear that its Jewish subjects had divided loyalties and widened an already deep breach.

CHAPTER 15

The Ordeals of Soviet Jewry

WITH HITLER DEAD and the war over, Stalin launched a
savage persecution of Soviet Jewry that overshadowed all
the injustices that had been heaped upon them by Czarism.
In 1948, the world-renowned Yiddish Art Theatre was
liquidated and its director, the dedicated Communist,
Solomon Mikhoels, died, ostensibly in an automobile acci-
dent, but probably by order of Stalin.[1] All other Jewish
cultural institutions were liquidated. The five outstanding
Yiddish writers, among them Itzik Fefer, who had served as
a Red Army Colonel in World War II, were arrested, in
four cases without any charges being made against them.
They disappeared from view and in 1952 were tried and
shot. Toward the close of the Stalin reign, virtually all
Jewish writers were in prison or dead.

Only one Jew, Lazar Kaganovich, survived on the Presi-
dium of the Central Committee of the Communist Party.

A purge of the Red Army eliminated 63 Jewish generals, 111 colonels and 159 lieutenant colonels during 1948-53. No Jew was appointed to an important command during the last years of Stalin's life.

The extent to which the Jewish presence was obliterated by official decree was revealed by the fact that Fadeev, who published *The Young Guard*, a novel about the Russo-German War, in 1951, and won the Stalin Prize for it, did not mention the extermination of Russian Jewry in its pages. In an earlier novel on the civil war that had followed the Bolshevik Revolution, Fadeev had made his hero a Jewish Red Army officer.[2] The closely supervised *Great Soviet Encyclopaedia* devoted 150 columns to "Jews" (*Evrei*) in its 1932 edition. The 1953 edition compressed these to four columns heaping vituperation on "national Jewish culture," which it characterized as an instrument of "rabbis and bourgeois" and of "our enemies."[3]

Nine distinguished Moscow physicians, six of them Jewish, were suddenly arrested and charged with having plotted to poison Stalin and other Soviet leaders as a preliminary to the overthrow of the Soviet regime. Stalin personally gave orders as to how the accused were to be interrogated and tortured and told Ignatiev, a high official of the secret police, "If you do not obtain confessions from the doctors, we will shorten you by a head." Stalin instructed the investigating judges to "beat, beat and, once again, beat."[4]

Jews in the Soviet Union and in the West feared that the fantastic "doctors' plot" was the preliminary to a massive purge of Soviet Jews and possibly to the deportation of Jewry in toto to some remote area in Siberia, where, like the Crimean Tatars, who had suffered similar deportation, they would be decimated by cold, disease, neglect, hunger and mistreatment and might vanish as a homogeneous people. That this dire result did not occur can be attributed to Stalin's death in 1953.

Knowledgeable Jews all over the world felt that, with Stalin's death, their most dangerous remaining enemy had been removed. But the left-wing Socialist and Communist Jews remained oblivious or indifferent to Stalin's true character and intentions. Thus, the leaders of the Mapam (United Workers) Party of Israel sent the following telegram:

"We lower our banners in sorrow at the passing of the great leader . . . captain of the world peace movement. His historic deeds will guide generations marching toward a regime of Socialism and Communism throughout the world."[5]

Stalin's anti-Semitism was a reflection of his paranoid fear of conspiracies against his life. It was also based on the growing Soviet conviction that the Jews were loyal at heart to Israel, rather than to the Soviet state, and that Israel was "an outpost of imperialism," or, in more realistic language, allied culturally, economically and politically with the West.

Khrushchev—Peasant Anti-Semite

Nikita Khrushchev continued Stalin's policies. What he lacked in paranoid fear, he made up for in a hostility to Jews in general. When he was sent to Galicia, after World War II, to settle certain intra-Communist Party squabbles, he denounced the organization for "treachery" and blamed this condition on the presence of "too many Jews" in the leadership.

Ten years later, Khrushchev lectured the Central Committee of the Polish Communist Party as follows:

"I believe that in Poland, too, you are suffering from an

abnormal composition of the leading cadres, as we had suffered from it. Now see what things are like in my country. . . . We have now got our affairs in good order. The percentage of high Jewish officials is now nil in my country —two or three per thousand."[6]

During the October 1956 crisis in Poland, Khrushchev flew to Warsaw to compel the Communist Party to toe the Moscow line. His first words to the recalcitrant Polish leaders were: "So you are going to help the Yids, are you?" Later, he added: "We have come to prevent you from delivering Poland into the hands of the Americans and the Zionists. . . . You have too many Abramoviches in your leadership."

Harrison E. Salisbury, former Moscow correspondent of the *New York Times* considered that much of the "creeping anti-Semitism" in the Soviet Union was due to Khrushchev's attitude, which reflected the hostility toward Jews characteristic of the Ukrainian border country and which he made little effort to conceal.[7] In an interview published by *Figaro*, Khrushchev attacked the Jews for "never considering they have learned enough" and for an intellectual bent which "tears them away from other occupations than those involving brain work."[8]

Khrushchev perpetuated and completed the purge of Jews from the high echelons of the Soviet State and Communist Party. In the early 1960's, the only powerful Jewish figure in these echelons was V. E. Dimchitz, First Deputy Chairman of the Planning Office. "Before World War II, Jews were heavily represented in the Supreme Soviet of the USSR. But by 1958, according to the Library of Congress Legislative Reference Service, "the figure had dropped to 0.25%. Jews were also under-represented in the Supreme Soviets of most Union Republics, especially in those where most Jews reside, the RSFSR, Byelorussia and the Ukraine.

At the lower local levels and that of the Union Republics, careers for Jews have been markedly limited by discrimination. For the higher executive positions, restrictions are universally acknowledged."[9]

Jews are considered, as Moshe Decter put it, "a security risk" and, for this reason, have been forced out of such sensitive areas as the Foreign Service and the armed forces.[10] This is again based on the phobia, dating from Stalinist days, that Jewish loyalty is primarily to Israel and that the Israeli diplomats in the USSR are espionage agents of the United States. As Vadim Bogoslovsky, a Soviet official attached to the United Nations, crudely expressed it, as reported by the New York Yiddish-language newspaper, the *Day-Jewish Journal:*

"Jews have a greater possibility of being seduced by foreign agents. Jews have a natural interest in and are not indifferent to Israel diplomats. The Israeli diplomats often go into the synagogues in Russia. They talk to the worshippers and make friends with them. They talk. They tell each other things. It happens that a Jew has a son who has an important post in a scientific research institute that is concerned with research in secret developments. The diplomat learns details and hands them over to his American friends. This is espionage."[11]

Jews in Russia are identified as such in the "internal passports" which they must carry about with them. They cannot escape their Jewish identification and merge into the general Soviet population.

The Khrushchev Purges and Executions

Between 1932 and 1962, the percentage of Jews in Soviet universities declined steadily from 13% to about 4% of total enrollment. The only high-income and high-status areas in which dejudaization did not occur were science and technology, where even Khrushchev recognized that the Soviets needed Jewish brains if they wanted to catch up with the United States.

The purpose was defined by one observer as eradicating "the Jewishness of the almost 3,000,000 Jews who live in the Soviet Union." The strategy used in trying to accomplish this was "the breaking down of morale, the slow strangulation of Jewish religion and culture, the steady erosion of all those special aspects of life that have meant so much to Jewish people." The observer, Rowland Evans, Jr., added:

"I came upon much evidence of this campaign during a recent trip through Russia—evidence of a sudden, grim increase in official anti-Jewish activity. The evidence strongly indicated that denunciation of the 'cosmopolitanism' and 'national narrow-mindedness' of Soviet Jews had advanced from the stage of propaganda harassment to the deadly serious stage of secret trial and imprisonment."[12]

One instance was the arrest in 1961 of Gedalia R. Pechersky, chairman of the Jewish religious community in Leningrad, on the charge of heading a "Zionist espionage ring," and his secret trial, conviction and sentence to twelve years in prison. Other Jewish leaders were tried and convicted with him; the chairmen of Jewish congregations in Minsk, Tashkent, Vilnyus, Kiev and Riga were deposed by governmental order and synagogues were closed all over the Soviet Union.

In March 1962, Bertrand Russell, Eleanor Roosevelt, François Mauriac and other internationally known figures protested the attempt by the Soviet government to extinguish Jewish religious and cultural life. The year before, the

Khrushchev regime had instituted the death penalty for crimes against property. This was followed by a rash of trials in which a "fantastically disproportionate number of Jews—60 to one—were sentenced to death by shooting."[13] The fact that many of the defendants bore Jewish names was stressed in the trials, and analysis of the trial records disclosed "an unmistakable pattern of hostility to Jews."[14]

These "crimes against property" ranged from theft and embezzlement to black market trading and the private manufacture of matzoth. Because of the over-centralization and colossal bureaucracy of the Soviet economy, gray market trading and surreptitious free enterprise were essential to the maintenance of production. Since Jews tended to be heavily concentrated in such areas as accounting and plant management, they were probably disproportionately involved in these activities. But all competent observers agreed that the ratio of Jewish to Gentile defendants in these trials was a fantastic distortion of the true state of affairs. The anti-Jewish bias in some of the trials was evidenced by the fact that the non-Jews would be sentenced to prison and the Jews to the firing squad for the same offenses.

The Jews of the West were slow to realize the profound extent and vicious character of the Soviet Government's campaign against its Jewish citizens. When the liberal magazine, the *New Leader*, devoted a special issue in September 1959 to Soviet anti-Semitism, "few persons were aware that the subject warranted special concern." Five years later, it called attention editorially to a Soviet pamphlet entitled *Judaism Without Embellishment* by Trofim Korneyevich Kichko, who was, like Nikita Khrushchev, a Ukrainian and who "seems to rank as a foremost Soviet sociologist of the Jews." This document was not some obscure gutter publication, but was issued under the auspices of the Ukrainian Academy of Science and hailed in a foreword by two members of that Academy as a "profound and substantial work . . . which contains a tremendous amount of factual material, conscientiously and scientifically analyzed . . . a valuable manual . . . [which] will assist wide circles of readers." This publication, with its cartoons "hauntingly reminiscent of Julius Streicher's *Der Stürmer*," was issued in an edition of 12,000 copies in Ukrainian.[15]

Some of the captions under the cartoons give a clear picture of what constitutes conscientious and scientific analysis for a Ukrainian academician. "The swindlers in religious articles brawl among themselves over the division of the spoils in the synagogue," one of them reads. Another asserts: "During the years of the Hitlerite occupation, the Zionist leaders served the Fascists." A third tells us that "all sorts of swindlers and cheats find refuge in the synagogue." Then there is a drawing of Israeli Prime Minister Ben Gurion, erasing the word "not" from the scroll containing the Mosaic injunctions against lying, stealing and committing murder.

Arthur Miller published a somewhat tepid protest against the Soviet campaign against Jewry.[16] Some 223 prominent Americans protested the decree under which 141 Soviet citizens, most of them Jews, had suffered death for economic offenses between May 1961 and April 1963. They urged the USSR to repeal the law on the grounds that "the conscience of mankind rebels against excessive and inhumane punishment." On December 2, 1963, Queen Elizabeth and Albert Schweitzer as well as six of his fellow Nobel Prize winners wrote Khrushchev expressing their "concern" over a wide range of anti-Semitic actions. A year previously,

the Soviet Premier had been subjected to hostile questioning on the same matter at a meeting of the outstanding
writers, artists and musicians of the Soviet Union. Even
more significant was the fact that Western Communist
Parties and their leaders publicly expressed a sharp disagree-
ment with Soviet conduct.

During the 1967 military struggle between Israel and the
Arab states, the Soviet press published blatantly anti-
Semitic cartoons. Thus, *Pravda* on July 4th depicted a Jew
holding hands with Hitler under the caption, "seeing eye
to eye." Despite Premier Kosygin's denials of this charge
when in America, there was reason to believe the Soviet
Union was reverting to the anti-Jewish hate propaganda
of the Khrushchev era.

Cultural and Religious Discrimination

The cultural and religious blackout afflicting Soviet Jews
entailed reducing the number of synagogues, serving a
population of three million, to less than sixty. Under
Kerensky's democratic government, there had been three
thousand. The State Publishing House refused to print
Jewish prayerbooks and the socialized bakeries would not
make *matzoth* for Passover, nor, of course, were Jews allowed to make their own for community sale, since that
would constitute "capitalist exploitation." The few synagogues open were described as incredibly shabby and under
police surveillance.

At a time when religious persecution of Christians was
lifting somewhat, the oppression of Judaism was being
accelerated. "For most Russians," Evans concluded, "life is
getting somewhat better. For the Jews, it is becoming
intolerable."[17]

The official organizations of American Jewry have stressed

the suppression of the practice of Judaism and this is understandable. Reprehensible as this suppression is, competent observers estimate that only about 1% of Soviet Jews are practicing believers in Judaism.[18] If this is so, the suppression imposes hardship merely on some thirty thousand members of the Jewish community.

A serious matter for Russian Jews is the fact that "we do not have our own newspapers in Moscow, Kiev, Minsk, or the other population centers; there are no Jewish libraries; there are no schools or courses for those who wish to study the Jewish language; there are no clubs, theaters, or any other centers of cultural activity; there is no public organization that concerns itself with the welfare of the Jewish population."[19]

Bertrand Russell, the British philosopher and pro-Soviet opponent of American foreign policy, called this letter to the attention of Aron Vergelis, editor of the Soviet magazine in Yiddish, *Sovietish Heimland,* and received the sort of intellectually contemptible reply that could have been expected from this Jewish spokesman for Soviet anti-Jewish policies. Russell replied:

"Your reply is equally lacking in scruple when it dismisses as a 'cold war' attitude, expressions of concern for Soviet Jews which exist in progressive, pro-Soviet, and also Communist circles in the West, and when it makes the ridiculous charge that the motive is the diversion of attention from 'the racist and anti-Semitic orgy rife in some countries across the water.' You cannot be unaware that the Communist Parties in Italy, France, United States, Canada, Scandinavia, Australia, and elsewhere have publicly criticized anti-Semitic literature in the USSR, discrimination against Jewish religion, and the depredation of Jewish culture."[20]

Since Khrushchev's Ouster

On October 15, 1964, Nikita Khrushchev was ousted from power. Since that time, executions of Jews for minor economic crimes have not been reported. The main preoccupation of American Jewish organizations has been with the absence of Jewish prayerbooks and matzoth, the insufficiency of synagogues, the lack of seminaries to train rabbis and the desolate state of Jewish cultural life.[21]

The condition of Soviet Jewry seems to have remained substantially unchanged. In February 1966, an interfaith mission to the Soviet Union reported that an atmosphere of "fear and insecurity" prevailed among Russian Jews. It added, according to the *New York Times*, that "there was fear of reprisal in the event Jews pressed for cultural and religious privileges. It reported that attendance at Russian Orthodox and Baptist churches was large and included youthful worshippers, but that Jewish congregations were made up of the elderly."[22]

In the previous fall, Moshe Decter reported minor modifications of Soviet policy, a softening of anti-Semitism and acquiescence in a modest revival of Jewish culture.[23] In July 1965, Dr. Nahum Goldmann, president of the World Jewish Congress, announced that Jewish leaders were holding unpublicized talks with Soviet leaders about the formation of a central body which could represent Soviet Jews in international Jewish affairs. He warned against violent attacks on the Soviet authorities, such as comparing them with the Nazis, claiming that any such action could end negotiations and stifle further progress.[24]

Most Eastern European countries permit Jews whose families were broken up by Nazi persecution to become reunited with them by emigrating. Until late 1966 at least,

Soviet policy was to issue exit permits in only a very small number of cases, generally to elderly people. Then on December 3, 1966 Premier Alexsei N. Kosygin made a statement at a press luncheon in Paris that Soviet Jews wishing to join their relatives abroad would be free to do so. This was received with cautious optimism by Jewish leaders in Israel and the United States. While a major change in policy seemed possible, American Jewish organizations pointed out that previous promises by the Soviet regime to liberalize treatment of its Jewish subjects had not been honored.

The same Jewish authorities who criticize Soviet anti-Semitism praise the policies of Communist Rumania toward its remnant of Jewish citizens as exemplary. In Poland, anti-Semitism, traditionally virulent, was reported on the increase in 1965. While the Polish Government bears no responsibility for this and has permitted Jews to emigrate to Israel, popular feeling is hostile. This is attributed, in part, to the prominent part Jews played in the Polish Communist Party leadership and the Polish Soviet state under Stalin and to the fact that Jews are also prominent in the theater, journalism, the movie industry, the universities and private trade. The average income of Polish Jews is believed to be "double that of non-Jewish Poles, or more."[25]

In May 1966, Israeli Foreign Minister Abba Eban went to Warsaw where he held conferences with Polish Foreign Minister Adam Rapacki and told the press that Israel was definitely seeking better relations with Poland. He said that "common suffering, common struggle and common rebirth" were factors cementing the friendship between Poland and Israel.

As for Soviet-Israeli relations, they did not exist in a vacuum, but were conditioned by Arab hostility to Israel and by the cold war between the Great Powers. "They would be better if the rivalry between the Great Powers became less intense, or if a greater sense of realism were to manifest itself in the attitude of the Arab States to Israel. Since neither of these situations is static, there is room here for acts of diplomacy."[26]

Events in Cuba soon made it seem most improbable that an era of good feeling was just around the corner, or that the Russian Jews were about to emerge from their long ice age of persecution. Cuba had seemed to be *sui generis* in the Communist world. About three-fourths of her ten thousand Jews had voted against Castro with their feet. The emigration was not due to discrimination against them, but was rather an expression of distaste for Communism. Cuba was the only Red country where Zionist groups could function openly. Judaism, Yiddish and Hebrew were still taught at Havana's Albert Einstein School, a Jewish institution which had been nationalized by the Castro regime.[27]

Then there was a rude awakening. When the Tri-Continental Conference of Anti-Imperialist Forces met in Havana in January 1966 to plan Communist subversion on a global scale, no Israeli group was invited. The so-called Israeli Peace Movement, composed of such organizations as the Maki (Communist Party of Israel) and the Mapam, which had distinguished itself a decade earlier by its sycophantic telegram on Stalin's death, protested this exclusion, announced that there were "anti-imperialist" forces in Israel eager to participate and chided the Conference for having surrendered to "the pressure of Arab chauvinism."

Worse was to come. A Conference resolution condemned "the existence of Israel in the occupied part of Palestine" and supported "the right of the Palestine Arabs to liberate their country within the frame of their natural right to self-defense."[28] This incendiary appeal for war against the state of Israel was made at a time of deteriorating Israeli-Arab relations and growing danger of armed conflict. It was recognized in Israel as a most serious matter and even the Mapam and Maki denounced the Conference action.

Meanwhile, the American Jewish organizations concentrated on such issues as the numbers of rabbis and synagogues permitted to function in the USSR, the state of the prayerbooks and synagogues and the baking of matzoth. This emphasis seemed to disinterested observers misplaced in view of the fact that Communist world policies (and those of the Soviet state which formulated them) called for a "war of liberation" which could mean the extinction of Israel and renewed slaughter of millions of Jews.

The Arab-Israeli War

The logical culmination of the destructive Soviet Middle East policies was the six-day Arab-Israeli War of June 1967 which decisively crushed Arab military power and, for the time at least, checkmated Soviet attempts to obliterate the state of Israel.

Between 1955 and 1967, the Soviet Union had supplied the Arab states with 2,000 tanks, 700 modern fighter and bomber planes, large quantities of field guns, specialized artillery, mortars, rockets and rocket launchers, ground-to-air and ground-to-ground missiles, together with naval craft, some of it with rocket-launching potential, including seven destroyers, fourteen submarines and 46 torpedo boats.[29] This menacing build-up of offensive weapons was greatly accelerated after Khrushchev's meetings with Nasser in

Egypt in May 1964, when the two chiefs of state pledged themselves to enduring "Arab-Soviet friendship." Imprisoned cadres of the Egyptian Communist Party were released, to emerge shortly thereafter as leading propagandists for "Nasser socialism" and war against Israel.

If American Jewish organizations were slow to grasp the full implications for Israel's national survival of this encroaching military encirclement, U.S. Embassy officials in Cairo were even slower. In fact, on the basis of conversations with them in Cairo in 1964, I would be inclined to characterize their attitude as incredibly myopic. This was perhaps not surprising in view of the fact that President Kennedy had named to the crucial diplomatic post of Ambassador to the United Arab Republic an ex-missionary named John Badeau, who had praised Nasser and written a eulogistic preface to the latter's shoddy version of *Mein Kampf*.[30] In his preface Ambassador Badeau hailed the Egyptian dictator's revolution as "the wave of the future" for neighboring Arab lands.[31]

As the years passed, the technological military advantage over Israel was heightened and the crisis moved from its latent toward its overt phase. Yet the Western powers remained complacent. The Soviet Government meanwhile consistently exercised its veto power in the UN Security Council to block all efforts at an amicable and constructive settlement of Arab-Israeli tensions and to prevent any censure of Syrian acts of terrorism and murder against Israeli citizens on Israeli soil. The Security Council was thus made aware of its impotence to take any restraining action against Arab aggression and, as this awareness sunk in, it ceased even to make the attempt.

The brilliant Israeli move against Egypt, Jordan and Syria in June 1967 revolutionized the balance of military power in the Middle East. Despite marked superiority in materiel and despite the presence of Soviet advisers in both the Egyptian and the Syrian armies, the defeat of the Arab coalition was one of the most sudden and spectacular in military history. Foreign Minister Eban claimed that, in the Sinai Peninsula alone, Egyptian forces abandoned over $2 billion worth of arms and equipment.[32]

The Israeli victory was widely regarded as one of spirit against matter, of intelligence and will against mere weaponry. After observing that "the Israelis are very patriotic, brave and skillful soldiers, brilliantly led," *Life* asked editorially: "What *is* the matter with the Arab armies?" Answering its own question with another, it queried rhetorically: "Was there ever a people so bellicose in politics, so reckless and raucous in hostility—and then so unpugnacious in pitched combat—as Nasser's Egyptians?"[33]

In the Sinai desert, the Soviet Union suffered one of its most serious diplomatic defeats. It lost, not merely several billion dollars in military materiel, but prestige before the world. It impaired its chance to dominate a region of great strategic importance. But the Soviet leaders will find it difficult to learn from this devastating experience since Marxism-Leninism demands that they consider all peoples innately equal in intelligence, initiative, fortitude, courage and other psychic values.

The West, however, is not under any similar compulsion. The Soviet debacle in the Middle East, like the Western debacle in tropical Africa, may result in a re-examination of the wisdom of any foreign policy predicated on the hypothesis that all peoples are equally capable of either self-government or self-defense. A possible implication of any such re-examination would be that the West reconstruct its foreign policy in backward areas to concentrate on the few islands of spiritual and intellectual strength in these seas of mediocrity. In the Middle East, Israel and, to a lesser extent, Lebanon would seem to be such concentration points. In sub-Saharan Africa, Rhodesia and the Republic of South Africa emerge as islands of order and progress, inhabited by people of high intelligence and love of country. Modern civilization can radiate outward from such areas of psychic strength and in time perhaps transform the backward regions. By contrast, American support of immediate independence for the Congo, Kenya and Nigeria—not to mention U.S. championship of the crusade of envy of these black states against white South Africa—has been almost as frustrating as the Soviet policy of showering modern arms on the spiritless *fellaheen* of Egypt.

The unequivocal Soviet support of the Arab aggressors during the six-day war had a profound shock effect on the American Jewish community. A more or less tolerant Jewish attitude toward the Soviet state was transformed overnight into one of outright and intense hostility. There was turmoil within the Communist Parties of the West. The Communist Parties of France, Finland and various other European states went so far as to criticize the anti-Israeli stand of the Soviet Union.

On June 20, 1967, twenty-one leading American Jewish organizations, but not the American Jewish Committee, published a scathing denunciation of Soviet policies toward Israel and Jewry in the form of a full-page advertisement in the *New York Times*. Entitled "An Appeal of Conscience to Mr. Kosygin," the declaration alluded to the Soviet characterization of Israel's successful defense as "Nazi aggression" and to *Izvestia*'s "lying charge that Israeli troops have shot down women and children in public executions."

"This powerful country, the USSR," the statement continued, "has never published a word of criticism about the Nazi war criminals who are actively mobilized in Cairo and Damascus in the war against the Jews. The Soviet Government has given unstinting support to the Arab States which disseminate the crude anti-Semitism of the 'Protocols of the Elders of Zion.'

"The very country which is preventing the development of Jewish life within its own borders, does not hesitate to fasten the hideous label of Nazism on the survivors of a small Jewish nation which lost a third of its members in Nazi atrocities.

"The accent of present Soviet propaganda is the accent of the Stalinist doctors' plot and the destruction of Soviet Jewish society. It is the accent of the Soviet anti-Semitic propaganda against Judaism, of the fever of Jew-hatred that periodically seizes the Soviet press. It means that the incorrigible anti-Semites who infest Russian society are again being given their hour."

The statement concluded with the hope that the Soviet Union would reverse its policies and "strive for a lasting peace in the Middle East" rather than seek to follow in the footsteps of Adolf Hitler.

The catalytic effect of the Soviet role in the Arab-Israeli War will extend beyond Jewish defections from the world Communist movement. The tone of Jewish organizations toward the Soviet regime and toward the Communist Parties which serve it has changed from one of gentle reproof to one of hostility. Naturally, fear of reprisals against Soviet Jewry and a desire to persuade the Soviet leaders to adopt a more civilized policy will serve as restraining forces. Nevertheless, there seems to be a growing realization among Jewish leaders that Soviet totalitarianism shares with the

Nazi Reich anti-Semitism, together with other social and political vices.

Within the Arab world, Egyptian hatred of Israel reached a fevered pitch only after the Nasser regime had shown its anti-elite character by cutting ties with the West, ousting from power Egypt's gifted Coptic minority and engaging in wholesale socialization. Similarly, Syria became the most strident voice in Islam for aggressive war against Israel only after the left-wing socialist Baath Party seized power in 1963. Three years later, the ultra-left military element within the Baath took over. Syria was transformed into a police state, equipped with concentration camps where the elite languished, while socialized enterprises were mismanaged by radical Army officers, discontented students and left-wing Arab "intellectuals" of various sorts.[34] Under Baath rule, Syria moved rapidly toward the status of Soviet satellite. Her people were compelled to exchange prosperity for poverty and freedom for bondage. Synchronized with this immense retrogression and the elimination of the Syrian elite was the emergence of socialistic Syria as the shrillest voice in the Arab world for an immediate war of extermination against Israel. In the Middle East, as elsewhere, anti-Semitism was directly correlated with collectivism and the destruction of a natural aristocracy by a gutter elite.

Underlying Purposes

Soviet policy toward its Jews is complicated by the existence of the state of Israel. The Kremlin has, over the years, supported the Arab world against Israel. The doctrinal reason for doing so is the conception of Arab aggression as "anti-imperialist" in character; the geopolitical motivation is to use this have-not area as a battering ram against Western defense ramparts. The pro-Arab, anti-Israeli policy of the USSR reinforces Soviet anti-Semitism and vice versa.

The Kremlin is uncomfortable with its Jews at home, but even more reluctant to let them emigrate. Should they be permitted to go to Israel, en masse, Arab resentment of Soviet permissiveness might result. Probably more important is the consideration that the Jews would be eloquent witnesses to the dreary life of the Soviet citizen, to the appalling inefficiency of the Communist productive system and to the pervasiveness of Soviet anti-Semitism. The main Jewish organizations would like to see Soviet Jews emigrate to Israel. This might significantly change the balance of power in the Middle East and it would counterpoise the tendency of Israel to become a state of Afro-Asian, rather than of European, Jews. From the American standpoint, the exodus of Soviet Jewry to any Free-World area would be immensely desirable as it would deprive the USSR of an element that has furnished the Kremlin with a disproportionate share of its best scientists.

Thus, a fundamental change in the situation of Russia's Jews presupposes one of two things. Either a drastic internal transformation of the Soviet system in the direction of freedom—something that is conceivable only in the long run—or else some far-reaching arrangement between the West or Israel and the Soviet state enabling Russian Jews to leave freely. Neither development seems on the visible horizon.

CHAPTER 16

Aspects of American Anti-Semitism

EVER SINCE GRAECO-ROMAN TIMES, fear of anti-Semitism has been a permanent preoccupation of Jewry. What is involved here is not merely dislike of Jews or social barriers against them, but an ideological movement (whether religious or political), of great virulence which may erupt under unknown conditions into massacres and genocide. To a large extent, Jewish political behavior, both in the United States and elsewhere, has been motivated by fear of its recrudescence. There seems, moreover, to be an intimate connection between Jewish radicalism and fear of anti-Semitism. Thus, it is a subject which can scarcely be glossed over in any study of the Jew in American politics.

There has been a prodigious amount of research into anti-Semitism in America and a great deal has been written about its motivations, the sort of people it attracts, the conditions under which it can become a mass movement, its pathological aspects, the psychological needs that it satisfies, the extent to which it is a reaction against specific Jewish traits, and so forth. Yet few findings have been scientifically established. In fact, the conclusions of one research study are often contradicted by those of the next. No clear and consistent pattern of either the habitual anti-Semite or the social conditions under which political anti-Semitism becomes a mass movement has emerged.

This would seem to be due to two reasons. The first is that the subject itself is inherently elusive. It would appear, in other words, that different sorts of people may become anti-Semites under different sets of conditions. If there are unifying and underlying elements in anti-Semitism in general, they have not been discerned and have certainly not been unequivocally established by social science research techniques.

The second difficulty is that some of the analysis—and particularly the theorizing about the relationship between anti-Semitism and the "authoritarian character structure" —has been highly subjective. Some of the psychologists and psychiatrists responsible for these studies have colored them with their own personal political and social prejudices. When subjects hold sets of opinions of which the investigators strongly disapprove, the former are frequently condemned for such traits as "rigidity," "excessive conformity," or a "debunking attitude" toward social and economic goals. Since the methods used in these studies are often highly subjective, there is no inbuilt protection against this sort of bias in their findings. Other studies have begun with the arbitrary assumption that all types of anti-Semitism must be symptoms of emotional disturbance and have hence concluded that the study of the prejudiced person should concentrate, not on "where he acquired the prejudice, but *why he needs it*."[1] An even more far-fetched view was that of Otto Klineberg that "prejudice exists because there is something to be gained by it. This gain is usually directly economic. . . ."[2] If this were true, American anti-Semitism would be most intense among the professionals and intellectuals, who face the brunt of Jewish competition, and least among the farmers and manual workers, who are not in competition with Jews to any significant extent. But the reverse is the case.

During the Nazi Era

During the thirties and forties, anti-Semitism was shockingly widespread in the United States. Since then, it has declined markedly.

The depth of this decline can be illustrated by a few examples of questions asked repetitively by public opinion polls. One of these was: "Have you heard any criticism or talk against the Jews in the last six months?" This question was asked samples of the non-Jewish population of the United States during twelve different years in 1940-1959. The percentage replying "yes" rose from 46% of the total in 1940 to a maximum of 64% in 1946, then declined to 24% in 1950 and to 12% in 1959.[3]

One measuring rod was the question: "If your party nominated a generally well-qualified man for President who happened to be a Jew, would you vote for him?" When this question was first asked, in slightly different form, in February 1937, 45% replied "yes" and 9% expressed no opinion. By 1958, 62% of the people polled expressed willingness to vote for a Jewish candidate and by August 1965, less than a year after the Goldwater defeat, this figure rose to 80%.[4]

In November 1938, *Fortune* published the results of a National Opinion Research Center (NORC) questionnaire concerning "hostility toward the Jewish people" in the United States. Nationally, 32.5% thought it was "growing," 52.5% considered it very slight and 15.0% didn't know. In cities with over a million inhabitants, more than twice as many people believed hostility was growing as did the people in towns with less than 2,500 population. The relationship of these opinions to anti-Semitism lies in the fact that people who dislike Jews are more prone to be aware of or to magnify hostility in others than are people who are either favorably inclined or neutral.

In 1942, 44% of the respondents to an Office of Public Opinion Research (OPOR) poll thought Jews had "too much power and influence in this country." In 1943, 33% of the people queried by the American Institute of Public Opinion (AIPO) thought that Roosevelt had appointed too many Jews to federal government positions. In the same year, almost 50% of those polled by NORC believed that Jews had "too much influence in the business world" and this percentage would rise to 57% in December 1944 and to 58% a year later.[5]

The feeling about Jews as neighbors depended on class and education. In 1955 and 1956, 5% of those polled by NORC stated that they would not like having Jewish neighbors at all. This negative reaction rose from 3% of the college-bred to 7% of those with only grammar-school education and reached 11% in the case of Negroes.[6] The hostility to Jews as neighbors was much greater than this among factory workers, as revealed by a study published by *Fortune* in November 1942. Some 72% objected to Negroes as residents of their neighborhood, 42% objected to Jews, 28% to Chinese and 4% to Catholics. Only 13% replied that it made no difference.

There was strong hostility to the admission of Jewish refugees from Nazi persecution. In November 1938, 71% of an AIPO poll registered disapproval of the admission of more Jewish refugees into the United States as permanent residents. When a similar question was asked in 1946, 72% disapproved.[7] Canada was somewhat more liberal on this topic, but not markedly so. In 1946, 61% of those queried opposed admitting Jewish refugees who had attempted to enter Palestine illegally and had therefore been interned by British authorities.[8]

This antagonism was not entirely due to anti-Semitism. In September 1944, NORC reported that 25% of American respondents opposed the admission of any foreigners at all, 46% opposed the admission of Jews, 59% that of Germans and 75% that of Japanese. Of the other national groups covered by the poll, English, Swedes, Russians, Chinese and Mexicans ranked ahead of Jews, in that order.[9]

Approval of Nazi oppression of Jews was more frequently encountered among workers than in the general population. In 1936, only 14% of those polled nationally believed Germany would be better off without the Jews as against 55% who believed she would be worse off. Two years later, 94% of those questioned by AIPO said they disapproved of the Nazi treatment of the Jews and only 6% said they approved. By contrast, a 1944 survey of the views of factory workers, mainly in war industries, disclosed that "over half the respondents condoned the Nazi measures" against Jews and "a large number of these even express[ed] unqualified approval."[10]

A *Fortune* poll published in November 1942 dealt with

intermarriage. The question asked was: "Are there any on this list that you would not consider marrying?" Negroes were rejected as spouses by 91.6% of the Protestants, 92.8% of the Catholics and 95% of the Jews. Chinese followed with a rejection rate of 70% to 80%. Jews were rejected by 51.6% of the Protestants, 58.8% of the Catholics and 57.8% of the Negroes. This was not entirely an expression of ethnic hostility, but was partly motivated by religious considerations. This is evident from the fact that 19.9% of the Protestants were unwilling to marry Catholics and 25.2% of the Catholics were averse to marrying Protestants.[11]

Who Are the Anti-Semites?

There is broad agreement concerning some characteristics of the typical American anti-Semite; wide difference of opinion concerning others. The higher the level of education, the less the prevalence of anti-Jewish attitudes. This seems to be a solidly established fact as far as the United States is concerned, but it is not universally true.

In Germany and Austria, for instance, the anti-Semitic movements, including the Nazis, seem to have appealed to people of higher than average education. In his authoritative study of the early decades of anti-Jewish political movements in the German-speaking world, Pulzer found that "the bulk of anti-Semitic support" derived from "the middle class and above all . . . a particular section of it—the middle and lower professional grades and the middle and small businessmen."[12] He cited as an example the occupations of the 18,184 members of the Pan-German League who lived in Germany in 1901. Of these 5,339 were described as professors and university lecturers, another 3,760 were artists, officials and teachers and some 4,905 were small business-men.[13]

In America, we find the opposite condition. In 1961, 83% of those with a college education were willing to vote for a Jewish candidate for President, but only 73% of those with a high school education and only 55% of those who had not gone beyond grammar school. Women were more willing to support Jewish presidential candidates than men. Some 76% of those in the 21-29 age bracket responded affirmatively as against only 62% of those over 50. This indicated that prejudice, as measured by this test, was declining. Catholics (82%) were significantly more tolerant in this matter than Protestants (66%). Since a Catholic presidential candidate with strong Jewish support had just broken the religious barrier to the White House, this difference was to be expected.

In an intensive interview study of anti-Jewish attitudes among 150 returned veterans of World War II, Bettelheim and Janowitz stressed educational difference. "The outspoken and intense anti-Semites did not differ appreciably from the tolerant subjects in either age or religion," they wrote, "though they did include slightly larger percentages of Catholics and older men. But there was a difference in educational levels. Only 26% of the intense and outspoken anti-Semites had some college education, a percentage half as large as that of the tolerant subjects."[14]

We cannot, however, assume that education in itself diminishes hostility. This was evidently not the case in Germany. The fact that education in the United States is strongly oriented against movements based on race hatred is probably the crucial factor. Thus, the withering of anti-Semitism is not necessarily the result of more knowledge; it is more likely to be the product of a specific sort of education. There are other contributory factors. The American anti-Semite may be typically a frustrated and disappointed person who feels that he has been given a raw deal by society. The undereducated provide much more than their fair share of these frustrates and failures. Finally, there is evidence that normal contacts on the basis of equality between Jews and non-Jews reduce hostility.[15] These equal-status contacts will be much more frequent on college campuses than elsewhere simply because Jews are so heavily represented on faculties and in student bodies.[16]

There is some evidence that the American anti-Semites tend not only to be worse educated, but mentally inferior and less successful. A 1951 study of the attitudes of high school seniors in a Midwestern city showed that the anti-Semites were from poorer home backgrounds, were less intelligent, were inferior in their school work and were less prominent in school activities.[17]

Hostility to Jews tends to be greatest in the Northeast and Midwest and least in the South. It is more common among the older than the younger age groups, more frequent among men than among women, and probably more characteristic of the great cities than of the smaller communities. Antagonism may arise whenever minorities become numerous enough to make the majority acutely aware of their presence and, accordingly, anti-Semitism tends to increase with the proportion of Jewish to total residents of any community.

A great deal of work has gone into the question of the relationship between social mobility and anti-Semitism. At least two authorities found that the "upward mobile" (typically children of manual workers who moved into the middle class) tend to be more hostile toward Jews than those who are stationary.[18] The theorizing behind this was that these people tend to take their working-class prejudices with them and to "overconform," because of uneasiness, to what they believe to be middle-class or upper-class norms. As a theory, this is unconvincing. Where the upper class frowns on anti-Semitism, "overconformity" will involve a change of opinion in a pro-Jewish direction. Moreover, Bettelheim found in his study of World War II veterans that the upward mobile element was more satisfied with life and hence more tolerant—both of Jews and in general —than either the downward-moving group or the stationary element.[19]

Proportionately, Bettelheim found, there was significantly more anti-Semitism among the "downstarts" than in either of the other two groups. This group was generally hostile, pessimistic about its future and quick to claim that it had a bad break in the armed services. The downward-moving group also tended to repudiate and reject such controlling institutions as the Veterans' Administration, the U.S. government and the political parties. Of those who accepted Jews, 67% accepted these institutions and only 8% rejected them. Among anti-Semites, only 23% accepted them and 49% rejected them.[20]

This is about what one would expect. People who are moving downward will inevitably seek to blame that fact on a bad break or unfair competition, rather than on their own inadequacies. Resenting their own deteriorating status, they will tend to be generally hostile. Since the Jews are the most rapidly and consistently upward-moving element in American society, they are natural targets for the enmity of the downstart.

In corroboration of this theory that anti-Semitism is often an expression of resentment of personal failure, Angus Campbell reported in 1952 that only 10% of those who expressed contentment with their own economic situation were anti-Semitic, whereas 38% of the economic malcontents were anti-Semitic.[21]

The "Authoritarian Personality"

There is an enormous literature on the "authoritarian personality" and cognate aspects of anti-Semitism. For instance, I have already cited the objective findings of one of the two Gough studies of anti-Semitism. Gough also reported that the anti-Semitic students were characterized by "a rigid, somewhat dogmatic style of thinking," by "a hostile and bitter outlook with rather transparent expressions of aggression," by "an 'underlying perplexity,' fearfulness, and feelings of estrangement and isolation," by "a tendency to 'debunk and discredit the abilities and achievements of others, to deflate and disrespect;' " by "debunking attitudes toward questions of political-social ideals and goals" and by "emphasis on nationalism, chauvinism, and conservatism."[22]

How does one measure these supposed traits objectively? For example a "debunking attitude" toward "political-social ideals?" Even in 1945, many Americans did not share the Administration's faith in the peace-loving intentions of Stalin's Russia, nor did they believe that the United Nations was on the verge of ushering in the Kantian era of perpetual peace. Under the Gough analysis, would they have been characterized as debunkers with "a hostile and bitter outlook with rather transparent expressions of aggression"? Would they also have been convicted of the triple crime of "nationalism, chauvinism and conservatism"? The trouble with studies such as these is that their findings are not objectively verifiable and have little precise meaning. The adjectives used to describe attitudes often shed more light on the political opinions of the investigator than on those of his subjects.

According to Adorno and associates, the authors of *The Authoritarian Personality*,[23] we can understand the anti-Semite by realizing that: "A basically hierarchical, authoritarian, exploiting parent-child relationship is apt to carry over with a power-oriented, exploitively dependent attitude toward one's sex partner and one's God and may well culminate in a political philosophy and social outlook which has no room for anything but a desperate clinging to what appears to be a strong and disdainful rejection of whatever is relegated to the bottom."[24]

Adorno also informs us that anti-Semitism is associated with "stereotopy; rigid adherence to middle-class values; the tendency to regard one's own group as morally pure in contrast to the immoral outgroup; opposition to and exaggeration of prying and sensuality; extreme concern with dominance and power (fear of Jewish power and desire for Gentile power); fear of moral contamination; fear of being overwhelmed and victimized; the desire to erect social barriers in order to separate one's own group from another and to maintain the morality and the dominance of one's own group."[25]

Much of this is self-evident and useless. We already know that people erect barriers in order to bring about group separation and that the anti-Semite believes his own stock morally better and fears Jewish power.

That which is not self-evident in the theory, however, is dubious in the extreme. Take, for example, the assertion that anti-Semitism is associated with "rigid adherence to middle-class values." Do Adorno and associates imagine that middle-class values include the repudiation of Christianity and

Christian ethics and the destruction of individual freedom and due process of law? On the contrary, the entire fabric of the free enterprise economy and representative government was the achievement of the middle class. This fabric was violently destroyed by the Nazis in Germany and the Bolsheviks in Russia. Hence, the statement is a reversal of the truth of the sort that is unhappily common among Socialist writers.

Consider also Adorno's assertion that a "basically hierarchial, authoritarian, exploiting parent-child relationship" is closely associated with anti-Semitism. There is a good deal of data to support the view that this was fairly prevalent in German families before and during the Nazi era. In fact, much of the unsubstantiated theorizing in the Adorno book is simply a rehash of some of the assumptions made about Nazism during World War II.[26]

To what extent, however, does this Germanic pattern of a generation or two ago apply to contemporary manifestations of anti-Semitism in America? In 1962, *Good Housekeeping* published an analysis of the character and background of twelve young men who tormented a Jewish family (the Bowmans) for sixteen months, bringing anguish and misery to neighbors who had never harmed them.[27]

Did they represent "rigid adherence to middle-class values," as Adorno and his associates would have predicted? Not quite. "One had been arrested for speeding and was arrested again, after indictment in the Bowman case, for drunken driving. Another had a record of truancy, tampering with an automobile and involvement in an auto theft. Two had been arrested for drunkenness. And one had a record of eighteen months of psychiatric treatment in a mental hospital after conviction of a sexual offense against a child."[28]

An astonishingly high proportion of the twelve had suffered major accidents, illnesses or physical disabilities, a syndrome which was also characteristic of the murderers described in Truman Capote's book, *In Cold Blood*.

The last thing one could say about the group was that they were the products of "hierarchical, exploiting parent-child relationships," to again quote Adorno's matchless English prose. In fact, five of the twelve came from homes broken by divorce. When asked why they had done it, one of them said:

"Our ages and neighborhood mostly. There are quite a few broken homes and parents with drinking problems. A lot of these kids drink, but that had nothing to do with it. *It's just that none of the parents knew what their sons were doing. Mine had no idea.* . . . My mother never had to work. But I'm an only child and *I guess my parents spoiled me.*"[29]

As Bruno Bettelheim points out, reducing the anti-Semite to a readily recognizable stereotype serves a psychological function for Jews. "It helps to overcome anxiety—since all anti-Semites are supposedly the same, one can approach them all with the same fixed 'plan'; it helps to safeguard self-esteem—since all anti-Semites are stupid, uneducated and depraved, what they think can be disregarded; thinking of them as inhumanly powerful also helps to protect self-esteem where one has to submit to them."[30]

More Constructive Approaches

Writing in *Psychiatry*, S. Tarachow suggests that the greatest single reason for hatred of the Jews is that they have always been nonconformists and dissenters. Like Mephistopheles in Goethe's *Faust*, they have been "the spirit that always denies." Without denial, doubt, dissent, experiment and questioning, there would be no forward movement of society and no freedom. This is recognized as part of the democratic creed. But in the authoritarian and totalitarian societies, the situation is very different. The Jews are hated and persecuted by the political rulers of these systems due to "the conscious or unconscious recognition by a tyrant that a tyrant is never safe so long as the smallest focus of dissidence exists. . . . Since the Jews were the most obviously nonconformist element in the community, they were the first to be attacked by an insecure authority."[31]

A similar view was expressed by Judd Teller. He suggested that anti-Semitism always increases during revolutionary periods. It may not be present in the initial phases, in fact, Jews may be prominent in the revolutionary leadership, but it is almost inevitable at some stage in the process.[32]

This view has a lot to recommend it provided one defines the word *revolution* carefully. Social revolutions are movements of such profound discontent with the existing order that they seek to change its entire power structure. Quite evidently, they attract, among others, power-hungry people who are suffering the pangs of downward mobility or who have much lower status than they believe they are entitled to possess. The revolutionaries include people whose reaction to this situation is abnormally intense and whose estimate of their chances for success within the existing order is highly pessimistic. Their followers are sufficiently discontented with the social order as it is to be willing to risk their lives to transform it drastically.

The revolution may be directed against the entire power structure of the ruling class, as was the Bolshevik revolution in Russia. Or else it may stress hatred of the Jews, as did the Nazi revolution in Germany, on the theory that the Jews are both the most incongruous and the most vulnerable element in the economic or political power structure. (To the extent that the revolutionary movement's leading cadres are composed of downward-moving or static elements, anti-Semitism of an intense sort is probable because the rapid Jewish social promotion arouses the hostility of the downstarts.)

In total revolutions, directed openly against the entire existing power structure, such as those led by the Communists, anti-Semitism may appear in either or both of two forms. During the years of revolutionary struggle, the counterrevolutionary forces may espouse anti-Semitism since they view it as a substitute incendiary appeal with which to win over the masses. (This was the case during the civil war in Russia of 1917-1920. It was the basis of Hitler's strategy of revolution. It was conceived by the German Socialist leader, August Bebel, as "the Socialism of the stupid," thus recognizing that it too was a revolutionary force.) The second form which anti-Semitism sometimes assumes in the total social revolution is a repression of Jews and Jewish institutions after the seizure and consolidation of power. The fundamental reason for this has already been stated. It is the incompatibility of the individualism, skepticism, propensity to dissent, superior intelligence and wider-than-average moral outlook of Jewry with the narrow ideals, leaden bureaucratic processes and egalitarian doctrines of the totalitarian society. The above refers to political anti-Semitism in its modern form and has little relevance to either social or religious hostility toward Jews.

The American Revolution of 1776 did not involve anti-Semitism at any stage in the process. The basic reason was that this was a liberal revolution, bent upon the enlargement of human freedom. In the American case, there was no desire for a general destruction of the social order or for a replacement of ruling elites by underdogs. Nor was there any desire to anticipate Nietzsche in bringing about a "transvaluation of all values." The destructive upheavals which contain within them the germs of anti-Semitism are not the liberal revolutions, but the totalitarian revolutions against liberty.

Albert Jay Nock, an unjustly neglected American individualist philosopher, once suggested that persecution of the Jews always originates in the masses and never "in an upper class movement." It is true that aristocracies and other ruling classes have not always succeeded in resisting mass pressure in this area, the outstanding example being the manner in which "the Spanish Inquisition was inflicted through popular pressure on kings and lords who both despised and feared it."[33]

The leading American Jewish organizations and a large part of American Jewry are obsessed by phobias of a recrudescence of anti-Semitism through the so-called radical right. They are engaged in misreading the present through the lenses of the past. With the Nazis reduced to a miserable, though no less despicable, remnant, Soviet and Chinese Communists have inherited the leadership of the forces dedicated to the destruction of free societies resting on democratic government, free enterprise and due process of law. Hence, whether willingly or not, they have also inherited leadership over the forces, latent and overt, of international anti-Semitism. The fact that Jewish survival is inextricably linked with the fate of Western Civilization should preclude the possibility of Jewish neutrality in this struggle. Any such neutrality should also be precluded by the Nasser-Soviet alliance and by its commitment to the military destruction of Israel.

CHAPTER 17

Jews, Negroes and Civil Rights

AN INTENSE EMOTIONAL COMMITMENT to the Negro drive
for total integration and total acceptance has been a conspicuous feature of American Jewish political behavior ever
since World War II. In the South particularly, this Jewish
commitment is regarded as notorious. In fact, one can
probably say that, to the extent that any modern political
anti-Semitism exists currently in the South, it is a reaction
against the prominence of Jews in pro-Communist and in
pro-Negro organizations.

In recent years, interesting changes in the stance of the
civil rights groups have begun to emerge. A reason for this
is that the colored leadership of the militant Negro organizations has begun to discover that the spate of legislation
enacted in their behalf under Presidents Kennedy and
Johnson has not fundamentally altered the economic con-

dition or remedied the social isolation of the vast majority of Negroes.

Accordingly, Negro militancy is striking out in new directions, directions which often disturb its white supporters, both Jewish and Gentile. Instead of demanding equality, the leaders of these pressure groups insistently clamor for special privilege. This is a view that Jews tend instinctively to reject, since the entire history of the Jewish struggle for emancipation is one that emphasizes equality of opportunity and advancement on the basis of merit alone. The Negro demand is reminiscent of such bygone institutions as the *numerus clausus* and other quota systems, which restricted the number of Jews having access to higher education and professional employment regardless of their ability.

The second new direction is toward the inchoate movement which extends from anti-war sentiment to appeasement of Communism and from appeasement of Communism to treason. It is exemplified by the unreasonable demand of Floyd B. McKissick, national director of the Congress of Racial Equality (CORE) that the United States abandon the war in Vietnam and divert the billions of dollars thus saved to Negro aid.[1] The view that American national interests should be sacrificed to the ravenous appetites of racial pressure groups was not likely to arouse much enthusiasm among white Americans, regardless of their political persuasion.

The third development has been a tendency to strike out in volcanic outbursts of blind violence and in seemingly senseless political demonstrations against whites in general. This paroxysmal behavior has grown rapidly since the Negro pressure groups ceased to be controlled by white liberals and became instrumentalities of Negro leaders backed by an aroused and organized colored membership. There is a consensus of testimony to the effect that Jews have been primary victims of the eruptions of savage violence in Harlem, Rochester, Watts and elsewhere. This is causing alienation and fear among American Jewry and these attitudes seem to be seeping gradually into the consciousness of the leaders of Jewish organizations.

Meanwhile, the irrational and anti-social behavior of the extremist Negro organizations generates widespread and deep-seated antagonism among the white people of both North and South. This antagonism remains invisible most of the time because of the overwhelming weight of official disapproval. Nevertheless, it exists and is probably growing. Every new demand of the Negro organizations and their white allies for legally enforced special privileges seems to many whites to constitute a new threat to American principles and hence adds to their pent-up feelings of resentment, fear and injury.

To the extent that American Jewry remains conspicuously identified with Negro militancy, it is bound to become a secondary target of this so-called white backlash. At a moment when the Jews seem to stand at the crossroads in relation to the Negro pressure groups, an examination of the history, development and rationale of this involvement is in order. The threads of this skein are tangled; the psychological aspects of the Negro-Jewish relationship are complex and baffling. On both sides, where love exists it is likely to be bound up with hatred. The complexity of motivations and attitudes is not lessened by the fact that some Jewish writers on the subject avoid candor because they do not wish to offend Negro sensibilities and because they do not wish to acknowledge their strong latent feelings of antagonism. On the Negro side, inarticulateness and incapacity for analysis often cloud the picture. Occasionally, however, a Negro writer such as James Baldwin expresses his searing hatred of the white race in honest and eloquent prose. The literate white world has listened to Baldwin, but not carefully enough. It has tended to regard him as an unhappy and wretched human being, carrying a burden of neurotic difficulties as well as the characteristic Negro reaction of self-hate. Hence, it has viewed Baldwin's writings on the race issue as an occasion for the display of sympathy. It might have been wiser to consider these outpourings of loathing and twisted envy as a warning.

How Jewry Became Involved

Jewish interest in the Negro as a submerged tenth of the American population dates back to the Civil War and Reconstruction era. This interest, however, was philanthropic and based on feelings of *noblesse oblige* rather than on any identification or desire for close association. Moreover, it was confined to a small minority of Jews. Julius Rosenwald, the merchandising genius who built up Sears, Roebuck & Company, gave millions to aid Negro education, but he was not involved in the activities of Negro pressure organizations. When the National Association for the Advancement of Colored People was organized in 1908, in reaction to a brutal lynching in Springfield, Illinois, the Northern liberals who were its moving spirits were William English Walling, Oswald Garrison Villard and Moorfield Storey, none of them Jewish.[2]

Jewish organizations were involved in the legal struggle against racially restrictive covenants of the 1920's, 1930's and 1940's. These covenants prohibited the sale or lease of real estate to excluded racial groups—generally Negroes, but sometimes Jews, Orientals and Amerindians as well. A particularly undesirable feature of these contractual provisions was that they almost always continued in perpetuity regardless of the changes in the desires of the neighborhood.

Jews regarded these covenants as pernicious instruments which permanently barred various racial and national groups from large parts of the United States. They supported a challenge to the constitutionality of the covenants, but the Supreme Court ruled in 1926 that they were private agreements which had nothing to do with the "due process" clause of the Fourteenth Amendment.[3] The legal battle continued and, in 1948, a Supreme Court which was considerably more sympathetic to the plight of the Negro in effect reversed this decision. It held that the covenants were valid private agreements, but that it was unconstitutional for the courts to enforce them.[4] Since unenforceable contracts are worthless, the racial covenant was destroyed.

After World War II, the major Jewish organizations were deeply concerned with preventing any recrudescence of the anti-Semitism which had just destroyed six million Jewish lives in Europe. The American Jewish Committee subsidized ambitious and far-reaching studies of anti-Semitism in all its aspects by such social scientists as W. Adorno, Marie Jahoda and Max Horkheimer. The consensus opinion that emerged within the leadership of the Jewish organizations was that prejudice is indivisible, that the main enemy is the "authoritarian personality" and that Jews could remain secure in the United States only by working to broaden the base of American democracy.

Is Prejudice Indivisible?

Before continuing with the chronological narrative, it might be well to pause and examine the validity of some of these assumptions. The first dubious assertion is the alleged indivisibility of *prejudice*. Now *prejudice* itself is a loaded word. The meaning it has with which we are here concerned, according to *Webster's New International Dictionary* (2nd edition), is "an opinion or leaning adverse to anything without just grounds or before sufficient knowledge." Thus, the very use of the term implies that those who hold negative views concerning Negroes, Jews or, for that matter, Anglo-Saxons, college professors, policemen or oboe players are necessarily either ignorant of the subject or irrational about it. A logical inference would be that holding a favorable judgment about any class of human beings must be equally a display of ignorance or stupidity, since the preference for one thing over another implies a comparatively negative judgment about that which is rejected.

The notion that negative views about racial, national, linguistic, class or occupational groups are necessarily *prejudicial* is always comforting to the minority which encounters this hostility. It conveys the pleasant implication that there can be no basis in fact for the negative judgment and that the trouble lies in the viewer and not in that which is viewed. This may be solacing, but it may also be dangerously unrealistic, for it suggests that the person encountering hostility need not examine himself and see whether by modifying his conduct he could remove it.

It also creates the tacit assumption that this "prejudice," being pathological and confined to the viewer and independent of the object viewed, will apply generally to everything alien. Accordingly, many students of anti-Semitism have dogmatically assumed that those who hold unfavorable opinions concerning Jews must hold similar views concerning Negroes and conversely. This leads to the further simplification that Jews and Negroes, since they are both groups which have generated a great deal of hostility, ought to be allies and experience a sense of identity.

I have dealt with this semantic problem at some length because it seems to me to illustrate a situation in which the careless choice of a word leads to a series of tacit assumptions which would never have been accepted if they had been explicitly stated. This is not the same as asserting that no "prejudice," in the dictionary sense of the term, exists against Negroes, Jews and others. Clearly, it does. But how much of the hostility is based on the mental pathology of the hostile person and how much on a realistic appraisal and rejection of a specific group? This is one of the questions the students of "prejudice" should have investigated and one does not begin an investigation, even in the social sciences, by assuming a specific conclusion.

The evidence in support of the proposition that "prejudice" is indivisible is shaky. Himmelhoch found that *Jewish* students who are "prejudiced" against one minority tend to be "prejudiced" against other ethnic minorities.[5] On the other hand, Pompilo studied college students and others and found that there was no relationship between anti-Jewish and anti-Negro attitudes.[6]

A highly significant study of anti-Semitism by Bruno Bettelheim and Morris Janowitz revealed that almost all subjects who were hostile toward Jews were also antagonistic toward Negroes. However, of those subjects who were tolerant toward Jews, only 15% were tolerant toward Negroes. Half of the people without any anti-Semitic attitudes, went beyond the stereotyped hostility to Negroes and were described as "outspokenly and intensely anti-Negro."[7]

The final point to make about this matter is that the South, which has a more negative attitude toward Negroes than the rest of the United States, is more favorably inclined toward Jews. It is interesting that this fairly obvious fact should be little known and very far from widely recognized. On the contrary, the highly prejudiced stereotype of the Southern white, who is customarily depicted on television and elsewhere as a decayed planter living on imaginary glory and vanished pretensions or else as a crooked, Negro-hating sheriff or perhaps as an incredibly ignorant red neck, suggests the very acme of intolerance of everything outside his county. We have here a case in which ideological preconceptions blind people to plain facts and I have found that even intelligent and well-informed Northern Jews habitually express astonishment or disbelief when they are told that the South is the least hostile region toward Jewry in the United States.

The comparative absence of anti-Semitism in the South is evidenced by public opinion polls. Since anti-Semitism in America has been steadily declining over the past 20 years, interest in the subject is waning and fewer polls are taken now than in earlier decades. Therefore, most of the evidence cited is not of recent vintage.

In 1940, a year in which pro-Nazi movements in the United States were at or near their all-time peak, *Fortune* magazine asked its readers: "Of the people now in the U.S. who were born in foreign countries, which nationality would you say had made the best citizens?" Seven national groups were listed: Germans, English, Scandinavians, Irish, Jews, Italians and French. Nationally, they ranked in precisely that order: the Jews were in fifth place. In the Southeast, however, the Jews were in third place, ranking behind Germans and English, but ahead of Irish, Scandinavians, Italians and French.[8]

An earlier poll, one taken by *Fortune* in January 1936,

asked: "Do you believe that in the long run Germany will be better or worse off if it drives out the Jews?" Some 14% of the nation believed that Germany would do better without Jews. This view was held by 16.1% of the Midwest, 15.1% of the Northeast, 14.7% of the Southwest, 14.3% of the Pacific coast, but by only 7.5% of the Southeast.

Another *Fortune* study, made ten years later, revealed that the Northeast was 28% more anti-Semitic than the nation as a whole, the Midwest 16% more so, the South 30% less so and the Far West 36% less than the national average.[9]

Finally, an analysis of the effect of the Eichmann trial revealed that it produced a more favorable attitude toward the Jews among 32% of all white Christians and a more favorable attitude toward the Germans in 5% of that group. The net effect of the trial was greater sympathy for the Jews in 22% of the Far Western sample, 29% of the Eastern, 34% of the Midwestern and 37% of the Southern. The small minority which was influenced in favor of Germany comprised 6% of the West Coast, 5% of the Midwest and South and 4% of the East.[10]

From Desegregation toward Miscegenation

Over the past ten years, the Negro pressure organizations and their white allies have continually enlarged their demands and changed their objectives, moving through successive stages, the boundaries of which were by no means clearly drawn or sharply defined.

The fundamental Supreme Court decision which declared racial segregation unconstitutional in American public schools swept aside such questions as the original meaning of the Fourteenth Amendment and the precise intentions of those who drafted and ratified it. The reason for this was that the only possible conclusion to be drawn from the historical record was that there had been no intention to interfere with racial segregation provided school facilities were equal. Instead, the Court devoted a good deal of space to the self-evident proposition that education in the twentieth century is "the very foundation of good citizenship," so much so that "it is doubtful that any child may reasonably be expected to succeed in life if he is denied the opportunity of an education."[11] The Court then proceeded to generalize on the basis of the testimony of nine social scientists. Of these "experts," four were employees or consultants of the NAACP and hence scarcely disinterested; another gave his evidence in such a misleading manner as to convince the Court of the exact opposite of the true facts; others would later be characterized by the Chairman of the Senate Judiciary Committee as "people who have a long record of affiliations with anti-American causes and . . . agitators who are part and parcel of the Communist Conspiracy to destroy this country."[12] The Court concluded that racial segregation by itself generated among Negro pupils "a feeling of inferiority as to their status in the community that may affect their hearts and minds in a way unlikely ever to be undone."

The Court's decision in the Brown case desegregated the public schools, but it did not forcibly integrate them. Moreover, the decision, by its very logic, seemed confined to institutions vital to good citizenship and success in life.

The Brown decision as such was consistent with the basic American doctrine of equality of opportunity and equality of rights. It did not strike down the neighborhood school. It did not suggest, either directly or by implication, that masses of Negroes with significantly inferior I.Q., scholastic aptitude and moral standards, should be forcibly injected into preponderantly white school districts in which neither they nor their parents lived.

The first significant amplification of the school desegregation decision was for the Supreme Court to apply it without argument to public parks, swimming pools, golf courses and cemeteries. This seemed odd unless the Court viewed these facilities as "the very foundation of good citizenship."

The second major amplification was the work of national, state and local governments. Negro pressure organizations, aided by their white liberal allies, demanded that "de facto ghettos" be abolished. Their abolition meant forced integration of residential areas inhabited exclusively, or almost exclusively, by white people. The reason for the existence of these residential areas was that these particular whites, rightly or wrongly, had strong objections to living in the same neighborhoods as Negroes. They were prepared to make considerable financial sacrifices to avoid this and would demonstrate repeatedly that they would rather sell their homes at a loss than remain in mixed neighborhoods.

These people were not doing anything revolutionary. They were merely exercising their right to choose their own associates. They were preponderantly of the working class or lower middle class. Upper-class intellectual liberals, who were enthusiasts for total integration, normally did not face this problem. They lived in areas from which all but a handful of Negroes were excluded because of high rentals and they sent their children either to upper-class public schools or to private ones, where one or two Negro pupils might be admitted as a token of integration.

Under pressure from Negro, Jewish and liberal organizations, states and cities proceeded to break down the "de facto ghettos" by busing Negro children to white schools, by starting public housing projects in white residential districts and by other devices. The federal government under President Johnson entered the picture by establishing a variety of bureaucratic agencies to grant preferential treatment to Negroes. These agencies were not satisfied with a finding that nobody was suffering discrimination because of race. They went far beyond that. In certain classes of Foreign Service employment, Chiefs of Mission were obliged to give detailed written explanations for their failure to fill vacancies with Negro candidates. Other government department heads had to report on the number of officials under them from "minority groups." Private business was placed under remorseless pressure to employ specified quotas of Negroes and to place them in middle- to high-echelon jobs regardless of their ability and qualifications. Public housing agencies and poverty program projects joined the great new game of seeing who could make the most impressive record in race mixing. The Department of Health, Education and Welfare issued guidelines to the nation's public schools which stipulated the speed at which classroom mixing of the races should occur.

Other institutions, particularly the colleges and universities, hastened to imitate or even outstrip the government. The result was that the American Negro found himself in a privileged and even pampered position. His apologists would attribute the meagerness of his progress to "lack of motivation on the part of many Negroes to improve their educational and occupational status," as the 1961 U.S. Commission on Civil Rights put it. Yet the Negro actually had stronger reasons for motivation than the average white.

In America, schools are free; public libraries abundant; relief available for all; even dull Negro children are paid by the federal government to study.

In my own alma mater, Columbia University, the authorities boast of scouring Southern high schools for Negroes with college potential and awarding scholarships "which frequently total more than $8,000" to Negroes "who would not have qualified scholastically for bare admission had they been white."[13] The policies of Princeton and other Ivy League colleges are equally discriminatory. When he taught at New York University, James Burnham found himself under pressure to mark Negro students two grades above whites for the same caliber of work. Professors who objected to giving C students A grades merely because they were colored were subjected to the combined pressure of the Dean's office, the NAACP and City Hall.[14] This dishonest, racist practice was praised as liberal by professors who would have sternly reproved students who got higher marks by cheating at examinations.

When the Negro graduates from college, sometimes with the assistance of undeserved scholarships and inflated grades, he is given preferential treatment in both governmental and academic jobs. Industry is strongarmed to give a similar preferential treatment, one repugnant to all American traditions of fair competition and impartial reward on the basis of merit. If the Negro professional, executive or official faces demotion or discharge, he is often able to allege racial persecution and to bring strong countervailing pressure on those who would presume to treat him on the basis of equality. Finally, Negro motivation should be particularly strong because, once he attains professional or middle-class status, the Negro stands much farther above the masses of his own race than does the white professional vis-à-vis the white masses.

The next stage in total integration was outlined in a guidelines report of the White House Conference on Civil Rights which met in June 1966. This report demanded that the United States Government commit itself to "racial integration as a goal." The critical element in this new strategy was "metropolitan planning," embracing white suburbs as well as black slums. Affirmative action to bring about racial balance in the schools, employment and residential patterns would be a prerequisite to federal financial assistance. Naturally, the residents of those cities and suburbs which resist this pattern would be stripped of federal aid, but at the same time forced to pay taxes to impose these total integration plans on other communities.

The reason for total metropolitan planning is conviction by the planners that, "The central cities will be anxious to utilize every available dollar, but the suburbs are likely to go right on siphoning off the more affluent whites and excluding the less fortunate and the non-whites."[15] This is a blueprint for an America in which there will be no place for the individualist to hide, no opportunity for the citizen to choose his own associates and no way for him to escape the regulation by the Leviathan state of vital aspects of what he once naively called his "private life." The only good thing that can be said for this blueprint for 1984 is that it has not as yet become United States Government policy.

But even this nightmare plan would probably not improve the lot of the Negro drastically. It would give him more government largesse, but not more self-respect. It would place him in better jobs, but it would not give him the mentality or competence to do those jobs well. It would increase the forced associations between the two races, but it is entirely possible that this sort of coerced fraternization would simply add to the volume of race hate.

The further the liberals travel along this road, the more evident does it become to the more intelligent of them that the road leads nowhere. Or, more accurately, it leads nowhere that any sensible, non-guilt-ridden, non-masochistic American would care to go.

This impasse was recognized several years ago by Norman Podhoretz, one of the leading Jewish intellectuals in contemporary America, a liberal-to-radical, of course, but a man with an independent mind which is not the captive of any closed doctrinal system. Although he is and was editor of *Commentary*, probably the most influential Jewish magazine in the world, he was not writing as editor but in an individual capacity. Podhoretz is able to acknowledge "the hatred I still feel for Negroes" and the motivation of his article is a desire to assuage and eliminate race hatred. His conclusion is:

". . . I think I know why the Jews once wished to survive (though I am less certain as to why we still do): they not only believed that God had given them no choice, but they were tied to a memory of past glory and a dream of imminent redemption. What does the American Negro have that might correspond to this? His past is a stigma, his color is a stigma, and his vision of the future is the hope of erasing the stigma by making color irrelevant, by making it disappear as a fact of consciousness.

"I share this hope, but I cannot see how it will ever be realized unless color does *in fact* disappear: and that means not integration, it means assimilation, it means—let the brutal word come out—miscegenation. The Black Muslims, like their racist counterparts in the white world, accuse the 'so-called Negro leaders' of secretly pursuing miscegenation as a goal. The racists are wrong, but I wish they were right, for I believe that the wholesale merging of the two races is the most desirable alternative for everyone concerned. I am not claiming that this alternative can be pursued programmatically or that it is immediately feasible as a solution; obviously there are even greater barriers to its achievement than to the achievement of integration. What I am saying, however, is that in my opinion the Negro problem can be solved in this country in no other way."[16]

Thus the end of the integrationist road is a morass. The best that a leading liberal Jewish intellectual can suggest is a process of massive and protracted crossbreeding which would cause a significant lowering of the nation's level of intelligence. In this manner, the United States might well become another nation of carnivals, of slums, of filth, of minor creative achievements and monotonous history, endowed perhaps with a handful of great men, but without anything approximating the powerful American creative elite that today exists. Tensions between whites and Negroes might in this manner be abated, but at the cost of genetic downgrading and biologically caused deterioration in inherited mental resources.[17] Is this the best the integrationist Jewish liberals have to offer?

To answer the question, we must return to basic and rudimentary things. What is the Negro problem? We are told that the basic problem is that, in virtually every society and in virtually every respect, he is at the bottom of the societary pyramid. But is there anything necessarily wrong with this? An older generation of American liberals would have answered:

"Yes, it is wrong if he is held down by lack of equal

opportunity. But if he is at the bottom because he is the least intelligent, the least productive and the least creative component of the population, then the bottom is where he belongs. And there is no point in being sentimental and saying that society should not have a bottom. For unless there is a bottom, there cannot be a top."

This seems reasonable, but it is countered by the contemporary liberal assertion that the Negro is at the bottom, not because of adverse genetic factors, but because he is condemned to have his children educated in "de facto ghettos" and because of the heritage of chattel slavery and other disadvantages. However, a very large part of the white immigrants into the United States were reared and educated in "de facto ghettos." This applied most obviously to Italians, Jews, and Chinese. Yet two of these groups today make a greater proportionate contribution to the American creative minority than does the Anglo-Saxon majority. Chinese, Italians and Jews enjoyed ample educational opportunities even when they studied with, lived among and were taught by other Chinese, Italians and Jews.

Thus, one returns to the fundamental biogenetic point: the Negro is not held back because of de facto segregation per se. The real problem is that, on the whole, he constitutes refractory material for the educational process. To a certain extent, his progress may perhaps be accelerated by placing him in a white environment, but when this is done the white children suffer educationally from his presence. Thus, the "environmental" consideration about school segregation assumes meaning only if one reverts to the basic factor of innate mental difference.

The Negro elite or, as the late W. E. B. DuBois called it, "the talented tenth," has made impressive intellectual, political and economic gains in American society. This group has benefited from school desegregation, but it is just as much the victim of campaigns to impose random race mixture on schools and residential districts as the white majority. The Negro elite is held back when it is compelled to associate with the most backward elements among the Negro masses. There is no reason why the intelligent Negro should be compelled to carry the stupid one on his back. A rational solution to the problem of differences in mental capacity would have been to see that racial desegregation of the public schools system was followed by immediate re-segregation on the basis of intelligence and learning aptitude and without regard to race.

Like other Americans, the Negro is entitled to equality under the law and equality of opportunity. Like other Americans, he is entitled to nothing more. If he is held down by external restraints, society should remove them. If he is held down by his own limitations, he should try to conquer them. If this is beyond his power, it is incumbent upon him to recognize and learn to live with his own limitations.

To a large extent, the recent outbreaks of Negro violence and the other bitter manifestations of black anger against the white race are the direct result of false expectations created by mass indoctrination of the colored with the mythology of twentieth century liberalism concerning race.

In short, the Negro has been persuaded that his unen-viable position in white society is due, not to his own short-comings, but to the oppression and injustice he has suffered at the hands of the white majority. He is promised that all this is to be changed through governmental action, social reform and official recognition of sins committed in the past. Yet, in a fundamental sense, there is very little change. Millions of Negroes remain slum dwellers, appallingly uneducated and unequipped for productive work, abnormally subject to the hazards of unemployment, periodically on relief, living in communities where crime is endemic.

When this group is taught that responsibility for its fate lies elsewhere than on its own shoulders the result is frequently explosive violence. This violence is inevitably directed against "whitey" because the liberals have propagandized the Negro into believing that his failures are due to neglect or oppression by the white man.

To the liberal Jewish intellectual, the possibility that the Negroes drift to the bottom of every society simply because they are inherently less capable than Caucasians and Mongolians is not an idea to be considered dispassionately, but a heresy to be rejected out of hand. This emotional attitude is reflected in a great spate of Jewish writing on the Negro problem. Discussing the plight of the Jewish liberal, who had always regarded the Negro as a faceless abstraction until the fact of integration made him face reality, Podhoretz writes:

"We find such people fleeing in droves to the suburbs as the Negro population in the inner city grows; and when they stay in the city we find them sending their children to private school rather than to the 'integrated' public school in the neighborhood. We find them resisting the demand that gerrymandered school districts be re-zoned for the purpose of overcoming de facto segregation; we find them judiciously considering whether the Negroes (for their own good, of course) are not perhaps pushing too hard; we find them clucking their tongues over Negro militancy; we find them speculating on the question of whether there may not, after all, be something in the theory that the races are biologically different . . ."[18]

And why not? Why should it be immoral to consider

the possibility that the races of man are different in respect of intelligence? We know that they differ fundamentally in color, in skin and hair texture, in sweat secretions, in soma-type, in capacity for survival in different habitats, in blood types and in dozens of other respects.[19]

The physical differences between races are caused primar-ily by evolutionary adaptation to habitat.[20] There is every reason to suppose that mental differences are created by the same process. In fact, if this is not the case with respect to human races, man constitutes an exception to a rule which prevails generally in the animal kingdom.[21] Prima facie, one would expect anyone who is scientifically minded to assume genetic differences in intelligence among different races unless shown preponderant evidence in favor of equality.

The Jewish syndrome concerning racial equality reflects the Nazi ordeal and the extermination camps. It is pre-dictable that this traumatic collective experience will affect the thinking and emotional reactions of world Jewry for decades to come. Yet it would be a great mistake to assume that the fundamental evil in Nazism was the denial of racial equality and it would be still more erroneous to equate Nazi race doctrine with social Darwinism. On the contrary, the Nazi doctrines on race were anti-scientific pseudo-mysticism, deriving from German romanticists of the nineteenth century who harped on blood and soil, on the "racial soul" and on other myths. The enormity of which Nazism was guilty was not that its views on race were wrong, as they were, but that its purpose was to oppress or exterminate those peoples it considered inferior. The antidote to Nazism is not an emotionally charged assertion that all races are equal or that race does not exist. It is a scientifically valid, dispassionate examination and exposi-tion of the real causes and nature of human differences.

The Moynihan Report

Distributed as a classified document by the U.S. Department of Labor, the so-called Moynihan Report or *The Negro Family: The Case for National Action* was leaked to the press and became the subject of widespread discussion throughout the summer of 1965. Its author, Daniel Patrick Moynihan, had been one of the brighter young sociologists advising the late President Kennedy. As junior author of *Beyond the Melting Pot*, he had acquired considerable knowledge of minority ethnic and national groups.[22]

Although he lacked competence in the field of genetics and ethnology, Moynihan asserted dogmatically: "Intelligence potential is distributed among Negro infants in the same proportion and pattern as among Icelanders or Chinese or any other comparable group." Professor Curt Stern, an eminent human geneticist and chairman of a National Academy of Sciences Panel on Biology and the Future of Man, stated at the Third International Congress of Human Genetics in September 1966 that "such statements lack a factual basis."[23] Another member of the National Academy, Professor Dwight J. Ingle of the Physiology Department of the University of Chicago wrote in *Science* in 1964: ". . . whether the average differences among races in test performance, school achievement and behavior have a genetic as well as an environmental basis is unresolved." After referring to Moynihan's brash dictum on the subject, Professor William B. Shockley of Stanford University, who was awarded the Nobel Prize in physics in 1956 for co-development of the transistor, pointed to the general recognition of "the environment-heredity uncertainty" by competent scientists and urged that this uncertainty be resolved by scientific investigation since failure to do so was "unfair to all concerned" and "irresponsible."[24]

Starting with his shaky premise of inherent racial equality with respect to brain, a premise which is less a conclusion from the evidence than an article of faith of the Kennedy-Johnson liberal establishment, Moynihan argued that a basic cause of Negro failure was the disintegration of the Negro family which in many cities was "approaching complete breakdown." Moynihan pointed out that about 25% of Negro births are illegitimate and that some two million of the nation's five million Negro families lack a husband. This, he asserted, leads to a matriarchal society and whenever a nation "allows large numbers of young men to grow up in broken families, dominated by women, never acquiring any stable relationship to male authority, never acquiring any set of rational expectations about the future—that community asks for and gets chaos. Crime, violence, unrest, disorder . . . are very near to inevitable."[25]

Predictably, Moynihan concluded that our society "richly deserved" the epidemic of Negro crime and violence from which it was suffering, because of its failure to step in and reconstruct the shattered Negro family. A basic question that remained unanswered was whether it is the business of government to reconstruct broken families. Nor did the Report reveal why the Negro male, unlike the Caucasian and Mongolian male, had so frequently failed to make the transition from the pleasure-role of sex to the responsibility-role of fatherhood. The basic issue, that of whether both the broken Negro family and the excessive Negro contribution to vice, violence and squalor were symptoms of innate psychic deficiency, had already been answered by Moynihan's dogmatic assertion about the equality of Negroes, Chinese and Icelanders.

On the basis of Census data, Moynihan reported that about 44.1% of all college-age Chinese and Japanese Americans were in college, as compared with 21.4% of college-age whites and only 8.4% of college-age Negroes. The corresponding Jewish figure was about 80%. He then pointed out triumphantly that what Jews, Chinese and Japanese have in common is "a singularly stable, cohesive and enlightened family life."

Unfortunately for this simplified approach, the Italian Americans have an unusually close-knit and harmonious family life and yet they are significantly under-represented in colleges. This Moynihan must be aware of since he and Glazer emphasized the point in their excellent study of New York City's motley population, *Beyond the Melting Pot*.[26] Similar considerations would apply to the Portuguese and Spanish stocks in the United States. In short, conceding the fact that a strong family life is conducive to moral conduct, identification with community and nation, positive goals, mental stability and perseverance and that the broken family is conducive to opposite traits, it does *not* follow that the family is either the only or the main factor behind the success or failure of different ethnic groups. Consider a specific area which Moynihan himself cites— that of college attendance. Americans of Southern European stock have strong family ties, yet are seriously under-represented in colleges and universities. Middle- and upper-class urban Americans of Nordic stock frequently come from broken families, yet are significantly over-represented.

In defense of his thesis, Moynihan asserts that in central Harlem, where a majority of Negro children have no fathers, the average I.Q. of sixth graders is only 86.3. At corresponding ages, Negro children with fathers show I.Q.'s which average 7.5 points higher. Moynihan assumes without adequate evidence that the broken family is the primary cause of the low intelligence quotient.

The fallacy here is obvious. Fathers who bring up their children are likely to be, on the average, considerably more intelligent than those who habitually desert them. Women who choose responsible men to father their children are likely to be superior to women who exercise no choice or who choose foolishly. Thus, the 7.5 point difference in I.Q. between the Negro children with and without fathers may be due, either partly or entirely, to the higher innate intelligence of the parents in the first group. Moreover, if we assume that the central Harlem children are about equally divided between those with and those without fathers, the average I.Q. of both groups would still be only 90. Sir Julian Huxley estimated that a population with a mean I.Q. 10 points below the national average would produce proportionately only about one-tenth as many very superior individuals (those with I.Q.'s of 160+) as the nation as a whole.[27]

Moynihan has been castigated in such radical-to-liberal magazines as the *Nation* and the *Christian Century*. He has been rebuked for criticizing the morality of the Negro family and has even been branded a racist. Floyd McKissick, a militant Negro organizer and agitator, attacked the Report because "it assumes that middle-class American values are the correct values for everyone in America. . . . Moynihan thinks that everyone should have a family structure like his own."

Moynihan has made several constructive suggestions for improving the Negro family structure. He thinks that idle Negro manpower should be employed in delivering the mails twice daily, thus increasing the self-respect and sense of responsibility of those thus engaged. He also urges that schoolteaching be made financially attractive to Negro men. The thought behind this is that fatherless Negro youth would thus acquire father surrogates in the classrooms and in that way perhaps develop positive and responsible attitudes toward society and toward social authority.

These suggestions seem to be good ones. If they succeeded in substantially reducing Negro pauperism, delinquency and crime, they would be well worth the extra cost to the taxpayer. However, no one should imagine that these or similar measures will prove a panacea for the Negro problem. There is no real evidence that strong family ties will bring groups with subnormal intelligence up to the norm. On the contrary, we know that gifted people from broken families often score high in intelligence tests, whereas ungifted people from stable and close-knit families often do poorly.

Jewish Identification with Negroes

Prima facie, this identification seems absurd. I have already pointed out that American and West European Jews tend to outperform other groups in intelligence tests and scholarship. In the Negro case, inferior performance is the rule. For almost half a century, the instrument of intelligence testing has been brought to bear on Negro-white differences, resulting in over 240 studies.[28] In seventeen comparative individual testings of randomly chosen whites and Negroes, Audrey M. Shuey found that the colored groups had average I.Q.'s ranging from 72 in four Southern cities to 89 in two border cities. In other words, the Negro *averages* were from mentally dull to borderline mental deficiency.[29] At the college level, Negro performance was even less impressive. At Howard University, probably the top colored institution of higher education in the nation, only

15% to 20% of the students equalled the nationwide college average.[30] In an effort to eliminate the influence of environmental differences, McGurk matched Negro subjects with a white control group of equal or worse socio-economic status. He found that the Negro score pattern remained well below the white and that no Negro scored as well as the top 9% of the whites.[31]

An analysis of 383,000 induction tests administered to the armed forces between June 1964 and December 1965 revealed that more than two-thirds of all Negroes, but only 18.8% of all whites taking the examination failed. These figures, which were released with the greatest reluctance by the Defense Department, showed that the highest failure rate was 85.6% for South Carolina Negroes as against a national Negro average failure rate of 67.5%.[32]

A comparison of the 1964-1965 tests with those of World War II showed that, despite the massive efforts to improve his housing, education, income and job opportunities, the Negro was rapidly falling behind. In World War II, 6.3% of the whites, but only 1% of the Negroes, were in Group I, or very superior. When the same nationwide comparison was made in 1964-1965, 7.6% of white draftees, but only 0.3% of Negro draftees, were in the same very superior group. The World War II (March 1945) figures showed that 39.7% of the whites, but only 7.4% of the Negroes, were in Groups I and II, very superior and superior. By 1964-1965, 39.7% of white draftees were still in the first two groups, but the Negro representation there had fallen by more than half—to 3.6% of the total.[33]

The broad picture was that almost 40% of the white draftees were in Groups I and II (very superior and superior), about a third in Group III (average) and about a fourth in Groups IV and V (inferior and very inferior). By contrast, less than one Negro in 25 rated in the superior and very superior groups and more than 75% of the Negroes tested were mentally inferior or mentally very inferior.[34] The Office of Education presentation of this material attributed the Negro shortfall to "America's erratic progress toward its elusive goal of educational equality."[35] What the data revealed was that a vast concentrated national effort to improve and accelerate Negro education had been associated with a spectacular decline in Negro mental achievement, below levels that had already been appallingly low. An increase in medication had been associated with a further relapse on the part of the patient. The prima facie inference to be drawn from the data seemed to be that the original diagnosis of under-education had been an incorrect one. Skeptics would suggest that the root problem was more likely to be deficiency of brain than deficiency of education and that, therefore, the higher educational standards were raised the greater would be the predictable gap between white and Negro test performance.

Regardless of whether or not the differences between the two races are due to genetic causes, it seems evident that they were not the result of some superficial handicap that could be easily or quickly removed. A century after emancipation, the Negroes, as a whole, had not caught up with the white majority to any significant extent. While there were gifted Negroes, who apparently resembled the gifted of other races, the evidence was that they occurred most infrequently.

Turning to other areas, the Negro masses remained impoverished by American standards, whereas the Jewish population was rich by the same criterion. The Negroes were under-educated, the Jews more highly educated than any other population group with the possible exception of the Chinese and Japanese. The Negroes were huddled in slums, from which they seemed unable to emerge. East European Jews started in the United States as slum dwellers, but swiftly moved into good residential districts.

Unlike the Jews, the Negroes contribute disproportionately to unskilled labor, to relief rolls, to unemployment and to crime. In 1960, proportionately 4.6 times as many Negro as white federal felony prisoners were received from courts, and this ratio has risen rather than declined after two decades of intensive efforts to improve those unfavorable environmental conditions which were supposed to be the causes of excessive Negro criminality.

The contrast between Jews and Negroes is equally marked in other areas. Alcoholism, narcotics addiction, sexual promiscuity and illegitimacy are much more frequent among Negroes than in the American white population. Among Jews, there is a very strong tendency to avoidance of heavy drinking and narcotics, and there is emphasis on monogamy and below-average illegitimacy rates. (The exception would be the small Jewish minority which has totally repudiated its cultural and religious heritage and which flaunts its nihilism. These Jewish beatniks are no more typical of American Jewry than the diabolists of the Middle Ages were characteristic of medieval Christianity.)

The unfavorable stereotypes of the two groups are almost equally far apart. The Jew is often characterized as excessively ambitious, pushing, shrewd, clannish, hardworking, over-intellectual, parsimonious and obsessed with making money. The Negro is more frequently seen as lazy, living from moment to moment, stupid, apathetic, dullwitted, spendthrift, flashy and paroxysmal.

The contrast between Negro and Jewish character structure could be further elaborated, but this would be redundant. Psychologically healthy people tend toward self-acceptance. They project this by forming close attachments and falling in love with people who are very like themselves. Hence, a feeling of deep rapport between Jews, as a group, and Negroes, as a group, would seem unnatural.

Often rapport is created by outside pressure. One frequent ploy is for Jewish organizations and their spokesmen to couple Jews and Negroes as common victims of discrimination by the American majority. The reason for creating this picture (which does violence to the facts) is to make Jews imagine that they are in the same boat as Negroes and hence should court their friendship and fight their battles. The result sometimes is that white non-Jews accept this spurious identification and extend their existing hostility toward Negroes to Jews as well.

The close Negro-Jewish relationship is also fostered by religiously and morally motivated pressure. As the Director of Jewish Communal Affairs of the American Jewish Committee put the matter in 1964:

"The issue of Negro equality is for Jews one of the utmost moment. As a religious group, we must decide whether our organized religious institutions will plunge actively into an effort to put our religious ethos to work in the society, and whether each of us truly means to live in accordance with the ethical demands of Judaism. . . . And as individuals, we must resolve the internal conflict between the desire we have always had for freedom and equality for ourselves and the knowledge that not acting to get it for others denies our own; only thus can we become whole."[36]

These lofty sentiments are characteristic of most of the Jewish literature of exhortation on the Negro question. The author does not bother to define what he means by either *freedom* or *equality*. Does *equality* include giving preferential treatment to an applicant for college education or for a professional job because his skin is dark? If it does, then

the entire historic Jewish struggle for equality of opportunity regardless of race has been in defiance of freedom
and against the principle of equality. Is it freedom for the
government to decree that the student bodies in public
schools must be mixed racially according to a bureaucrati-
cally approved formula regardless of the preferences of the
people directly concerned? And by *equality* does the author
mean equality of opportunity, which can be established by
law, or equality of ability, which is either a fact or a fiction,
but which cannot be legislated or imposed by anybody?[37]

Jewish Attitudes toward Negroes

The Jews have long been in the forefront of the struggle
for Negro demands. "We are no Johnny-come-latelies,"
writes Rabbi Richard C. Hertz in *Ebony* for December
1964. "We had a head start in the civil rights race. After
World War II, the Jewish civic protective agencies—the
American Jewish Committee, the Anti-Defamation League,
Jewish community councils and all the others—were in the
forefront of the battle."

This Jewish effort was based primarily on a moral imperative. The Jews, in short, did not need the Negroes. The
Negroes *did* need the Jews.

Norman Podhoretz, who lived as a boy in a racially mixed
neighborhood where Negro boys regularly beat up Jewish
boys, writes perceptively about his own attitudes toward
Negroes. After observing that the psychologists tell us "that
the white man hates the Negro because he tends to project
those wild impulses that he fears in himself onto an alien
group which he then punishes with his contempt," Podhoretz continues:

"So with the mechanism of projection that the psychologists talk about: it too works in both directions at once.

There is no question that the psychologists are right about what the Negro represents symbolically to the white man. For me as a child the life lived on the other side of the playground and down the block on Ralph Avenue seemed the very embodiment of the values of the street—free, independent, reckless, brave, masculine, erotic. I put the word 'erotic' last, though it is usually stressed above all others, because in fact it came last, in consciousness as in importance. What mainly counted for me about Negro kids of my own age was that they were 'bad boys.' . . . The Negroes were *really* bad, bad in a way that beckoned to one, and made one feel inadequate. . . . To hell with the teacher, the truant officer, the cop; to hell with the whole of the adult world that held *us* in its grip and that we never had the courage to rebel against except sporadically and in petty ways."[38]

Tł ɛre is, I believe, a good deal of truth in this, but it is a truth that could perhaps be expressed somewhat more clearly and somewhat more sharply. Podhoretz, I take it, is not writing about those whites who are constructively interested in helping Negroes solve their problems, nor is he talking about normal whites who have friendly relationships with normal Negroes.

He is talking about a form of perverse love, in which the white man empathizes with the Negro only to the extent that he conceives of the Negro as a force for destruction and a force for evil. He is talking about those whites who despise the successful, middle-class and professional Negroes who have adopted white American values, and consider them "Uncle Toms." He is talking about the sort of white "liberal" who has no interest in doing anything for oppressed minorities in general, who ignored the plight of the self-reliant, intelligent and hard-working Japanese

Americans of World War II and who has no interest in the desperately impoverished American Indians whose condition is infinitely worse than that of the Negro. He was not interested in the Japanese Americans because these people shared and exemplified the values which have made America what it today is. He is not concerned about the Indians because they are passive and inwardly self-sufficient.

He esteems the Negro to the extent that he considers him a battering ram with which American middle-class society can be smashed. In his association with Negroes, he chooses the morally depraved, the pathologically rebellious, those without any moral restraints, and seeks to imitate or excel them in their vices. He often embraces the cult of dirt and the practice of totally indiscriminate promiscuity or of promiscuity which is discriminating only in the sense that its purpose is self-degradation.

We are dealing with the love of evil, or the love of what is imagined as evil. It has a very long history and originated many centuries before the Satanists and worshippers of the Anti-Christ of the Middle Ages.

Thus, we are talking about rebelliousness and moral nihilism. Those impelled in these directions are generally warped by self-contempt and without fundamental self-respect (often rightly so). To the extent that Negroes follow movements infected by this pathological type of white, they are being led down a blind alley. Any gain which the Negro makes in his ability to cope constructively with the problems he faces in modern society will simply alienate white supporters of this type and send them off in search of a new symbol and moral pretext for acting out their anti-social impulses.

"There are the writers and intellectuals and artists," Podhoretz writes, "who romanticize Negroes and pander to them, assuming a guilt that is not properly theirs. And there are the white liberals who permit Negroes to blackmail them into adopting a double standard of moral judgment, and who lend themselves—again assuming the responsibility for crimes they never committed—to cunning and contemptuous exploitation by Negroes they employ or try to befriend."[39]

These attitudes are not, of course, specifically Jewish. They are part of the pathology of a certain type of liberal white Negrophile. As such, they apply to Jew and non-Jew alike.

Negro Attitudes Toward Jews

In recent years, American Jewish organizations have viewed the swift rise of Negro anti-Semitism with mounting alarm. A bibliography on Negro-Jewish relations, published by the American Jewish Committee in March 1966, reveals this growing anxiety.[40]

"When the Negro hates the Jew *as a Jew*," James Baldwin wrote in 1948, "he does so in much the same painful fashion that he hates himself."[41]

A 1964 article is summarized as chiding Negro leadership "for its lackadaisical reaction to growing anti-Semitism among Negroes."[42] Another takes the existence of growing anti-Jewish sentiment among Negroes for granted and warns that this may cause Jews to withdraw from the Negro movement.[43] Still another reports that "anti-Semitism among Negroes is a stark reality which can no longer be ignored:"[44] In a survey of a small, almost entirely Negro institution, the colored students are described as exhibiting "markedly prejudiced and authoritarian attitudes directed particularly against Jews, Orientals . . . and non-Negro foreigners."[45]

Negro hostility toward Jews has a long history. At one

time, Negro anti-Semitism "formed one of the major themes of the Negro press. . . ." In an interesting study of the Negro in politics, James A. Wilson gives a good deal of attention to Negro-Jewish hostility.

"The founder of the *Chicago Defender*," he writes, "was suspicious of Jews, and that paper contained many uncomplimentary references to them." During the military struggle between Jews and Arabs which ended with the establishment of the state of Israel, "many prominent Negroes sided with the 'colored' Arabs in their fight against the 'white' Jews."[46]

Wilson reports that the Negroes suspected that the Jews wanted to help them for ulterior and selfish motives. When a group lacks self-respect, it is likely to reject offers of friendship or assistance because it cannot conceive of anyone liking it enough to want to do anything for it.

Still according to Wilson, the Jews were feared as being really interested in drawing Negroes into the "left-wing movement."[47] They were called hypocrites because they talked race brotherhood, but excluded Negroes from their private lives. Negroes characterized Jews much as did other anti-Semites, calling them "clannish," "grasping," "pushy," "merciless" and "greedy."[48]

A traditional cause of, or pretext for, Negro anti-Semitism is that a large proportion of the businesses in the black ghettos are Jewish-owned and a considerable proportion of the landlords in these slums are also Jewish. These Jewish businessmen and property owners are habitually referred to as "blood suckers" by Negroes and accused of making their money in the colored districts and then moving to fine new houses in lily-white suburbia.

Dr. Eric Lincoln, a Negro sociologist, complains that, in Jewish stores in colored districts, "there isn't a black face behind a single counter. . . . [The Jew] will open a liquor store. . . . Soon he follows his Negro customer home and buys the flat he lives in. By that time, the Jew is providing the Negro with his food, his clothes, his services, his home and *the whiskey he has to have to keep him from hating himself.*"[49]

The answer to all this is fairly obvious, but not obvious to the more backward Negroes. The Jewish (and non-Jewish) merchants charge Negroes higher prices because they have to contend with more pilfering, more vandalism, more bad debts, the ever-present threat of violence and the distinct possibility of full-scale riot. If the high prices brought windfall profits, competition would come into the area and pull prices down. No great American fortune was ever amassed by storekeeping in a Negro slum.

C. Belzalel Sherman, in an article which I have already cited, gives a straightforward answer to this chronic Negro complaint of economic oppression by Jewish merchants.

"One wonders whether the lackadaisical reaction of Negro leadership to the mounting anti-Semitism among Negroes is not tied up with the failure of the Negro community to do more in the direction of self-improvement. We hold no brief for the Jewish landlords and storekeepers, but we are aware that they have come to their present, unenviable station in Harlem the hard way. It was not so long ago that life for them was not much better than life is now for most Negroes in this city. Tenement houses on the Lower East Side were at the turn of the century not superior to the present slums in Harlem. Work in sweatshops and peddling in unfriendly neighborhoods was no less debilitating than the occupations in which unskilled Negroes are currently engaged. Social Security and unemployment insurance were non-existent. Devoid of political power, the Jewish immigrants were subjected to disabilities and 'police brutality' to a far greater extent than the Negro demon-strators of our days. Nor were physical attacks on Jews lacking; and discrimination in housing, employment and education was a daily occurrence. Still, this did not stop the Jews from making valiant attempts to pull themselves up by their own boot-straps."[50]

The most obvious retort to the charge that Jews move out of residential districts as soon as Negroes move in is that middle-class Negroes also do everything in their power to move out of colored districts. Neither group believes there is any virtue in exposing one's family to slums, vice and the constant threat of violence.

Here again, Sherman discusses the real issue with an hon-esty and directness that is in refreshing contrast to the breast-beating and morally exalted tone of so many Jewish spokesmen. He refers to the case of a community of Ortho-dox Jews in Brooklyn who found that, when Negroes moved into their area, their women were subjected to the danger of being robbed, raped or even murdered. These Orthodox Jews organized their own volunteer defense corps, called the Maccabees, which cooperated with the police in attempt-ing to restore decency and order.

Sherman observes that "we are still confronted with the sad fact that crime *does* increase when Negroes enter a neighborhood. The Lubavitcher *hassidim* did *not* run away when Negroes moved into the Crown Heights area in Brooklyn; and surely there is no more peaceful group in the world—did *that* exempt them from unprovoked attacks? Should they, too, be forced to move, as is quite likely, who in all fairness would find it in his heart to accuse *them* of racism? We all admire self-sacrifice, but this does not give us the right to demand heroic sacrifices of a whole commu-nity, especially when the sacrifices are in vain."[51]

Understandably disturbed about the growth of Negro anti-Semitism, which he believes is percolating up from the lower-class to the middle-class Negroes, Nathan Glazer makes the bizarre proposal that Jewish philanthropic agencies concentrate their resources on Negroes. His argument is that the Jews are so successful that they no longer need these agencies.

Glazer's proposal is simply a variation on the perennial American illusion that friends can be bought. Our foreign policy often seems to be based on the naive notion that rich and productive peoples can escape the envy and hatred of poor and incompetent ones by largesse. Often the result has been to make the poor nations feel guilty toward their benefactors and hence more hostile. Having obtained something for nothing, they rationalize that this is their right and, if they are not given more and more, they denounce the rich nations that support them in idleness as exploiters. "Noble on the surface," Sherman observes concerning Glazer's proposal, "such suggestions are in reality a disservice to the Negro community, whose crying need is self-improvement as part of its fight for equality."

The Black Muslim movement is outspokenly and violently anti-Semitic. This fact has been underplayed by the Anti-Defamation League, whose ostensible *raison d'être* is to fight anti-Jewish propaganda and activity, probably out of fear that publicizing Black Muslim views on this matter would sour a large part of the Jewish population on the so-called Negro struggle for freedom. In February 1962, George Lincoln Rockwell, the late leader of the American Nazi Party, addressed an audience of 5,000 at the Chicago Convention of Elijah Muhammad's "black supremacy" movement. On this platform, he hailed Muhammad as "the Adolf Hitler of the black man" and added that Muhammad was "trying to do what I am trying to do." Since both politicians were trying to bring about total segregation of the Negroes, this observation was more truthful than most of the Nazi agitator's assertions.

Glazer points out that the recent Negro riots in Watts and other urban areas were not the spontaneous outbursts of sans-culotte fury of a few decades ago. They were organized and led by agents of the more militant and lawless Negro organizations. The wholesale destruction of Jewish businesses in the black ghettos can no longer be regarded as just a by-product of mindless mob action. It takes on the characteristics of organized anti-Semitism of a very dangerous sort.

The sacking of Jewish stores in the Watts district of Los Angeles was so extensive that the *Jewish Daily Forward* referred to these riots as "pogroms." The only Negro store that was wrecked in the Philadelphia race riots of 1964 was owned by a man called Richberg. The Negroes thought he was a Jew.[52]

At a 1966 "speakout" in Greenwich Village, two Negro intellectuals disowned the "martyrdom" of Michael Schwerner and Andrew Goodman, two young Jews who were murdered in connection with pro-Negro civil rights action, on the grounds that they had gone to Mississippi to "assuage their conscience." When a member of the audience protested and referred to the Jewish victims of Nazism, a colored jazz musician named Archie Shepp observed that he was "sick of you cats talking about six million Jews." LeRoi Jones, a black writer with a repertoire of four-letter words, told the primarily Jewish audience that "our enemies" included most of those who were listening.[53]

Previously, Jones had been known chiefly for a dirty, but dull, play called *The Toilet.* In the January 1966 issue of *The Liberator,* a little magazine of Negro extremists, Jones blossomed out as the leading Negro anti-Semite. His poem

Black Art referred to "the slimy bellies of the owner-jews" and "cracking steel knuckles in a jewlady's mouth." Jones' hatred was not, however, confined to such a limited object as Jewry. He called for "poems that wrestle cops into alleys and take their weapons leaving them dead with tongues pulled out and sent to Ireland." There are also lines about "dope selling wops" and "mulatto bitches whose brains are red jelly stuck between Elizabeth Taylor's toes."[54] Much of the blank verse is too obscene to be reproduced here; all of it shows an almost total dearth of talent, and the poem as a whole merely reveals the volcanic power of self-hatred and self-contempt when it is externalized and directed at all those who are more successful and more constructive than its author.

On February 3, 1966, Clifford A. Brown, an official of the Congress of Racial Equality (CORE), told Jews in Mt. Vernon, N.Y., that "Hitler made one mistake when he didn't kill enough of you." Will Maslow, executive director of the American Jewish Congress, resigned from the national board of CORE a few days later because of that organization's "tepid and ambiguous response" to Brown's comment about Hitler.[55] A New York spokesman for CORE reacted to the protests against anti-Semitism with the statement: "We are sick and tired of white politicians telling us who our leaders should be."[56]

After the 1967 Arab-Israeli War, the Student Non-Violent Coordinating Committee (SNCC), an extremist black power organization strongly under Communist influence, resorted to violent and mendacious denunciations of the Israeli army and people. In Atlanta on August 15, 1967, SNCC leaders Featherstone, Wise and Minor charged Jews with "imitating their Nazi oppressors" and Israel with resorting to "terror, force and massacres." While this sort of thing may be partly attributed to Red influence and perhaps desire for Soviet subsidy, the emergence of Negro anti-Semitism into the open reflects black sympathy with Arab incompetence and envy of Jewish achievement.

Some Fundamental Issues

Perhaps the main cause of the growing cleavage between Negroes and Jews is that the Jews have fought for Negro equality of opportunity only to discover that this is not what the Negroes want. "The Negro anger," Glazer writes, "is based on the fact that the system of formal equality produces so little for them. The Jewish discomfort is based on the fact that Jews discover they can no longer support the newest Negro demands. . . ."[57]

What the Negroes are asking for today is not, as Glazer imagines, "radically new"; it is as old as the concept of caste. It is the notion that each group is entitled to "its fair share" without regard to its ability or its contribution to production. The new Negro revolution is essentially a return to the old concept of a society based upon status. It is a formula for rewarding the incompetent, for stultifying progress, for quickfreezing innovation and for reverting to a Diocletian or Byzantine conception of man's relationship to the state.

Glazer does his best to see the Negro's point of view and to try to explain that peculiar perspective to his largely Jewish audience. Understanding is always desirable, but it should not be tantamount to acceptance.

American Jews have fought hard for a recognition of the Negro's right to equality of opportunity and for his right to attend schools which are not segregated on the basis of race. Unfortunately, in a display of masochistic sympathy for the underdog, they have gone much further than this. They have supported enforced race-mixing in the schools to the detriment of educational standards and they have backed enforced race-mixing in residential districts to the detriment of public safety.

American Jews today have a golden opportunity. It is an opportunity to get off the merry-go-round, to say, "this far and no further," to totally dissociate themselves from unreasonable Negro demands for special privileges. This means reverting to the sound principle that privileges entail duties, that those who consume should also produce, that men are not entitled to equality, but to the far more precious gift of equality of opportunity, that the future does not belong to the common man, but to the uncommon man.

The fundamental reason for this dissociation is principle. But there are also reasons grounded in expediency. His fervent support of unreasonable Negro demands has exposed the Jew to two types of anti-Semitism: the antipathy of those who oppose total integration and the hostility of the Negroes themselves. That the first antipathy would be assuaged by a Jewish withdrawal from the entire Negro racist movement with its noisy clamor for more and more special privileges needs no comment. That it would also reduce anti-Jewish antagonism among the Negroes themselves will not seem equally self-evident to most readers.

A great deal of light was shed on this problem by Dr. Alvin F. Poussaint, a Negro psychiatrist, who reported in May 1966 to the Atlantic City annual meeting of the American Psychiatric Association on what happens to white girls when they go South to work as civil rights organizers.

Observing that the main area of disturbance is the relationships between white women and Negro men, Dr. Poussaint said:

"The white woman has been the supreme 'tabooed object' for the Southern Negro male. Suddenly, he finds a white girl working side by side with him who accepts him as a person.

"How is he to deal with the mixture of feelings of adoration, fear and hate for the cherished symbol of the 'Southern way of life'? His first reactions are generally those of fear and uneasiness in her presence. He first treats her with great deference, but views her with distrust. He may adore her 'whiteness' and hate her at the same time as the symbol of his oppression. . . .

"Because of the rage he feels toward the white world and the white woman as the 'forbidden fruit,' the Negro man, consciously or unconsciously, will come to view sexual intimacy with the white girl as a weapon of revenge against white society."

A white female civil rights worker, after a year in the South, told Dr. Poussaint:

"I think that Negroes really *do* feel that they are inferior and therefore feel that any white woman who associates with Negroes is really less than the 'all-American,' respected woman in white society and that something is wrong with her or she is just down here for sex with Negro men."[58]

In a sensational article in the *New York Times Magazine*, which aroused a storm of comment both pro and con, Eric Hoffer pointed out that the root of the Negro problem is the Negro's lack of self-respect or self-esteem.

"Despite the vehement protestations of Negro writers and intellectuals," Hoffer wrote, "the Negro is not the white man's problem. On the contrary, the white man is the Negro's chief problem. As things are now, the Negro is what the white man says he is—he knows himself only by white hearsay. That which corrodes the soul of the Negro is his monstrous inner agreement with the prevailing prejudice against him."[59]

Regardless of whether the words "monstrous" and "prejudice" are appropriate—that is to say, without considering whether or not the Negro's lack of self-esteem is well-based, Hoffer has pointed to the crux of the problem, one that probably precludes any satisfactory solution.

Groups which lack self-respect and view themselves with hatred project this hatred outward. Secretly considering themselves unlovable, they despise those who love them and regard this love as proof of inferiority.

These hostile feelings are not normally extended, or at least not intensely extended, to groups which treat the self-hating element with justice and consideration, but without any attempt at intimacy or identification. There is abundant evidence that, during the Mau Mau troubles in Kenya, the first planters to be murdered in hideous fashion were those who had been most liberal in race relations, most ostentatiously friendly and informal with their Kikuyu plantation hands. The attempt at identification aroused defensive hostilities of a deep-seated nature, which were not aroused by those planters who behaved with justice, kept the black workers at a distance and followed the rule of noblesse oblige.

The complex Jewish relationship to the militant Negro movement is subject to the same tensions, ambiguities and generalizations. The fundamental solution for the Jews is disengagement. It means a moratorium on empty moralistic twaddle, an end to the cant and claptrap about equality of talents and an end to the search for some special alliance and empathy between the two groups. Once the emotional binge is over, Jews can look at the Negro problem with sober, morning-after eyes and support those measures, and only those measures, which will help the Negro to advance by his own efforts and be of benefit to the nation as a whole.

CHAPTER 18

Israel, Zionism and Assimilation

A FREQUENT ISRAELI COMPLAINT against American Jews
is that there is no Zionist movement in the United States.[1]
By this they mean that American Jews give Israel valuable
moral and financial support, but take no direct part in building it and feel no allegiance toward it. The complaint reflects a basic contradiction between three incompatible concepts of the nature of the state of Israel—contradictions
which have plagued not merely Israel, but American Jewish
organizations as well.

The first of these concepts, one that has completely gone
by the board and is accepted today only by groups that are
insignificant in terms of both numbers and power, was that
advanced by the late Dr. Judah L. Magnes, president of
Hebrew University in Jerusalem. Magnes envisioned Israel
(or Palestine) as a multi-racial, multi-national, multi-lingual
state, one that might unite Jew and Arab in a common

effort to transform the Middle East into a region in which the masses could move toward a more civilized life. In this concept, Palestinian Jews would have played a role traditional to that of Jewry: they would have served as fertilizing agents and transmission belts from one civilization to another. This concept has been swept aside by events.

A second view was that Israel should serve as a refuge and homeland for those Jews who chose it. This is the concept upheld by the vast majority of American Jews. It involves no issue of dual loyalty or divided allegiance. Naturally, American Jews can be expected to have deeper emotional and sympathetic attachments to Israel than to other foreign countries, just as Irish Americans retain their love for Eire, but do not in the process lessen their loyalty to the United States.

The third concept, one that has at times been advanced by the chiefs of state of Israel in strident and unambiguous tones, is that Israel is the homeland of all Jews, that they owe it their primary allegiance and that it is the duty of all Jews to abandon the lands in which they live and come to the new Jewish state—to work for it, live under its laws and, if necessary, defend it. The explosive implications of this position for the relationship of American Jews to the United States are self-evident. Whenever it was enunciated, particularly when this was done in the extreme fashion chosen by former Israeli Prime Minister David Ben-Gurion, responsible organizations of American Jewry repudiated it in unequivocal terms.

Cutting across these incompatible concepts of the relationship of the Israeli nation to Jewry was a different issue. If Israeli citizenship is automatically and instantly available to every Jew as his birthright, then it becomes important to know how Israel defines the word *Jew*. Is the basic distinction one of religious belief, marked perhaps by synagogue attendance or by some ritual such as circumcision, or is it a matter of common descent from the same subracial stock? And, if the latter, how can American Jews unequivocally support the concept of a Jewish homeland, run by Jews, while denying South Africa's right to *Apartheid* or the right of the white American South to avoid integration?

Ben-Gurion and the Ingathering

"The basis of Zionism," Ben-Gurion declared in 1950, "is neither friendship nor sympathy, but the love of Israel, of the state of Israel. . . . It must be an unconditional love. There must be a complete solidarity with the state and the people of Israel." Similarly, Dr. Nahum Goldmann, then president of the World Zionist Organization, declared in 1959, that "American Jews must have the courage to openly declare that they entertain a double loyalty, one to the land in which they live and one to Israel."[2]

In his address to the World Zionist Congress in December 1960, Dr. Ben-Gurion, who was then Prime Minister of Israel, declared:

"Since the day when the Jewish state was established and the gates of Israel were flung open to every Jew who wanted to come, every religious Jew has daily violated the precepts of Judaism and the Torah by remaining in the Diaspora.[3] Whoever dwells outside the land of Israel is considered to have no God, the sages said."[4]

Ben-Gurion continued with the observation that Jewry in America faced as mortal a danger as it did in the Arab or Soviet worlds. There it was menaced by "death by strangulation," whereas "in the free and prosperous countries, it faces death by a kiss—a slow and imperceptible decline into the abyss of assimilation."

The American Jewish Protest

As early as 1949, the American Jewish Committee sent a delegation to Israel, headed by its president, Jacob Blaustein, to confer with Prime Minister Ben-Gurion and reach an understanding with Israeli authorities on the matter of divided loyalty. The following year, with the approval of the Israeli Cabinet, Ben-Gurion made a solemn declaration that:

"The Jews of the United States, as a community and as individuals, have only one political attachment and that is to the United States of America. They owe no political allegiance to Israel. In the first statement which the representative of Israel made before the United Nations after her admission to that international organization, he clearly stated, without any reservation, that the State of Israel represents and speaks only in behalf of its own citizens, and in no way presumes to represent or speak in the name of the Jews who are citizens of any other country. We, the people of Israel, have no desire and no intention to interfere in any way with the internal affairs of Jewish communities abroad. The government and the people of Israel fully respect the right and integrity of the Jewish communities in other countries to develop their own mode of life and their indigenous social, economic and cultural institutions in accordance with their own needs and aspirations. Any weakening of American Jewry, any disruption of its communal life, any lowering of its status, is a definite loss to Jews everywhere and to Israel in particular."[5]

In reply, Blaustein stated that the American Jewish Committee would continue to help Israel "solve its problems and develop as a free, independent and flourishing democracy." He added that "American Jews vigorously repudiate any suggestion or implication that they are in exile. American Jews—young and old alike, Zionist and non-Zionist alike—are profoundly attached to America." Rebutting Ben-Gurion's frequent complaints that American Jews had refused to emigrate en masse to Israel and his often expressed belief that only in Israel could Jews enjoy true security, Blaustein said: "To American Jews, America is home. There, exist their thriving roots; there, is the country which they have helped to build; and there, they share its fruits and its destiny. . . . They further believe that, if democracy should fail in America, there would be no future for democracy anywhere in the world, and that the very existence of an independent State of Israel would be problematic. Further, they feel that a world in which it would be possible for Jews to be driven by persecution from America would not be a world safe for Israel either; indeed it is hard to conceive how it would be a world safe for any human being."

This exchange of views appeared to settle the matter. From Ben-Gurion's standpoint, however, it seems to have been merely an enforced concession to the representatives of the richest Jewry on earth at a time when Israel desperately needed financial support. In 1959-1960, Ben-Gurion again attempted to speak for the world's Jews and again exhorted American Jews to leave their country and become Israeli citizens. A new AJC delegation was sent to Israel and in 1961 Prime Minister Ben-Gurion and Mr. Blaustein reaffirmed their earlier statements. With Ben-Gurion's fall from power, the statement of principles was reasserted by

Ben-Gurion's successor, Prime Minister Eshkol. Since then, the issue has diminished in importance.

Arabs and Oriental Jews

The vehement complaint of Ben-Gurion against American Jews for shirking their supposed duty to emigrate and take up Israeli citizenship was not an expression of irrationality or petulance. He and the other founders of the new state had hoped that it would attract European and American Jews in sufficient numbers so that it would remain basically a Western society. They faced the prospect of being swamped by masses of ignorant Afro-Asian Jews whose rampant reproduction habits would inevitably make them the majority element. "The Moroccan Jews took a lot from the Moroccan Arab," Ben-Gurion once observed, "and I don't see much we can learn from the Moroccan Arabs. The culture of Morocco I would not like to have here. And I don't see what contribution Persians have to make."[6]

Jews of Afro-Asian stock are already a majority in Israel, primarily because the expected exodus from the West did not materialize. Jewish survivors of the Nazi holocaust did enter Palestine, to be sure, soon after World War II. The Jews of Britain, the United States and Latin America, however, in their overwhelming majority stayed where they were, remaining citizens of the countries in which they had been born and where they had struck roots. Migration to Israel meant a new language and culture, a harder and more dangerous life and generally a lower standard of living. Hence, their attachment to Israel remained sentimental and financial. As far as the large Jewish population of the USSR was concerned, there may well have been a general desire to emigrate to Israel, but this was sternly prohibited by the

Soviet authorities. In the Balko-Danubian area, governmental policies were more liberal, but the Jewish population had been practically wiped out.

Hence, the great exodus of Jews from the Asian and African Middle East soon became the only significant source of Israeli immigration. As of 1966, about 10% of the population of Israel was Arab in origin and either Muslim or Christian. Of the remaining 90%, a majority was of Afro-Asian stock (including Jews born in Israel of Afro-Asian parentage). Since this element is much more fertile than European Jewry, the Oriental majority will predictably become greater with each succeeding year.

The implications of this demographic change have never been clear to American Jewry, but they are painfully clear to the leaders of Israel. As early as July 1951, Iraqui Jews organized a mass demonstration against "race discrimination" in Israel.[7] A race riot in the Wadi Salib slum of Haifa in July 1959 involved a four-day melee between the "White Jews" of European origin and the "Black Jews" of Afro-Asian stock. Eleven policemen were wounded and 32 rioters were arrested.

A 1961 study of kindergarten and first and second grade pupils in Israeli schools showed that the average I.Q. for European children, as measured by the Wechsler Intelligence Scale for Children (WISC), was 104.4 as against 94.2 for Oriental Jewish children. The basic correlation was between I.Q. and area of origin, rather than between I.Q. and socio-economic status of parents. Moreover, the more these Oriental Jewish children were exposed to the excellent Israeli educational system, the greater the gap between their I.Q. and that of the Jewish children of European origin. As Moshe Smilanksy put it, ". . . there was a continuous decline in the level of the intelligence of the children tested, starting with the nine- to ten-year-olds and reaching a peak at the age of fourteen with the completion of elementary school."[8]

Sarah Smilanksy observed "statistically significant deterioration" in the I.Q.'s of Jewish children from Afro-Asian countries from the first year of school forward, whereas Jewish children of European origin made normal, or better than normal, progress. In short, the learning pattern of the "Black Jews" was comparable to that of Negroes in the United States. In both cases, the I.Q. gap increased steadily with age and academic level.

Of the 162,000 Israeli illiterates, 137,000 are Orientals. While over half the first-graders in Israeli schools are Afro-Asians, they are eliminated so rapidly that they constituted only 16% of the twelfth-grade student body and only 7% of the university student population. Some 43% of the North African and 34% of the Middle Eastern Jews in Israel do unskilled labor as against 17% unskilled laborers for Israeli Jews as a whole.[9]

The conditions and performance of the Israeli Arabs are as bad or worse. In the early 1960's, there were widespread complaints of lack of textbooks and teachers, job discrimination and the absence of Arabs in civil service jobs. In 1961, 88% of all Arab secondary-school pupils failed their examinations.

Blood-group investigations by A. E. Mourant and others would indicate that the Jews of Yemen and the rural Jews of Morocco are not Jews at all from an ethnic standpoint, but are the descendants of Arabs and Berbers converted to Judaism. This condition may be present elsewhere in the Afro-Asian Jewries. To the extent that it is not, the shortfall in learning capacity is probably caused by the fact that the Jewish institutional complex of selective breeding for intelligence, which I have described at length elsewhere,[10] never really took hold in the Middle East.

In any event, we seem to be dealing with fundamental genetic differences, which cannot be wiped out by improvements in education, preaching about brotherhood or propaganda in favor of intermarriage.

In fact, from the biogenetic standpoint, the future of Israel appears somber. It seems fated to become an Oriental country, that is to say, to become a land inhabited by a population, the majority of which resembles the masses of North Africa and the Middle East. This condition will no doubt be masked for many years by the fact that the ruling element will continue to be the European Jewish minority. Yet, as this minority dwindles, its foothold must become more and more precarious. To the extent that Israel becomes such a Middle Eastern nation, it will lose much of its attraction for those Western Jewries which today give it such enthusiastic and dedicated support. Regardless of their theories about racial equality, Western Jews are not likely to feel any real identification with Afro-Asian populations which in many respects resemble fellaheen. Thus, even if it establishes its military security against the ever-present threat of invasion by its neighbors, Israel faces the prospect of being swamped by its own internal proletariat and hence gradually becoming more and more demographically similar to its neighbors.

Increasing discontent among Israel's Afro-Asian Jews, the expression of this discontent in mounting Oriental crime and delinquency, the eruption of "race" riots and the coalescence of Afro-Asian Jewry into an oppositional political force—all these tendencies make the leaders of the new state intensify their efforts to bring about assimilation of the two Jewries. Yet assimilation through intermarriage could be the kiss of death. It could nullify the effects of two thousand years of selective mating among European Jews for intelligence.

Assume, for example, that the true I.Q. difference between the two major groups of Jews is the 10% observed at the kindergarten and first- and second-grade levels. Assume further that European and Afro-Asian Jews are roughly equal in number and that completely random mating occurs. We could then expect a drop of five I.Q. points from the present level of European Jewish children. Under some assumptions, a decline of as little as one and one-half I.Q. points will cause a decrease by one-third in the number of highly gifted children born—those with I.Q.'s of 160 or better. Under slightly different assumptions, the decline at this level will be even greater. The first calculation is that of Sir Julian Huxley, the second is based on assumptions introduced by Sir Cyril Burt.[11]

Once it becomes evident that trends in Israel threaten the continued existence of Jewish intelligence, a radical rethinking on the topic of equality can probably be expected from American Jews. If it is biogenetically necessary that Israeli Jews preserve their genetic heritage and their society against mixture with either Arabs or the descendants of Arab converts to Judaism, then it is difficult to demand the enforced blending of Negroes and whites in American schools and American residential districts in proportions prescribed by the state, assuming the unspoken purpose is that which Podhoretz enunciated, namely, that they subsequently blend in bed.[12] Nor is it easy to continue to condemn South Africa and Rhodesia for forms of white rule which have brought African natives a degree of prosperity and security that has never been present in those countries which they ruled themselves. It becomes difficult for American Jewish liberals to condemn the policy of Australia for whites only as "fascist" or for them to urge a United Nations invasion of South Africa so that that prosperous country may be turned over to majority Negro rule and allowed to revert to barbarism. If such liberal measures are just by democratic standards, the intelligent American Jew may ask himself, then would not democracy for Israel consist in letting it be overwhelmed by Arab and other Afro-Asian masses so that it might resume the condition of stagnation and squalor in which it wallowed between the Islamic conquest and the Jewish return.

I have no illusion that these transvaluations of values will be made quickly, but I think the rising tide of demographic crisis in Israel may serve as an impetus for American Jewish re-examination of the basic problems of equality and freedom.

Assimilation and American Jewry

American Jewry faces the prospect of eventual extinction as a significant coherent group because of low fertility and rising assimilation through intermarriage. Jewish fecundity is much lower than that of either Catholics or Protestants. To a large extent, this is due to the fact that the Jewish population in the United States is overwhelmingly urban, high income, highly educated, conversant with birth control devices and devoid of religious convictions against using contraceptives. On the basis of present fertility and mortality rates, American Jews are approximately maintaining their numbers while the nation as a whole is experiencing rapid population growth. Thus, Arthur T. Jacobs, of the Union of American Hebrew Congregations, has estimated that by the year 2000, American Jews will constitute 1.6% of the population as against the 1960 figure of 2.9%.[13] The low fertility of American Jewry is merely one facet of a much larger problem—the comparative infertility of the elite elements of Western civilization. The consequence of a continuation of this pattern must inevitably be a decline in the mental potential of each generation from the one which preceded it. This decline is not always revealed by intelligence tests, since better education, greater familiarity with the tests and improvements in living conditions tend to raise scores from one decade to the next. Nevertheless, a real genetic impoverishment of the intellectual resources of mankind seems, almost imperceptibly, to be occurring.

Most studies of Jewish intermarriage have emphasized the comparatively low overall rates. Thus C. B. Sherman concluded that, in view of the extent to which the Jewish community has become culturally assimilated, the remarkable thing about the intermarriage rate is that it has been so small. Glazer and Moynihan in *Beyond the Melting Pot* similarly found that American Jews, in contrast to the successful Jewries of Western Europe, characteristically marry within their own group.[14]

More recent and more detailed studies do not bear this out. A survey by Rosenthal, cited elsewhere, showed that during 1953-1959 only 57.8% of the marriage licenses applied for by Jews in Iowa listed both spouses as of the Jewish faith. In Washington, D.C., the same authority estimated that the intermarriage rate among Jews was 1.4% for the first (foreign-born) generation, 10.2% for the second and 17.9% for the third.

It is the intellectual elite of Jewry that is most prone to intermarriage. Thus, a study by Rabbi Henry Cohen showed that 20% of Jewish faculty members at the University of Illinois, but only 6.5% of Jewish townspeople, were married to Gentiles.[15] An investigation of psychoanalysts by A. B. Hollinshead and F. C. Redlich showed that 83% of them were Jewish and that 64% of Jewish analysts were married to non-Jewish spouses.[16]

An estimated 70% of the children born to mixed couples are not brought up as Jews. The rising trend of intermarriage has caused great concern within Jewish organizations and among rabbis. Yet, ironically, it is one of the products of precisely the measures they have successfully fought for. The mixed fraternity, the country club open to Jews and Gentiles alike, the knocking down of the barriers to Jewish advancement in the American corporation have all operated to make intermarriage more attractive and more frequent. Probably the main barrier to such marriages today is Judaism and, among the Jewish college youth at least, this is a feeble force. Thus, a National Opinion Research Council (NORC) poll of 35,000 graduates of 135 colleges revealed that 13% of the Jewish subjects said they had no religious faith and another 60% said they were lax in religious observance.[17]

Observation would suggest that those American Jews who intermarry do so very frequently with members of the non-Jewish intellectual elite. To the extent that this is the case, there is no reason to suppose that these marriages produce less gifted children than purely Jewish marital unions. Jewish leaders, however, consider it deplorable that Jewry and Judaism should have managed to preserve their identity through millenia of persecution, despite the most harrowing ordeals and ghastly epidemics of genocide, only to face the possibility of gradually being killed by kindness and destroyed by freedom.

CHAPTER 19

Church and State

FROM THE 1940's TO AT LEAST 1965, Supreme Court decisions progressively stretched the meaning of that part of the First Amendment to the Constitution which defines the relationship of government to organized religion. By a gradual, but glacially powerful process, the separation between Church and State was sharpened; the list of religious practices and observances banned in the public schools and in other governmental institutions was lengthened, and both education and government were increasingly secularized.

The mighty engine of change in this area has been the Supreme Court. However, the Court can act only when cases come to it on appeal. Hence, the instigators of these successive reinterpretations of the Constitution have been those individuals and organizations which bring suit to force public authorities to divorce themselves from one religious observance after another.

Public opinion polls reveal that many of these Supreme Court decisions have been and are strongly opposed by substantial majorities of the American people. They have caused bitter and deep-seated resentment among devout parents who wish to send their children to public schools but who also wish them to receive an education from which religion is not totally excluded. This resentment has been particularly widespread against Supreme Court decisions striking down non-denominational prayers and barring Bible readings in the public schools.

The most prominent and powerful of American Jewish organizations have been energetic and uncompromising instigators of measures to bring about total separation of Church and State. The suits are frequently initiated and financed by the American Jewish Congress and the Anti-Defamation League. The parents who bring suit are, as a rule, Jews, Unitarians and Universalists, atheists or agnostics. The extent of the involvement of organized American Jewry in these matters is not a secret affair. It is plainly revealed and in fact proclaimed in the *American Jewish Year Book*, the official annual publication of the American Jewish Committee. Year after year, this publication devotes what must seem to many of its readers an exhorbitant amount of space to the details of the legal battles in the campaign to further the cleavage between organized religion and government. Often it enumerates the cases in which some of the plaintiffs were Jewish or in which their legal argument was buttressed by *amici curiae* briefs prepared by Jewish organizations.[1] In the 1965 edition of the *Year Book*, 85 pages are devoted to "Civic and Political" issues, of which 22 deal with "Church and State."

Before proceeding further, it seems important to point out that neither the entire American Jewish community nor all of its organizations support this campaign. Thus, when the American Jewish Congress opposed the Education Act of 1966 because it provided for assistance to students taking courses in denominational institutions of higher education, as well as in other colleges and universities, this stand was vigorously opposed by Rabbi Amos Bunin, chairman of the Executive Committee of the National Society for Hebrew Day Schools and by other Jewish leaders. Rabbi Bunin testified as follows before the Senate Subcommittee on Education:

"The American Jewish Congress does not represent the religious community. It ill behooves this organization to try to protect the religious freedom of the Jewish community or, for that matter, of other faith groups, when that religious leadership endorses the bill and sees in it no threat whatsoever to religious freedom and, on the contrary, expects the strengthening of religious freedom to emerge from the enactment of the bill."[2]

The voice of Rabbi Bunin, however, was a minority voice in American Jewry. His organization was far weaker in money, political influence and membership than the American Jewish Congress. As for the American Jewish Congress, its leadership has been so uncompromising in its determination to prevent any federal subsidy for students desiring a religious education that it broke with the overwhelming majority of Catholic and Protestant groups which supported the 1965 Education Act. The Congress found itself part of a motley alliance of fanatically anti-Catholic organizations and little societies of free thinkers.

In December 1966, the American Jewish Congress joined with the American Civil Liberties Union and two organizations of parents and teachers to challenge the constitutionality of the 1965 Elementary and Secondary Education Act.

Suits in Federal and New York State courts demanded an injunction against spending federal funds on parochial and other denominational schools as being in violation of the First Amendment. The leaders of the Jewish organization, Shad Polier and Leo Pfeffer, said they expected the suits to be tested by the Supreme Court in the fall of 1968. The Very Reverend Eugene J. Molloy, chairman of the Committee of Non-Public School Officials of New York City, which claimed to represent 450,000 Catholic, Protestant and Jewish children in denominational schools, expressed confidence that the courts would "defeat these reactionary efforts and protect the rights of the children involved."[3]

Commenting on the American Jewish Congress in the May 11, 1966 issue of the *National Catholic Reporter*, John Leo made some observations that reflect a widespread Catholic attitude. "For Catholics," he wrote, "all the bad guys are in the American Jewish Congress and all the good guys in the American Jewish Committee. This may be, as the hard-hearted rumor has it, because there has been a de facto division of duties, the Committee working more with Catholics while the Congress works more with Protestants who are not over-fond of Catholics. Whatever the truth of this, all I know is that I cringe whenever I meet, or even read anything by an official of the American Jewish Congress. On the night of the Pope's visit to New York, I had the misfortune to be on a TV panel with Shad Polier, chairman of the American Jewish Congress' national governing council, who put on the most dazzling all-round offensive performance I have ever had to squirm through. I further note that he is still at it. Just this week he announced that use of tax funds for church schools has 'robbed public education of desperately needed funds and subverted the most basic institution of American democracy.' Has this become

the standard rhetoric of the Congress? Or shall we discuss
the sticky inter-group issues without accusing each other of
robbery and subversion?"

The preponderant attitude of American Jewry toward religious observances in the schools and toward public support
of either religious educational institutions or the religious
education of individual students is part.of the much broader
spectrum, or syndrome, of Jewish political behavior in the
United States. The first problem is how this intransigent
position arose. The second is to define the scope of Jewish
political activity in this area. The third is to discern and
evaluate the emergence of a new and more constructive
approach to the Church-State issue by the American Jewish
community. Before approaching any of these problems, a
brief summary of the evolution of the constitutional doctrine of Church and State separation in America seems in
order.

Religion and the Bill of Rights

Our forefathers were concerned primarily with the danger that the federal government would give preference to
one religious denomination over another and, by so doing,
find itself at loggerheads with the states. When James Madison introduced his draft of the First Amendment to the
Constitution to Congress, the part referring to religion read:
"The civil rights of none shall be abridged on account of
religious belief or worship, nor shall any national religion
be established, nor shall the full and equal rights of conscience be in any manner, or on any pretence, infringed."
The House, the Senate and a conference committee of both
Houses boiled this down to the wording incorporated in the
First Amendment, namely: "Congress shall make no law

respecting an establishment of religion, or prohibiting the free exercise thereof. . . ."

In his authoritative interpretation of the intent of the framers of the Constitution, Mr. Justice Story pointed out that the purpose of the provision was, "not to discredit the then existing State establishments of religion," but to "exclude from the National Government all power to act upon the subject."[4] He added that there had been no thought of denying preference to Christianity:

"Probably at the time of the adoption of the Constitution, and of the amendments to it now under consideration, the general if not the universal sentiment in America was, that Christianity ought to receive encouragement from the state so far as was not incompatible with the private rights of conscience and the freedom of religious worship. An attempt to level all religions, and to make it a matter of state policy to hold all in utter indifference, would have created universal disapprobation, if not universal indignation."[5]

In 1802, President Thomas Jefferson wrote in a letter to a Baptist group in Danbury, Connecticut, that the objective of the First Amendment in the sphere of religion had been to erect "a wall of separation between Church and State." This phrase, since it conforms to contemporary liberal thinking on the matter, has in recent decades become almost as authoritative as the words of the First Amendment themselves and one finds the *American Jewish Year Book* occasionally scolding such a benighted institution as the Supreme Court of Florida for not being bound by it. Yet this communication was only one of many thousands which Jefferson wrote in the course of an unusually long and active life. Neither the nature of the occasion nor the quality of the audience required a profound constitutional interpretation.

Three years later, when Jefferson read his Second Inaugural Address, he spoke with the precision appropriate to a state paper which he knew would go down in American history. Here he defined the scope of the First Amendment in a very different and much more restrictive fashion. "In matters of religion," he declared, "I have considered that its free exercise is placed by the Constitution independent of the powers of the general government."

This original interpretation of the First Amendment was probably too narrow for a nation that was evolving from a religious toward a scientific view of the world. The first revolutionary change in interpretation came in the case of Benjamin Gitlow, a Communist leader who had been tried and convicted under a New York criminal syndicalism law which made it a crime to advocate the overthrow of the American government by force and violence. Gitlow's attorneys challenged the constitutionality of the law and the case went to the Supreme Court.

The first issue was whether freedom of speech and freedom of the press were guaranteed against state laws, as well as against federal law, by the First Amendment. Speaking for the Court majority, Mr. Justice Sanford delivered the revolutionary pronouncement that they were so guaranteed. "We may and do assume that freedom of speech and of the press—which are protected by the First Amendment from abridgment by Congress," he declared, "are among the fundamental personal rights and 'liberties' protected by the due process clause of the 14th Amendment from impairment by the states."[6] A few years later, this doctrine was applied to the provisions of the First Amendment concerning religion.

This enlargement of constitutional scope was followed by a series of decisions which gradually raised the barrier set up by the First Amendment between State and Church. In 1947, a narrow majority of the Supreme Court held that

New Jersey communities were entitled to give free transportation to children attending parochial schools. However, it added the following warning as to what local authorities were not entitled to do:

"Neither a state nor the Federal Government can set up a church. Neither can pass laws which aid one religion, aid all religions, or prefer one religion over another. Neither can force nor influence a person to go to or to remain away from church against his will or force him to profess a belief or disbelief in any religion. No person can be punished for entertaining or professing religious beliefs or disbeliefs, for church attendance or non-attendance. No tax in any amount, large or small, can be levied to support any religious activities or institutions, whatever they may be called, or whatever form they may adopt to teach or practice religion. Neither a state nor the Federal Government can, openly or secretly, participate in the affairs of any religious organizations or groups and vice versa."[7]

During the next few years, the Supreme Court had to decide on various "released time" cases—that is to say, state or local laws by which children, whose parents wished them to have religious instruction, were given time off from classes for that purpose. The Court struck down one such arrangement in a famous Illinois case and upheld another in an equally well-known New York decision.[8] It was a matter of drawing a precise line and seeing whether or not these local systems stayed within it. It is of some interest that in the New York case, Mr. Justice Douglas, generally regarded as ultra-liberal, expressed these views:

"When the state encourages religious instruction or cooperates with religious authorities by adjusting the schedule of public events to sectarian needs, it follows the best of our traditions. For it then respects the religious nature of our people and accommodates the public service to their spiritual needs. To hold that it may not would be to find in the Constitution that the government shows a callous indifference to religious groups. That would be preferring those who believe in no religion over those who do believe."[9]

An Evolving Jewish Pattern

The Jewish attitude toward the separation of Church and State was based on the collective memory of centuries of religious persecution. Prior to the modern era, it had been a general rule that, where the Church dominated the State, Jews had been peculiarly subject to the hazards of humiliating discrimination and, in some instances, to imposed quarantine, expropriation and exile. Where the State had been secular, however, Jews had generally enjoyed greater equality of rights and opportunities under law. Religiously speaking, the Jews were in a unique position vis-à-vis the Christian Church, one that could not be compared with that of the Chinese and Japanese, for example. They were not merely non-believers in the divinity of Jesus Christ; they were in part the descendants of people who had taken part in the Crucifixion.

As early as 1904, the Central Conference of American Rabbis (CCAR) took a strong stand against the indoctrination of pupils with the Christian religion in public schools. As Rabbi Joseph Krauskopf put it: "Let us be Protestants or Catholics, agnostics or Jews in our churches or homes; in our public institutions, however, let us be Americans."[10]

At his instigation, a standing committee was set up by the CCAR to cast a vigilant eye on the use of the public school system for sectarian purposes. The Central Conference nevertheless shied away from legal action to test the constitutionality of the religious instruction then current, feeling no doubt that this was an area fraught with great danger and potentially disagreeable repercussions. "Defeat in such matters is so baneful that the risk of it had rather not be incurred," the standing committee reported.

In 1939, however, the CCAR injected itself into legal action to defend the right of the Jehovah's Witness sect to violate state laws compelling school children to salute the American flag. The Witnesses taught their children that this was a form of idolatry contrary to the teachings of the Bible. Some two thousand children were expelled from schools in 31 states and hundreds of incidents of violence against members of the sect were reported. The American Civil Liberties Union, backed by the CCAR, argued that the state laws which compelled salute to the flag were unconstitutional because they prevented the "free exercise" of a religion. In 1943, the Court upheld the plaintiffs.

From then on, Jewish organizations took an increasingly active stand to enforce and deepen the separation between Church and State. To summarize all of these struggles would be tedious and unrewarding. A few highlights of the activities of Jewish organizations in this area during the 1960's will serve to illustrate the sort of policies advocated and the conflicts and tensions generated.

Prayer in the Schools

In 1951, the New York State Board of Regents approved a 22-word, non-denominational prayer for reading in the public schools. Its text was: "Almighty God, we acknowledge our dependence upon Thee and we beg Thy blessings upon us, our parents, our teachers and our country."

This Regents' prayer was challenged by five parents of

New Hyde Park school children, two of whom were Jewish, one Unitarian, one Ethical Culture and one agnostic.[11] Although this prayer did not conflict with the tenets of Judaism, organized American Jewry was virtually unanimous in its support of the plaintiffs. The American Jewish Congress, the Jewish War Veterans, the Jewish Labor Committee, the Anti-Defamation League of B'nai B'rith and the rabbinical associations of Orthodox, Conservative and Reform Judaism joined in supporting an *amici curiae* brief to the Supreme Court.

On June 25, 1962 the U.S. Supreme Court by a six to one majority held that the Regents' Prayer was unconstitutional. "It is not part of the business of government," Mr. Justice Black said for the majority, "to compose official prayers for any group. . . . Neither the fact that the prayer may be denominationally neutral, nor . . . that its observance . . . is voluntary can serve to free it from the limitation of the Establishment Clause. . . ."[12]

The long dissent by Mr. Justice Potter Stewart called attention to the fact that the United States armed forces have chaplains, to the words "under God" in the Pledge of Allegiance and to the "In God We Trust" legend on pennies as evidence that total separation between Church and State was never intended and has not been consummated.

"I cannot see how an 'official religion' is established by letting those who want to say a prayer say it," Justice Stewart observed. "On the contrary, I think that to deny the wish of these school children to join in reciting this prayer is to deny them the opportunity of sharing in the spiritual heritage of the nation."

The nationwide reaction against the decision was spontaneous and convincing testimony to the intensity of religious feeling in the United States. Former President Herbert Hoover called for a Constitutional Amendment to establish "the right to religious devotion in all governmental agencies—national, state or local." Forty-nine amendments to the Constitution were sponsored by Congressmen in 1962 alone, all designed to strip the Supreme Court of the power to eliminate religious teaching and religious emblems. Congressional mail ran heavily against the Supreme Court.

Senator Samuel J. Ervin (Democrat from North Carolina) charged that the Court had "made God unconstitutional" and Representative George Andrews (Democrat from Alabama) added: "They put the Negroes in the schools, and now they've kicked God out."

Catholic spokesmen were almost unanimously opposed. Cardinal Cushing described the Court's action as "fuel for Communist propaganda." Cardinal Spellman charged that it struck "at the very heart of the Godly tradition in which America's children have for so long been raised." The *Pilot*, organ of the Boston Archdiocese, said that the decision had been the work of a "small clique of minorities—Ethical Culturists, Humanists, Atheists and Agnostics, assisted by certain secularist Jews and Unitarians."[13]

Letters to the press were generally opposed and expressed "horror," "disbelief" and "shock." In July, the Governors' Conference voted unanimously, with only Governor Rockefeller of New York abstaining, to call upon Congress for laws to make possible "free and voluntary participation in prayers in our schools. . . ." The National Association for the Advancement of Colored People backed the Supreme Court decision as did such leading Negro newspapers as the *Amsterdam News*, *Chicago Defender* and the *Pittsburgh Courier*.

From January 1963 on, Congressmen tried to get the

resolutions for Constitutional Amendment heard by the House Judiciary Committee. Its chairman, Emanuel Celler, a diehard New York liberal, did all in his power to prevent hearings, but, when faced by 167 signatures behind a discharge petition and mounting protest mail, finally yielded.

Hearings were held in the spring and summer of 1964. Public opinion polls revealed overwhelming support for an Amendment validating school prayer. Thus, the Gallup Poll found in August 1963 that 70% opposed the Supreme Court's outlawry of Bible reading and prayer in the public schools, 24% approved and 6% had no opinion. A Louis Harris poll in the last days of the 1964 presidential campaign, at a time when Barry Goldwater's defeat was almost universally predicted, found that 88% of the respondents supported Goldwater's stand in favor of permitting voluntary school prayer.[14]

The great majority of Protestant leaders opposed any such Amendment; the minority consisted mainly of Fundamentalists. The Jewish groups were stoutly opposed. Oddly enough, no Bishop of the Catholic Church testified in favor of the proposed Constitutional Amendment and both *America* and the National Catholic Welfare Conference opposed it.[15]

While the hearings were in progress, public indignation petered out and the mail received by Congress began to run against the proposed Constitutional Amendment. Further action ceased and the proposed change became a dead letter.

The issue of anti-Semitism was raised by the liberal Jesuit journal, *America*, in a September 1962 editorial entitled "To Our Jewish Friends." Predicting that the attitude of certain leaders of Jewish organizations in forcing the issue of school prayer would cause incidents of hostility to Jews in general, *America* stated that it had noted "disturbing

hints of antisemitic feelings" since the decision. The magazine did not criticize American Jewry in general, but blamed
the leaders of the CCAR and UAHC (rabbinical congregations) and of the American Jewish Congress for precip-
itating the conflict. Leo Pfeffer, the counsel for the American Jewish Congress, was the only Jewish leader attacked
by name.

"We wonder," *America* asked, "whether it is not time for
provident leaders of American Judaism to ask their more
militant colleagues whether what is gained through the
courts by such victories is worth the breakdown of community relations. . . . What will have been accomplished
if our Jewish friends win all the legal immunities they seek,
but thereby paint themselves into a corner of social and
cultural alienation."

This friendly and temperate warning from a Catholic
magazine known for its sympathy toward Jews and Judaism
was characterized by Joachim Prinz, the president of the
American Jewish Congress, as a threat. "It is a sorry day for
religious liberty in the United States," Prinz declared,
"when an effort to protect the guarantees of the First
Amendment should evoke thinly veiled threats of antisemit-
ism from so respectable a journal of opinion as *America*."
Mr. Prinz was apparently either unwilling or unable to dis-
tinguish between predicting an event and advocating it.

Banning Christmas

In widely scattered areas of the country, Jewish organizations stirred up intense hostility by trying to abolish Christmas and Easter celebrations in the schools.

In New Haven, the school authorities invited the local
Jewish Community Council to participate in a joint Christ-

mas-Hannukah celebration. The latter declined, at the same time protesting "any form of public sponsoring of religious exercises, celebrations and festivals within America's public schools. . . ."

A local Protestant minister retaliated by condemning American Jews for "becoming so divisive that they refuse to listen to the prayers and songs of another's faith." The Knights of Columbus organ, *Columbia*, also protested, though more mildly.

The New Haven school system bowed to the demands of the Jewish Community Council and agreed that there should be no celebration. It was deluged with abusive letters and phone calls, many of which were described by First Selectman DeNicola as "nasty" and "sickening." After a violent, furious mass meeting, the school authorities backtracked a second time and agreed to hold the same Christmas celebrations as in previous years. The Christian clergy, both Protestant and Catholic, appealed for tolerance of "our Jewish friends" and the flare-up of anti-Semitism, caused by the doctrinaire stand of the Jewish Community Center, subsided.

The Jewish Community Center of Washington, D.C., made a similar demand earlier in 1962 and nearly created a similar situation. It urged school boards to cease celebrating religious holidays in the public schools. School Superintendant Carl F. Hansen flatly rejected the proposed elimination of Christmas carols and pageants, stating that to yield to the Jewish Community Center would "create an artificial separation between events within and outside the school . . . difficult to reconcile with the purposes of education."

The anti-Semitism generated by the Washington, D.C.,

episode was apparently confined to sometimes abusive letters to newspaper editors, the great majority of which were hostile to the Jewish Community Center's position.

Meanwhile, Jewish, Unitarian and agnostic parents protested the celebration of religious holidays in the Miami public school system. The Florida Supreme Court rejected the plaintiffs' demand as "just another case in which the tender sensibilities of certain minorities are sought to be protected against the allegedly harsh laws and customs enacted and established by the more rugged pioneers of this nation. . . ." On June 1, 1964 the Supreme Court of the United States overruled this intemperately phrased decision without hearing argument. This created widespread resentment among Florida parents.

Winds of Change

Meanwhile, the attitude of the more enlightened Jewish organizations was readjusting to the changes that were occurring within the Christian churches.

The World Council of Churches at its Third Assembly in 1961 urged its "member churches to do all in their power to resist every form of anti-Semitism," adding: "In Christian teaching, the historic events which led to the Crucifixion should not be so presented as to fasten upon the Jewish people of today responsibilities which belonged to a 'corpus humanity' and not to one race or community."

Pope John XXIII and his successor Paul VI met with leaders of the United Jewish Appeal. Pope John introduced himself as "Joseph, your brother." The Ecumenical Council proposed a decree on November 20, 1964, ordering Catholic preachers and scholars to "never present the Jewish people as one rejected, cursed or guilty of deicide. All that happened to Christ in His passion cannot be attributed to the whole people then alive, much less to those of today."

After almost a year of intra-Church debate, a compromise decree was promulgated by the Council on October 28, 1965. While deploring both anti-Semitism and the branding of the Jewish people as deicides, it was somewhat more circumspect than the original decree in its formulation. The final decree read: "The Jewish authorities and those who followed their lead pressed for the death of Christ; still, what happened in His passion cannot be charged against all the Jews, without distinction, then alive, nor against the Jews of today. Although the Church is the new people of God, the Jews should not be presented as rejected by God or accursed as if this followed from Holy Scriptures."

A scholarly analysis of the meaning of contemporary Catholic doctrine concerning the relationship of Jewry to the Crucifixion by Fr. Arthur B. Klyber, C.Ss.R., emphasizes that the Church never branded the Jews as deicides. In the first place, "Nobody can kill God, for Divinity is eternal: only the HUMAN BODY of Jesus could die." Guilt applied only to those individual Jews, chiefly their leaders, who urged Christ's death and Catholics should remember that "any sin committed by any Jews in the actual Crucifixion was already forgiven by the Messiah while He hung on His Cross."[16]

Rabbi Arthur Gilbert, who has devoted a large part of his adult life to creating closer cooperation between the American leaders of Christianity and Judaism, wrote: "Here in America, both Catholic and Protestant educators have reviewed their religious school texts and are now rewriting them to assure a greater measure of understanding of Jews

and Judaism. Any reference to Jewish suffering as a consequence of the crucifixion of Jesus is to be excised; for church
teaching is that Christ was killed by the sinfulness in the
hearts of all men and he is continually crucified when men
harbor hatred against their brothers. Anti-Semitism is a sin
against God and man, therefore, and cannot be counten-
anced by the church."[17]

Closely related to the movement for Christian unity is
the fact that groups of Christian and Jewish clergy "now
meet monthly in 55 cities of the United States to discuss
issues of religious freedom; and with the cooperation of
educational associations, national denominational bodies,
and academic institutions, new approaches to the problems
of religion in education and the financing of education are
being explored."[18]

All this is bringing about changes in the attitude of the
dominant Jewish organizations, although the changes are
not likely to be rapid.

Another ingredient in the change is the growing realization by both Christian and Jewish leaders that a society of
alienation and *anomie*,[19] in which all the institutions which
attempt to develop ethical or religious awareness are attacked and denigrated, continuously throws off psychopathic personalities. These are individuals of deficient super-
ego, or conscience, but not necessarily of low intelligence.
In a well-integrated society, they are restrained from committing moral enormities by the force of religious and
social censure as well as by the fear of punishment.[20] In
our society, these restraints have been dangerously weakened. The lay school and the broken family generally teach
neither religion nor ethics. The perhaps excessively understanding attitude of modern psychiatry enables the criminal
to gain attention, sympathy and even renown which he

might not have enjoyed had he stayed within the law. The protective labyrinth the Supreme Court has created for the procedural protection of the arrested suspect and the tendency of many parole and prison agencies to be more concerned with the rehabilitation of the psychopathic criminal than with the protection of his potential victims makes punishment less swift and inevitable than it used to be and hence weakens this deterrent.

Another consideration is growing governmental control over education. Under the Kennedy and Johnson Administrations, the federal government, or rather its executive branch, managed to expand into almost every area of American life, assuming unprecedentedly large and ill-defined regulatory powers. In this vast, glacier-like and, in some respects, surreptitious process of assumption of power, the Supreme Court served as a moving force and the Congress alternated between ineffectual opposition and rubber-stamping.

It was self-evident that education would not be immune from this process. On the contrary, it was of crucial importance both to the nation and to the Establishment. The vital role of education in every aspect of American advance had become increasingly evident after World War II and the key importance of ideological indoctrination through academic institutions was equally apparent. In what proportions these two considerations were mixed in the enormous program of federal aid to education presented by the Johnson Administration in 1964 and 1965 is a question that lies outside the scope of this book.

The Administration circumvented and flanked the rigid doctrinaire opposition to all public aid to religious education by a series of ingenious expedients. It assisted the plight of the overcrowded, financially weak and inadequately staffed parochial schools by enabling their students to attend the public schools for non-religious courses. This permitted the parochial schools to concentrate their comparatively slender human and material resources more intensively on religious education. It financed the construction of classrooms and other facilities for the non-religious courses and departments of private denominational institutions. It assisted not only Catholic but also Protestant and Hebrew schools with free lunch programs and surplus property disposal. The federal program of aid to educational libraries should similarly benefit all qualified schools and colleges regardless of whether they are public or private, religious or secular.

Finally, the Education Act of 1965 provided for the subsidization of students seeking an education. This program was open to those attending any qualifying institution and hence included church schools. The expedient of financing the student, rather than the educational institution, had previously been adopted in the post-World War II GI Bill of Rights, which assisted veterans in financing their continued education and specialized training.

As these vast programs assumed shape, the leaders of American liberalism faced the dilemma of choosing between their intransigent anticlericalism and their love of the Leviathan state. Most chose love. On May 1, 1963 Walter Lippmann urged federal aid for all schools, religious and private as well as secular and public, in a CBS nationwide television program. With a rare outburst of common sense, the *New Republic* of March 2, 1963 observed:

"The national interest is in better education for *all* children, regardless of race, creed, or parental income. Nobody needs to send his child to a private school, but millions do. No useful purpose is served if these children grow up knowing less history or less chemistry than children who attend public school. Ignorance, not the Catholic hierarchy, is the enemy."[21]

The majority of the Protestant churches shifted to this more relaxed view of the problem. In 1964, the General Convention of the Protestant Episcopal Church reversed a policy that had been in force for fifteen years and supported the inclusion of denominational schools in "general public-health and public-welfare programs, such as, among others, the provision of standard text-books and of equal bus transportation."

In broader terms, Protestant leaders began talking, not about the "wall of separation" between Church and State, but about "separation *and interaction.*" A new approach on the part of all three major religious groups was also dictated by economic necessity. In an America of schools lavishly subsidized by the federal government with funds collected from taxpayers, private institutions which opposed this aid faced the prospect of withering on the vine. They would find it virtually impossible to compete in classrooms, laboratories, libraries, equipment and teachers' salaries with the subsidized institutions. Parents, who are obligated by law to support those institutions on which the federal government chooses to shower largesse with its tax receipts, will not be attracted by the prospect of paying large tuition fees as well to private schools whose facilities are inferior. This creates almost irresistible pressure on all denominational educational systems to apply for federal aid and, having applied, they are not likely to attack the entire system as unconstitutional and repugnant to American traditions. They have to get on the band wagon if they want to survive.

But the new emerging attitude is much broader than a mere bread and butter issue. We find Jewish leaders such as Rabbi Balfour Bricker arguing that, since Judaism has a unique contribution to make to America and to the world, it is desirable that Jewish preparatory schools under Reform auspices be fostered. The implication is that religious pluralism is an eminently desirable feature of the American educational and religious scene. While this statement may seem self-evident, it runs diametrically counter to the older, traditional Jewish view that "we are firmly committed to our public school system as the bulwark for preserving America's democratic heritage" and that "as a network of parochial schools mushrooms, support for public schools would constantly be diluted."[22] The hard-core "Church-State-bitter-ender" Leo Pfeffer expressed this view in testimony for the American Jewish Congress on the 1965 Education Act as follows: "Use of Federal funds to finance parochial schools would . . . gravely endanger the continued existence of the public school system" and cause its "fragmentation."[23]

The newer Jewish view is that America's strength derives from diversity, not uniformity. This has always been the approach of some of the more religious Jewish organizations, such as the Agudath Israel of America, whose vice president, Rabbi Morris Sherer, told the Senate Subcommittee on Education that "our Founding Fathers never intended our children to be raised in a monolithic educational strait jacket. . . ." It is the view of both Christian and Jewish scholars who occasionally speak of the three great religious systems deriving from the Old Testament as streams flowing from the same river. It is the view of such scholars of Judaism as Rabbi Arthur Gilbert, who has written a thoughtful analysis of the areas in which Judaism adds to Christianity and those in which the reverse is the case.[24] With this rapidly evolving religious consensus, which is very far from being a submergence of doctrinal differences in a politically acceptable, but intellectually disreputable, formula, it is not remarkable that Senator Abraham Ribicoff recently predicted that the Supreme Court will "indicate a much wider area of permissiveness than is now in effect" for public support to private education.

This development will be heartening to all true conservatives because it is a trend away from the emphasis on uniformity and equality and toward the stress on individuality and the vast importance of the uniqueness of each human being.

CHAPTER 20

American Jews and the
Conservative Movement

THE PROBLEM with which this book began was why are
most American Jews liberal-to-radical in their political attitudes. A survey of the evidence suggested several reasons
why this stance was illogical and contrary to the self-interest
of American Jewry as a whole. Before proceeding to discuss
the prospects of a Jewish turn toward conservatism, it might
be worthwhile to recapitulate some of these reasons briefly.

The first, and perhaps the most impressive, point is that
American Jews are an economic, political, educational and
cultural elite. This is so to an overwhelming extent. Since
America as a whole is more prosperous, better educated and
politically more powerful than any other nation on the face
of the earth, it is possible to think of American Jewry as an
elite within an elite. In short, its position is extraordinarily,
one might even say uniquely, privileged.

On the other hand, Jews are subject to some forms of discrimination and are keenly aware of that fact. Jewish organizations are quick to publicize such inequities as the underrepresentation of Jews in such power and prestige positions as the top administration of colleges and universities and the leading echelons of public utilities and other corporate enterprises. Their protests against such exceptional situations create a false impression, in the mind of Jew and Gentile alike, of widespread anti-Jewish discrimination and serve to obscure the fairly obvious fact that, taking the entire area of American leadership into consideration, the Jews do better than any other ethnic group.

Another point that may be raised is that American Jews, as a whole, do not behave like members of an elite. Certainly, they have not, as a group, acquired the manners and assurance that are the hallmarks of an established upper class. This is characteristic of nations and peoples who rise suddenly to wealth and power. The eighteenth century English gentry complained of the crude manners of Anglo-Indian nabobs just as Paris, more than a century later, both thrived upon and despised the Argentine meat barons. An excess of wealth over manners is the mark of a rising elite; one of manners over wealth of a declining one.

Elite behavior, however, is far more a matter of basic political attitudes than of manners or assurance. In free societies, elites are normally characterized by their conservatism. While all classes benefit from political and economic freedom, those elites whose position is based upon ability benefit more than the others. To the extent that they are also intellectual elites, they have an additional reason to be conservative since the two great essentials of an environment in which intellectual activity flourishes are order and freedom.

Elites should not, however, defend every *status quo* nor

should they be opponents of all social change. The true conservative welcomes progress whereas the standpatter is often the midwife of unnecessary revolutions. A selfish defense of one's own class interests to the exclusion of those of society as a whole is incompatible with true conservatism. It conflicts with the entire elite conception of *noblesse oblige* and runs counter to the axiom of every viable elite, that privileges carry responsibilities.

The incongruity in the Jewish attitude toward American politics, then, is not the acceptance of change, but rather the denial of continuity. In its extreme form, that is to say in the subversive movements, it is a dedication to the destruction of the entire social order and its free institutions. To the extent that Jews are still not accepted in some of the better social clubs, a probable contributory reason is the profound Jewish ambivalence that creates uneasiness and distrust among all classes. This ambivalence is a feeling of being both part of the elite and, at the same time, outside it and pariahs. The former attitude reflects current economic and social realities, the latter, traumatic memories of prior oppression. As time passes, these traumatic memories are being increasingly relegated to a nightmare past lived in foreign countries under undemocratic and brutal governments. As these memories fade and as their irrelevance to American conditions becomes increasingly self-evident, the Jews should function with greater assurance as part of an unalienated American elite.

The second major characteristic is Jewish awareness and fear of anti-Semitism. In these pages, I have tried to show that anti-Semitism in its virulent political form is almost invariably associated with social revolutionary movements. That is to say, it is primarily an attitude of the discontented and frustrated elements in society, who are often motivated by envy and who seek to bring about a fundamental change in the power structure. The change desired is to replace the actual elite with a pseudo-elite, which is frequently composed of people with mediocre abilities and meager successes. Thus, movements of anti-Semitism tend to be directed also against the upper classes. For the same reason, the upper classes and the elites are hardly ever involved in anti-Semitism and as a rule oppose it. .

In the twentieth century, these revolutionary movements seek to impose heavily bureaucratized systems. Freedom of economic action is generally destroyed together with the democratic process and basic political rights. The state becomes all-important; unquestioning obedience to the state becomes the supreme duty. Such totalitarian systems, whether Nazi or Soviet, inevitably suppress and, where possible, destroy those elements in society which question authority, which cherish personal freedom and which find their own values within themselves—in short, the elites, including both the upper classes and the Jews.

A cardinal Jewish political error has been to assume that the anti-Semitism habitually associated with egalitarian and totalitarian systems of the left is an "accidental" factor—that is to say, a phenomenon due to special conditions which are transitory or due to misunderstandings which can be removed by communication. Actually, anti-Semitism is intrinsic to these systems. This is the case because they represent a crude form of economic and political organization, requiring docile masses whose minds can be shaped by the state. In these societies, the uncommon man, whether Jew or Gentile, aristocrat or peasant, is a latent threat to the social order. Such societies have no room for the spirit of doubt. In the free society, doubt is the leaven of progress; in the slave society, it is a crime.

Let me put this another way. To the extent that the Socialist system remains true to its principles, it eradicates financial gain as an incentive for work.[1] Yet only a small minority of the human race will work steadfastly and efficiently for altruistic reasons. Accordingly, substitute incentives must be devised. These invariably include intense social approval for those the state considers productive and intense social disapproval for those it deems slackers, idlers or saboteurs. In order for these psychic incentives to work at all, they must be intensified. This presupposes governmental control over public opinion to such an extent that lotus eaters and those engaged in activities of which the state disapproves cannot find any niche in society in which they will be tolerated. The directed economy thus presupposes a monolithic public opinion. Docile people, whose mental equipment is so limited that they never really think for themselves on fundamentally important matters, make the ideal citizens of the Socialist society. Obviously, the dissenter, the path breaker and the man who is not afraid of being in a minority (and who in fact would rather be scorned for saying what he believes to be true than praised for uttering what he knows to be a lie) are undesirables in the regimented state. More than this, anyone who habitually applies scientific method and Aristotelian logic to the problems that confront him is a potential security risk simply because he cannot be relied upon to accept whatever he is told by higher authority.

A powerful force driving Jews toward radicalism is a sense of alienation from American society. This is not specifically a Jewish problem, but appears to be characteristic of almost all the middle-class and intellectual elements who adhere to the so-called New Left. I am not going to go into the possible causes of this sense of alienation and *anomie* beyond offering the purely subjective and unsubstantiated opinion that the excessive softness of modern life in middle-class America may have a lot to do with it. Where desires are satisfied as soon as they are born, life tends to be bland. Where one does not have to struggle to preserve it, life may seem of little value.

Be that as it may, American Jews seem to be more susceptible to the disease of alienation than American Gentiles, as is evidenced by their disproportionate presence in the ranks of the left wing and subversive rabble. One related factor would seem to be self-imposed Jewish apartheid after the religious reason for it has disappeared. The disintegration of religious faith often causes a frantic search for substitute secular faiths. To the extent that the latter express alienation and the desire to huddle in a psychic ghetto, they often espouse values at variance with those of the majority and coalesce in a congregation or political party with the characteristics of a *despised elite*.

The *despised elite* is not, of course, truly despicable. It is an eschatological religion of the underdog or of those who feel it necessary to identify with the underdog. It suffers persecution in the here-and-now, while nourishing itself on the assurance that it will triumph, rule and demonstrate its superiority over the Philistines in the hereafter. The early Christians were in some respects such a *despised elite*, as are the Communists in those countries where they are efficiently persecuted.

In the secular religions of the *despised elites*, the Godhead is some force or class or race or element which visibly represents the antithesis of all the values which society respects, but which is depicted as being morally superior, as having an invisible goodness or wisdom or power which will enable it to inherit the earth. Thus, Bishop Vasco de Quiroga, who left the sophisticated society of Spain to come to the Tarascan Indian country of Michoacán as *visitador* in 1533, a few years after the conquest of Mexico, reported that his Indian charges "walked in the manner of the apostles" and that their society was "like the primitive Golden Age, which, because of our malice and cupidity, became one of iron...."[2]

In the 1930's, it was the proletariat that was supposedly destined to topple the mighty and to transform society, taking it through successive shower baths of blood into an immaculate utopia. But the dream vanished. "Now that the masses have actually risen to power," writes Jeffrey Hart, "the old romantic vision has faded; it is no longer possible even to the political Left to imagine that the teamsters or even the steelworkers are going to save us all from bourgeois corruption. The Negroes have become the heirs of that old emotion. Like the old working class, they *have* been victimized; and therefore—'therefore' is the illogical step— they are the repositories of virtue and their claims are absolute. The Negro has even inherited some of the mythic-sentimental attributes of the proletariat: warmhearted spontaneity, solidarity outside the law, superior sexuality, natural generosity. We have been asked by Norman Mailer, for example, to become 'white Negroes.' "[3]

If the Negro, as the avenging force of history, is romanticized, the picture drawn of the *despised elite* is equally mawkish. "In their depth of feeling for each other and for their cause, in their simplicity and courage," wrote Martin Duberman concerning the Student Nonviolent Coordinating Committee agitators and organizers, "they stand out against a purposeless, sterile backdrop in something truly like heroic outline, showing us what might be hoped for when the barriers artificially separating people are broken down.... Intimacy among them has been allowed to ripen through constant contact and mutual reliance, and has been further intensified by common dangers and goals."[4]

Much the same sort of stuff was written about Fidel Castro's equally grubby band of terrorists and guerrilleros.

The contemporary barometer of alienation, in its active form, is white submergence in the black racist movement. This is, of course, very different from taking measures to assist Negroes in overcoming unjust prejudice and their own shortcomings. The essence of the difference is that the alienated white intellectual seeks to identify himself with and acquire those characteristics among Negroes which are vicious and antisocial. The responsible white intellectual, on the contrary, attempts to aid Negroes in overcoming these traits.

The alienated posture of the New Left and the extent to which it borders on treason are illustrated by the case of the Students for a Democratic Society. "Perhaps the only forms of action appropriate to the angry people are violent," wrote Tom Hayden, SDS founder and drafter of its first official statement. "Perhaps a small minority, by setting ablaze New York and Washington, could damage this country forever in the court of world opinion."[5] "To damage this country forever"—what a splendid goal for an American! To set cities ablaze—what an appropriate approach for a society of "democratic" students!

Another man of the New Left, a certain M. S. Arnoni, editor of *The Minority of One*, sees the entire history of the United States as an "aboriginal combination of sin and myth." By tortuous reasoning, he proves to his own satisfaction that our handling of the Indians or the Viet Cong ranks morally below Hitler's of the Jews. At a Berkeley Vietnam teach-in, he was cheered by students when he urged them to volunteer as fighters for the Viet Cong.

Not to be outdone in violence or hatred for a government which had showed the deplorable judgment of subsidizing

him with public funds, the Negro poet LeRoi Jones, pon-
tificating as a military expert, declared that guerrilla war-
fare "makes nuclear bombs *obsolete*." In bizarre English,
Jones predicted that, if America went to war, "the Chinese
or the Russians would run them back across the ice into
those weird caves of their species' childhood."[6]

One of the reasons for the Jewish presence in movements
of the sort represented by the three persons just quoted is
an habitual and deep-seated distrust of conservatism. The
Jews have had an historic fear of nationalism which, on the
European Continent, has often been associated with anti-
Semitism. The fact that conservatives are generally nationalistic therefore arouses Jewish fear and distrust. In the United
States in the 1930's and 1940's, a large part of the conservative movement was isolationist—a position which was interpreted by many Jews as one of indifference to their fate
under Hitler. In addition, the Nazi, fascist and anti-Semitic
element attempted to smuggle itself into the conservative
movement, using anti-Communism, opposition to Roosevelt and isolationism as its credentials. With the destruction
of Nazism, Jewish fears of renewed persecution tended to
become fixed on the dead past. There was much preoccupation over a possible recrudescence of Nazism. The pro-
Soviet Nasser movement in Egypt was seen as a revival of
Hitlerism rather than in its true light as a left wing authoritarian system with strong Soviet affinities. Since the Soviet
Union was able to persecute its Jewish population savagely
without espousing an anti-Semitic ideology, American Jews
tended to ignore or underestimate this threat to the Jewish
remnant in Eastern Europe. A final factor was that, while
the conservative movement willingly accepted Jewish support, the liberal forces did so ostentatiously.

The Promise of Conservatism

Most conservatives consider the state to be the only organization in modern society which has the power of almost limitless coercion against its subjects. They are distrustful of all such universal, coercive institutions and would vastly prefer particular and voluntary ones in which compliance was based upon free consent. Where a choice exists between uniform regulation by a single state authority and diverse systems of regulation by many such authorities, the conservative normally prefers the latter. He will argue that a diversity of such systems enables the individual to choose those which suit his requirements, that it creates variety in development and institutional patterns and that it provides a means of determining through observation which of these patterns best serves human needs. The liberal, by contrast, is often distinguished by a mania for uniformity. Whether the issue is federal vs. state power, public vs. private schools, or some other variant of the same problem, he will predictably support the centralizing tendency, do what he can to suppress the diversity of social life in favor of a bland uniformity and seek to place all citizens in a Procrustean bed.

Unfortunately, we live in an era of world conflict, in which the lethal potential of nations is increasing at an accelerating rate. The consolidation and application of world power to maintain peace and freedom therefore become vital to the survival of civilization. As the greatest world power ever known, the United States faces the alternatives of either assuming the responsibilities which that power gives her or else abdicating and, in so doing, placing world power by default in unworthy or evil hands.

It may be unrealistic to expect any diminution in the powers of government over the individual in the near future. The proliferation of population in disregard of the availability of foodstuffs and other resources has ceased to be a long-term prospect and threatens to erupt in chronic famine on a continental scale. This is only one of many major world problems which suggest that the role of government is more likely to increase than diminish. Air and water pollution are similar, though less dire, hazards. It is not likely that mankind will become toilet trained against soiling his biosphere if the task is left to the voluntary action of small and backward peoples. The depletion of world resources and extermination of rare fauna and flora are, again, areas in which international control seems the only alternative to permanent impoverishment of man's living space. Control of the proliferation of nuclear energy for military purposes is another critical problem. All these issues are magnified by the presence of Communist regimes, yet are independent of the cold war and would persist even if Communism vanished tomorrow.

The conservative differs from the liberal in that he regards an increase in governmental restraints as justifiable only by necessity. He differs in opposing the advance of uniformity and the denial either that each individual is unique or that that quality of uniqueness is important. Those conservatives who accept the need for international political cooperation are not likely to be enthusiastic over an egalitarian United Nations in which voting power is totally divorced both from real power and from political responsibility. Conservatives may accept the proposition that the United States must protect the world against those outbreaks of disorder and subversion which threaten the entire infrastructure of international stability, but they are not likely to see this task as a crusade to bring democracy to mankind. Since the conservative believes in the diversity of man, he is more concerned with history and tradition than with ideological abstractions, prone to view the needs of different human societies as uniquely determined by their background and heritage and distrustful of all simple and universal solutions.

If the advance of society depends overwhelmingly on the gifted minority which is able to devise and operate the production complexes, the educational systems, the institutions and the cultural and creative processes of the nation, then the greatest failure of Socialism is that it cripples the gifted minority and chains its creative powers.

It has become an article of the liberal creed that every man should be given the vote and every effort should be made to get out the vote. Regardless of the voter's stupidity, ignorance, apathy or lack of civic responsibility, he should be dragooned to the polls. The underlying assumption would appear to be that citizenship is a biological rather than a political attribute. The Greeks believed that a certain proportion of the population was bound to consist of "idiots" (that is to say, of those whose interests were limited to the private sphere), that these "idiots" were too narrow in vision to form part of the *polis,* and that a free society should discourage them from voting.

Perhaps the essential difference between conservatives and liberals is the difference between those who believe in elites and those who believe in masses, between the uncommon and the common man, between those who favor freedom and those who uphold security, between those who have roots and respect continuity and those who are flotsam and restlessly seek change, between the unique man and the mass man. The social position, character and capacity of American Jews place them unequivocally in the first category.

Notes

CHAPTER 1

1. George Gallup, "Party Ties Return to Pre-LBJ Vote," *Miami Herald*, December 14, 1966, p. 21A. Gallup also disclosed that 55% of the Protestants, but only 35% of the Catholics and 25% of the Jews, backed Republican candidates. White voters were split evenly between the two parties, but 81% of the non-whites favored the Democratic nominees. Republicans had 52% of the vote in communities with fewer than 50,000 inhabitants, but polled only 43% to 44% of the vote in larger cities. There was a slight tendency for older voters to support Republican office seekers, but there was no difference in the voting patterns of the two sexes.

2. Wesley and Beverly Allinsmith, "Religious Affiliations and Politico-Social Attitudes," *Public Opinion Quarterly*, 1948, No. 12, pp. 377–389.

3. The survey covered 2,332 Catholics, 1,344 Baptists, 720 Lutherans, 2,053 Methodists, 571 Episcopalians, 923 Presbyterians, 362 Congregationalists and 515 Jews.

4. Lawrence H. Fuchs, *The Political Behavior of American Jews* (Glencoe, Illinois: Free Press, 1956), pp. 84–85.

CHAPTER 2

1. In *The Geography of Intellect*, a book co-authored by Stefan T. Possony, (Chicago: Regnery, 1963), and in *The Creative Elite in America* (Washington, D.C.: Public Affairs Press, 1966).

2. Weyl and Possony, op. cit., p. 136.

3. *Examen de Ingenios* (Investigation of Intelligence). The title suggests that Huarte was a pioneer of sorts in psychology. Quoted from Américo Castro, *The Structure of Spanish History*, translated by Edmund L. King, Copyright 1954 by Princeton University Press, pp. 468–469.

4. Carnegie Institute of Washington, Washington, D.C.

CHAPTER 3

1. Quoted by Howard M. Sachar, *The Course of Modern Jewish History* (Cleveland: World, 1958), p. 161.

2. Castro, *op. cit.*, p. 95.

3. The quotation is from Castro's summary, *op. cit.*, p. 523.

4. For example, García de la Riega, Nicolas Díaz Pérez and Otero Sánchez.

5. The Spanish original of Don Fernando Colombo's biography is lost, but the Italian version of 1571 remains.

6. Cecil Roth, *The Jewish Contribution to Civilization* (Cincinnati: Union of Hebrew Congregations, 1940), pp. 87–88.

7. The quadrant itself was invented by Jacob ben Mahir ibn

Tibbon (1230–1312), a Jewish professor at the University of Montpellier.

8. Hugo Bieber, "The Jewish Contribution to the Exploration of the Globe," in Dagobert D. Runes, *The Hebrew Impact on Western Civilization* (New York: Philosophical Library, 1951), p. 707.

CHAPTER 4

1. "The Two Cradles of Jewish Liberty" in *The Golden Land*, Azriel Eisenberg, editor (New York: Yoseloff, 1964), pp. 28–40.

2. Roth, *op. cit.*, p. 34.

3. John Doyle, "The First Century of English Colonization," *Cambridge Modern History* (Cambridge: 1907), Vol. VII, p. 35.

4. Abraham A. Neuman, "The Influence of Hebrew Scriptures on Puritanism" in Eisenberg, *op. cit.*, pp. 41–45.

5. Quoted by Howard M. Sacher, *The Course of Modern Jewish History* (Cleveland: World, 1958), p. 162.

6. Sachar, *op. cit.*, pp. 164–165.

7. Joseph L. Blau and Salo W. Baron, *The Jews of the United States, 1790–1840* (New York: Columbia University Press, 1963), Vol. I, p. 10.

8. *Ibid.*, Vol. I, p. 12.

9. *Ibid.*, Vol. I, p. 13.

10. Article VI, Clause 3.

11. Blau and Baron, *op. cit.*, Vol. II, p. 318.

12. Fuchs, *op. cit.*, pp. 34–35.

13. Blau and Baron, *op. cit.*, Vol. III, pp. 924–955.

14. *Ibid.*, Vol. III, p. 929.

15. *Ibid.*, Vol. I, p. 86.

16. *Ibid.*, Vol. III, pp. 804–805.

17. Sachar, *op. cit.*, pp. 107–111.

18. *Ibid.*, p. 174.

19. According to Fuchs, *op. cit.*, p. 33.

20. *History of the Rise and Fall of the Slave Power in America* (Boston: Osgood & Co., 1872), 3 Vols.

21. Thaddeus Stevens posthumously became a hero of American Communism which recognized his destructive spirit as kindred.

22. Edmund Silberner, *Scripta Hierosolymitana*, pp. 380–381, as quoted in Zygmund Dobbs, *The Great Deceit* (West Sayville, N.Y.: Veritas Foundation, 1964), p. 123. Dobb's volume is a valuable source on anti-Semitic aspects of the Socialist movement.

23. Dobbs, *op. cit.*, p. 121, citing Silberner.

24. Dobbs, *op. cit.*, p. 135, quoting Silberner, "Fourier on the Jewish Question," *Jewish Social Studies*, October 1946, pp. 248–249.

25. Vernon Louis Parrington, *The Beginnings of Critical Realism in America* (New York: Harcourt, Brace & Co., 1927), p. 43.

26. Isaiah Berlin, *Karl Marx* (New York: Galaxy, Oxford University Press, 1959), p. 184.

27. Max Geltman, "A Little Known Chapter in American History," *National Review*, October 5, 1965, p. 866.

28. *Ibid.* Geltman adds that Friedrich Engels, Marx's alter ego, had "hailed the gutter literature of the French anti-Semite 'Satan' who inflamed the passions of the mob with his pamphlet, *Rothschild I, King of the Jews.*"

CHAPTER 5

1. William B. Ziff, "The Jew as Soldier, Strategist and Military Adviser," in Runes, *op. cit.*, p. 741.

2. It should be added that these discriminatory provisions were not specifically anti-Jewish, but applied to all who denied the divinity of Christ.

3. In 1861, at a time when both Northern and Southern passions were running high, D. Francis Bacon, a distinguished physician, who had been a student at Yale with Benjamin, publicly charged that the latter had been forced to leave because he had been caught stealing cash and jewelry from fellow students. There are various inconsistencies in this account, which, moreover, seems at variance with all we know of Benjamin's career and character. Yet, despite the fact that the accusatory article, entitled "The Early History of a Traitor," was widely circulated in both North and South during the Civil War, Benjamin steadfastly refused to comment on it or refute it. Whatever the real facts may be, it seems clear that he left Yale involuntarily and under discreditable circumstances.

4. The machinery Benjamin installed at Bellechasse in Plaquemines Parish south of New Orleans in the 1840's was still in use half a century later. Burton J. R. Hendrick, *Statesmen of the Lost Cause* (Literary Guild of America, 1939), p. 165.

5. Speech on December 31, 1860 on the eve of secession.

6. Hendrick, *op. cit.*, pp. 155–156. The reason to question the authenticity of the anecdote is that a similar one was told about Disraeli's rejoinder to an opponent in the House of Commons.

7. William Howard Russell, *My Diary North and South* (London, 1863), Vol. I, p. 254.

8. He burned all the letters he received and spent the last days of his life incinerating everything that might have aided his biographers. As for his private life, he married Natalie St. Martin in a Catholic church in 1832. She left him in the 1840's with their only surviving child, Ninette, emigrating to Paris. Benjamin supported them there in lavish style, but seldom saw them. He had no other known romantic attachments.

9. Lawrence H. Fuchs, *The Political Behavior of American Jews* (Glencoe, Illinois: Free Press, 1956), pp. 38–39.

10. Margaret L. Coit, *Mr. Baruch* (Boston: Houghton, Mifflin Co., 1957), pp. 12–13.

11. Hendrick, *op. cit.*, pp. 9–10.

12. Fuchs, *op. cit.*, pp. 34–35.

13. Kenneth P. Williams, *Lincoln Finds a General* (New York: Macmillan, 1956), Vol. IV, p. 165.

14. *The Official Record of the Rebellion*, Vol. XVII, Part 2, pp. 421–422.

15. Hudson Strode, *Jefferson Davis: Confederate President* (New York: Harcourt, Brace & Co., 1959), pp. 347–348.

16. The Department of Tennessee, which Grant commanded.

17. Jewish Publication Society, Philadelphia, 1954.

18. Williams, *op. cit.*, p. 178, finds Korn's conclusions unwarranted and dismisses Jesse Grant's testimony on the grounds that he was not in a position to know the facts.

19. Quoted by Carl Sandburg, *Abraham Lincoln, The War Years* (New York: Harcourt, Brace & Co., 1939), Vol. II, p. 37.

CHAPTER 6

1. Cincinnati, 1901. Quoted by Sachar, *op. cit.*, p. 169.

2. John S. Billings, *Vital Statistics of the Jews in the United States, Census Bulletin* (December 1890).

3. Summarized by Nathan Glazer, "Social Characteristics of American Jews," in Louis Finkelstein (editor), *The Jews, Their History, Culture and Religion* (New York: Harper & Brothers, 1960), 3rd edition, Vol. II, p. 1,701.

4. The Straus brothers founded R. H. Macy & Company.

5. Fuchs, *op. cit.*, p. 49.

6. *The New Era, Workers' Newspaper* and the *The Forward.*

7. She is best known for her sonnet, "The New Colossus," engraved on the Statue of Liberty.

8. E. Digby Baltzell, *The Protestant Establishment* (New York: Random House, 1964), p. 56.

9. Erich E. Hirshler, editor, *Jews from Germany in the United States* (New York, 1955), p. 59.

10. Bret Harte was the grandson of a Jewish sailor who fought on the American side in the War of 1812.

11. Richard Hofstadter, *The Age of Reform* (New York: Vintage, 1955), pp. 77–82.

12. *The Rise of American Civilization* (New York: Macmillan, 1927), Vol. II, p. 210.

13. Quoted by Hofstadter, *op. cit.*, p. 64.

14. *Ibid.*, p. 67.

15. "The Myth of Populist Anti-Semitism," *American Historical Review*, Vol. 68, No. 1, October 1962, pp. 76–80.

16. He was ruled insane and unable to conduct an intelligent defense and hence was never brought to trial.

17. *The Problem of Civilization Solved* (Chicago, 1895), pp. 319–320.

18. Martin Ridge, *Ignatius Donnelly, the Portrait of a Politician* (Chicago: University of Chicago Press, 1962), pp. 263–264.

19. Quoted by Ridge, *op. cit.*, p. 337.

20. Both statements were made in 1899. They are quoted by Ridge, *op. cit.*, p. 395.

21. By comparison, a similar sanguinary novel by Jack London on worldwide class war, *The Iron Heel*, 1907, has no Jewish characters and no references to the Jews. The salient difference is that London was a half-Nietzschean Marxist.

22. Quoted by Edward Flower, *Anti-Semitism in the Free Silver and Populist Movements and the Election of 1896*, Columbia University unpublished M.A. thesis, p. 27. Hofstadter, *op. cit.*, p. 80.

CHAPTER 7

1. *Report of the U.S. Industrial Commission*, 1910, XV, p. 284. Cited in Nathan Glazer, "Social Characteristics of American Jews 1654–1954," in *American Jewish Year Book 1955*, p. 12. Glazer's article is an invaluable source.

2. *Ibid.*, p. 13.

3. *Report of the U.S. Industrial Commission*, pp. 325–327.

4. Herman D. Stein, "Jewish Social Work in the United States (1654–1954)," in *American Jewish Year Book 1956*, pp. 25–26.

5. Nathaniel Weyl, *The Creative Elite in America* (Washington, D.C.: Public Affairs Press, 1966), pp. 94, 207.

6. This situation would be reversed in the 1920's and the Jewish birth rate would continue to be considerably lower than the Protestant or Catholic rate from that time to the present.

7. Glazer, *op. cit.*, p. 1705.

8. Issue of March 30, 1894. Cited in John Higham, "Social Discrimination against Jews in America, 1830–1930," *Publication of the American Jewish Historical Society*, Vol. XLVII, No. 1, September 1957, p. 9 of reprint. This valuable study was initiated "at the request of the American Jewish Committee and carried out with its generous support."

9. Oscar and Mary F. Handlin, "The Acquisition of Political and Social Rights by the Jews in the United States," *American Jewish Year Book 1955*, p. 74.

10. Higham, *op. cit.*, p. 12.

11. Allegedly including the sign, "No Hebrews or Dogs Allowed."

12. A. H. Rhine, "Race Prejudice," *Forum*, III (1887), p. 441. The quotations are from Higham's summary, *op. cit.*, p. 12.

13. *Ibid.*, p. 15.

14. *Ibid.*, pp. 21–22.

15. Howard E. Freeman and Gene Kassebaum, "Exogamous Dating in a Southern City," *Jewish Social Studies*, XVIII (1956), pp. 55–60. Cited in Eric Rosenthal, "Studies of Jewish Intermarriage in the United States," *American Jewish Year Book 1963*, p. 11.

16. Marshall Sklare and Marc Vosk, *The Riverton Study* (New York: American Jewish Committee, 1957), pp. 37, 42.

17. Rosenthal, *op. cit.*, pp. 15–53. Rosenthal summarized studies which showed that American Jews of Western European parentage are more prone to marry non-Jews than those of Eastern European parentage; that native-born Jews of native-

born American parentage are most disposed to intermarriage, and that foreign-born Jews are least so disposed. Those Jewish men who marry Gentiles average considerably higher incomes than those who marry Jewish women.

18. Emphasis supplied. Rabbi David Kirshenbaum, *Mixed Marriage and the Jewish Future* (New York, 1958), pp. 82–83. Quoted by Rosenthal, *op. cit.*, p. 14.

19. John P. Roche, *The Quest for the Dream* (New York: Macmillan, 1963), p. 95. This 50th anniversary volume of the Anti-Defamation League of the B'nai B'rith was copyrighted and financed by that organization. At the time, Dr. Roche was national chairman of Americans for Democratic Action and occupied the Morris Hillquit chair as Professor of Labor and Social Thought at Brandeis University. While not unprejudiced and not always accurate, this volume is of value if used with caution.

20. John Leo, "Some Jewish Messes in the Social Arena," *The National Catholic Reporter*, May 11, 1966.

21. Harry Golden, *A Little Girl Is Dead* (Cleveland: World, 1965), p. 8.

22. The quoted descriptive words are from Golden, *op. cit.*, pp. 7–8. The last two charges were contained in the testimony of the madam of an Atlanta house. Any juror of average intelligence should have disregarded them on the grounds that proprietors of brothels only testify against their clients when the police put pressure on them.

23. Golden, *op. cit.*, pp. 137–138.

24. Quoted in Rabbi Arthur Gilbert, *A Jew in Christian America* (New York: Sheed and Ward, Inc. ©, 1966), p. 43. Italics in the original.

25. Quoted in Golden, *op. cit.*, p. 220. Watson was, of course, not referring to Athens, Greece, but to Athens, Georgia.

26. Letter from Louis Marshall to the editor of the *Boston Herald*, November 9, 1927.

27. The *Jeffersonian*, August 26, 1915.

28. C. Vann Woodward, *Tom Watson, Agrarian Rebel* (New York: Macmillan, 1938), p. 486.

29. *Ibid.*, p. 486.

CHAPTER 8

1. Fuchs, *op. cit.*, pp. 52–53.

2. *Ibid.*, p. 58.

3. *Ibid.*, p. 63.

4. *Ibid.*, p. 64.

5. Charles Alexander, *The Ku Klux Klan in the Southwest.*

6. Seymour Martin Lipset, "An Anatomy of the Klan," *Commentary*, October 1965, pp. 74–83.

7. Fuchs, *op. cit.*, p. 67.

8. The civil rights legislation enacted to benefit Negroes and other minority groups under the Kennedy and Johnson Administrations would almost certainly have been declared unconstitutional by the Supreme Court of the early 1930's.

9. In the spring of 1933, Roosevelt would scuttle the London Economic Conference, thus setting back the prospects for international monetary cooperation for a decade.

10. Fuchs, *op. cit.*, pp. 71–73.

11. Keith Sward, *The Legend of Henry Ford* (New York: Rinehart & Co., 1948), p. 146.

12. *Ibid.*, pp. 93–94.

13. Although he was probably the richest capitalist in the United States, Ford told the *Detroit News:* "Do you want to know the cause of war? It is capitalism, greed, the dirty hunger for dollars. Take away the capitalist and you will sweep war from the earth." Sward, *op. cit.*, p. 86.

14. Sward, *op. cit.*, pp. 110–115.

15. *Ibid.*, pp. 103–105. These questions and answers are not consecutive.

16. *Ibid.*, p. 147.

17. Sachar, *op. cit.*, pp. 340–341.

18. William B. Ziff, "The Jew as Soldier, Strategist and Military Advisor," in Runes, *op. cit.*, pp. 750–751.

19. Lawrence W. Levine, *Defender of the Faith: William Jennings Bryan: the Last Decade 1915–1925* (New York: Oxford University Press, 1965), pp. 257–258.

20. Sward, *op. cit.*, p. 151.

21. Reprinted in Eisenberg, *op. cit.*, pp. 338–339.

22. Sward, *op. cit.*, pp. 461–462.

CHAPTER 9

1. Daniel Bell, "The Background and Development of Marxian Socialism in the United States," in *Socialism and American Life*, editors: Daniel Drew Egbert and Stow Persons (Princeton: Princeton University Press, 1952), 2 vols., Vol. 1, p. 296.

2. Morris Hillquit, *Loose Leaves from a Busy Life* (New York, 1934), p. 44.

3. Waldo Frank in *Commentary*, July 1947, p. 44. Quoted by Bell, *op. cit.*, p. 244.

4. Bell, *op. cit.*, p. 283.

5. *Ibid.*, p. 310.

6. *Ibid.*, p. 309.

7. Charles Edward Russell, *Bare Hands and Stone Walls* (New York, 1933), p. 288. Quoted by Bell, *op. cit.*, pp. 313–314.

8. Roche, *op. cit.*, p. 61.

9. Statement by Marx Lewis to the writer, December 28, 1966.

10. Theodore Draper, *The Roots of American Communism* (New York: Viking, 1957), pp. 188–191. The standard source for the early years.

11. Theodore Draper, *American Communism and Soviet Russia* (New York: Viking, 1960), p. 191.

12. (New York: Harcourt, Brace & World, 1961), pp. 130–131; 220–223.

13. Report of the Committee on the Judiciary of the U.S. Senate (81st Congress, 2nd Session), *The Immigration and Naturalization Systems of the United States* (Washington, D.C., 1950), pp. 783–784.

14. *The Creative Elite in America*, pp. 102–103.

15. Bella Dodd, *School of Darkness* (New York: Kennedy, 1954), p. 130.

16. Glazer, *op. cit.*, pp. 224–225.

17. Melech Epstein, *The Jew and Communism* (New York: Trade Union Sponsoring Committee, 1959), Chapter 28, and Glazer, *op. cit.*, pp. 151–152.

18. August 31, 1939.

19. Cited by Max Nomad, *Political Heretics* (Ann Arbor: University of Michigan Press, 1963), p. 310.

20. Irving Howe and Lewis Coser, *The American Communist Party: A Critical History (1919–1957)* (Boston: Beacon Press, 1957), p. 402.

21. *Ibid.*, p. 404.

22. Glazer, *op. cit.*, pp. 164–165.

CHAPTER 10

1. Roche, *op. cit.*, p. 163.

2. Arthur M. Schlesinger, Jr., *The Politics of Upheaval* (Boston: Houghton Mifflin Co., 1960), p. 550.

3. *Ibid.*, p. 77.

3-A. *Ibid.*, pp. 17–18.

4. *Redbook*, March 4, 1935.

4-A. Schlesinger, *op. cit.*, pp. 557, 627.

4-B. *Ibid.*, p. 629.

5. According to the *Oxford English Dictionary*, the ultimate source, there is no such word.

6. Nathaniel Weyl, *Treason* (Washington, D.C.: Public Affairs Press, 1950), pp. 320–325.

7. These figures are analyzed in detail by Seymour Martin Lipset in "Three Decades of the Radical Right," *The Radical*

Right, Daniel Bell, editor (Garden City: Doubleday, 1963), pp. 380–390.

8. Kenneth S. Davis, *The Hero: Charles A. Lindbergh and the American Dream* (Garden City: Doubleday, 1959), p. 38.

9. *Ibid.,* pp. 347–348.

10. *Ibid.,* p. 397.

11. Norman Thomas thought Lindbergh "not as anti-Semitic as some who seize the opportunity to criticize him." Davis, *op. cit.,* p. 412.

12. Fuchs, *op. cit.,* p. 176.

13. In *The Radical Right, op. cit.,* pp. 391–421.

14. Lipset, *op. cit.,* p. 361.

15. *Ibid.,* p. 415.

CHAPTER 11

1. Arnold Forster and Benjamin R. Epstein, *Danger on the Right* (New York: Random House, 1964), p. xii.

2. *Intermountain Jewish News,* May 27, 1966.

3. *Danger on the Right,* p. 49.

4. *Ibid.,* p. 63.

5. Statement by Lord Malcolm Douglas-Hamilton to the writer, made in July 1962.

6. Epstein and Forster, *Report on the John Birch Society 1966* (New York: Random House, 1966), pp. viii–ix.

7. Seymour Martin Lipset, "The Source of the Radical Right" in *The Radical Right,* Daniel Bell, editor (Garden City: Anchor, 1964), pp. 423–435.

8. *Ibid.,* p. 435.

9. *Danger on the Right, op. cit.,* p. 26.

10. Mark Sherwin, *The Extremists* (New York: St. Martin's Press, 1963), p. 67.

11. Donald Janson and Bernard Eisman, *The Far Right* (New York: McGraw-Hill, 1963).

12. Sherwin, *op. cit.,* p. 68.

13. April 1961 *Bulletin* of the John Birch Society.

14. *Danger on the Right*, p. 31.

15. *Report on the John Birch Society, 1966*, pp. 26–27.

16. Colin Cross, *The Fascists in Britain* (London: Barrie and Rockliff, 1961).

17. *Report on the John Birch Society 1966*, p. 1.

CHAPTER 12

1. Fuchs, *op. cit.*, p. 79.

2. Such incidents as President Truman's widely publicized offer to punch the nose of a music critic who had written unkindly concerning his daughter's singing ability did not help.

3. Harry S. Truman, *Memoirs*, Volume II, *Years of Trial and Hope* (Garden City: Doubleday, 1956), p. 185.

4. *Op. cit.*, p. 80.

5. Herbert H. Hyman and Paul B. Sheatsley, "The Political Appeal of President Eisenhower," *Public Opinion Quarterly*, Vol. XVII, No. 4 (Winter 1953), pp. 443–461.

6. Lucy S. Dawidowicz and Leon J. Goldstein, *Politics in a Pluralist Democracy: Studies of Voting in the 1960 Election* (New York: Institute of Human Relations Press, 1963), p. 88.

7. Fuchs, *op. cit.*, pp. 84–85.

8. *Ibid.*, pp. 86–90. However, the Austro-German sample was small.

9. Dawidowicz and Goldstein, *op. cit.*, p. 89.

10. Eugene C. Lee and William Buchanan, *Western Political Quarterly*, Vol. XIV, No. 1 (1961), p. 319.

11. Dawidowicz and Goldstein, *op. cit.*, pp. 66–67.

12. *Ibid.*, p. 65.

13. Lucy S. Dawidowicz, "Civil Rights and Intergroup Tensions," *American Jewish Year Book 1965*, p. 168.

14. *Ibid.*, pp. 172–173.

15. Dawidowicz and Goldstein, *op. cit.*, p. 78.

16. *New York Times*, November 17, 1965.

17. *Ibid.*, November 26, 1965.

18. *Ibid.*, January 15, 1966.

19. Perhaps it is superfluous to say that this a point which the American Jewish Congress did not make.

20. Bona fide pacifists were excused from military service anyhow and hence were not at issue.

21. *New York Times*, February 23, 1966.

22. *Ibid.*, February 27, 1966.

CHAPTER 13

1. Nathaniel Weyl, *The Battle Against Disloyalty* (New York: Thomas Y. Crowell, 1951), p. 29.

2. Colin Clark, *The Conditions of Economic Progress* (London: Macmillan, 1940), p. 84.

3. My calculation. National income estimated by National Industrial Conference Board, General Price Indexes by Snyder-Tucker.

4. "Jews In and Out of New York City," *The Jewish Journal of Sociology*, III: 2 (December 1961), pp. 254–260.

5. Herman P. Miller, *Rich Man, Poor Man* (New York: Thomas Y. Crowell, 1964), pp. 121–122, citing Donald J. Boggue, *The Population of the United States* (Glencoe: Free Press, 1959).

6. William Attwood, "The Position of the Jews in America Today," *Look*, Vol. 19, No. 24 (November 1955), pp. 27–35.

7. Simon Kuznets, "Economic Structure and Life of the Jews," in *The Jews, op. cit.*, Vol. II, p. 1,641.

8. Nathan Glazer, "Social Characteristics of American Jews," in *The Jews, op. cit.*, Vol. II, p. 1,707.

9. *Ibid.*, p. 1,715.

10. Nathan Goldberg, "Occupational Patterns of American Jews," *The Jewish Review*, Vol. III, No. 1 (April 1945) and Vol. III, No. 3 (October-December 1945).

11. Melvin M. Fagen, "Jewish Workers in New York City," Committee on Economic Adjustment Information Service, *Notes and News*, January 3, 1938, pp. 7–8.

12. Eli E. Cohen, "Economic Status and Occupational Structure," *American Jewish Year Book 1950*, p. 65.

13. *Idem.*

14. The Cities were: Camden, Charleston, Gary, Indianapolis, Los Angeles, Miami, Nashville, New Orleans, Newark, Newark suburbs, Passaic, Port Chester, Trenton and Utica.

15. Glazer, *op. cit.*, p. 1,719.

16. *Ibid.*, p. 1,720.

17. Weyl, *The Creative Elite in America*, pp. 99–101.

18. Benjamin R. Epstein and Arnold Forster, *Some of My Best Friends* (New York: Farrar, Straus and Cudahy, 1962), pp. 209–216.

19. Lewis B. Ward, "The Ethnics of Executive Selection," *Harvard Business Review*, March-April 1965, unpaginated reprint. About 80% of American Jews of college age went to college in 1964, or proportionately three times as many as non-Jews.

20. *Ibid.*

21. Lewis B. Ward, "Do You Want A Weak Subordinate?". *Harvard Business Review*, September-October 1961, p. 6.

22. Weyl, *The Creative Elite in America, op. cit.*

23. Marion K. Sanders, "The Several Worlds of American Jews," *Harper's*, April 1966, p. 61.

24. Where this is the underlying factor, it is cruel mockery to tell the drop-out that he should prolong his formal education in order to earn more money later on. Very often, lack of intelligence is the underlying cause of both truncated education and subsequent low earning power and lowly economic status. This cannot be remedied by mere school attendance.

25. L. M. Terman and M. H. Oden, *The Gifted Child Grows Up* (Stanford: Stanford University Press, 1947), p. 298.

26. Alvin Chenkin, "Jewish Population in the United States, 1964," *American Jewish Year Book 1965*, p. 146.

27. Ernest Havemann and Patricia Salter West, *They Went to College* (New York: Harcourt, Brace & Co., 1952), pp. 187–189.

28. Weyl, *The Creative Elite in America*, pp. 92–104, 223–232.

29. Mensa is an international organization open to all persons, and only to those persons, who score in the first 2% of the population in intelligence tests. It had (December 1966) about 11,000 members in the United States.

30. Listings in the 1961 *Directory of Medical Specialists*. Any such listing is an indication of high ability in a specialized area of the medical profession.

31. Weyl, *The Creative Elite in America*, pp. 34–40.

32. Keith Sward, "Jewish Musicality in America," *Journal of Applied Psychology*, December 1933, pp. 675–712.

33. Max Weber, *Ancient Judaism*, translated and edited by Hans Gerth and D. Martindale (Glencoe: Free Press, 1952).

34. H. Rosenthal, "Die Musikalität der Juden," *Int. Zscht. f. Indiv-Psych.*, IX (1931), pp. 122–131.

35. Sward, *op. cit.*, pp. 695, 697.

36. Weyl and Possony, *op. cit.*, p. 144.

37. These Jewish Nobel prize-winning scientists are: in physics, Bloch, Feynman, Michelson, Rabi, Schwinger, Stern and Wigman; in chemistry, none; in medicine and physiology, Block, C. F. Cori, G. T. Cori, Erlanger, Gasser, Kornberg, Landsteiner, Lederberg, Lipmann, Muller and Waksman.

CHAPTER 14

1. This summary of Pestel's views is taken from Salo W. Baron's *The Russian Jew*, Macmillan, 1964, p. 32, a lucid, perceptive, scholarly and virtually indispensable book.

2. *Ibid.*, p. 180.

3. *Ibid.*, p. 166.

4. In 1887, the Russian Government restricted the number of Jewish students in institutions of higher learning to 10% of the student bodies in the Pale of Settlement, 3% in St. Petersburg and Moscow and 5% elsewhere.

5. I have discussed this point in more detail in *The Geography of Intellect* and *The Creative Elite in America*.

6. The last true Romanov was Peter III, the husband of

Catherine the Great, murdered with her connivance in 1762. Peter was impotent or sterile and Catherine's heir, Paul, was sired by one of her lovers.

7. Baron, *op. cit.*, p. 170.

8. *Ibid.*, p. 171.

9. Günther Nollau, *International Communism and World Revolution: History and Methods* (New York: Praeger, 1961), p. 58.

10. Leonard Shapiro in *Slavonic and East-European Review*, XL, p. 165. Quoted by Baron, *op. cit.*, p. 203.

11. Baron, *op. cit.*, p. 204.

12. Robert Payne, *The Life and Death of Lenin* (New York: Simon & Schuster, 1964), p. 485.

13. I. N. Steinberg, *In the Workshop of the Revolution* (New York: Rinehart, 1953).

14. Victor Serge, *Memoirs of a Revolutionary, 1901–1941* (New York: Oxford University Press, 1963), pp. 121, 124, 153.

15. Baron, *op. cit.*, p. 208.

16. Bertram D. Wolfe, *Strange Communists I Have Known* (New York: Stein and Day, 1965), pp. 207–222.

17. *Ibid.*, p. 210.

18. William Henry Chamberlain, *The Russian Revolution 1917–1921* (New York: Macmillan, 1960), Vol. II, p. 234.

19. Baron, *op. cit.*, pp. 290–291.

20. Hugh Seton-Watson, *From Lenin to Khrushchev* (New York: Praeger, 1965), p. 170.

21. Corliss Lamont, *The Peoples of the Soviet Union* (New York, 1946).

22. Baron, *op. cit.*, p. 304.

23. Weyl and Possony, *op. cit.*, p. 161.

CHAPTER 15

1. Baron, *op. cit.*, pp. 314–315.

2. *Ibid.*, p. 317.

3. *Ibid.*, p. 322.

4. Nikita Khrushchev, *Secret Report to the 20th Congress of the Communist Party of the Soviet Union (CPSU)*, February 24–25, 1956.

5. Used as campaign literature by the Herut-Liberal bloc against the Israeli Eshkol Administration, which is based on the Mapai (Labor Party), but has an "alignment" with the Mapam.

6. Committee on the Judiciary, United States Senate, 89th Cong., 1st Sess., *The Soviet Empire: A Study in Discrimination and Abuse of Power*, prepared by the Legislative Reference Service, Library of Congress, p. 62, (hereafter referred to as *The Soviet Empire*).

7. Harrison E. Salisbury, *A New Russia?* (New York: Harper & Row, 1962), pp. 73–74.

8. Quoted in *The Soviet Empire*, p. 63.

9. *Ibid.*, p. 63.

10. Moshe Decter, "The Status of Jews in the Soviet Union," *Foreign Affairs*, January 1963, p. 429.

11. *New York Times*, February 10, 1962, p. 8. Bogoslovsky denied making this statement, but the reporter, Gershom Jacobson, gave him the lie. The authors of *The Soviet Empire* believed Jacobson.

12. Rowland Evans, Jr., "The Kremlin's Persecution of Jews," *Saturday Evening Post*, undated 1962 reprint.

13. S. Andhil Fineberg, "The Plight of Soviet Jews," *The Christian Century*, April 1, 1964.

14. *Ibid.*, quoting Roscoe Drummond in the *New York Herald Tribune*.

15. "Missing Voice," *New Leader*, March 16, 1964.

16. Arthur Miller, "Thinking Aloud: On Obliterating the Jews," *New Leader*, March 16, 1964.

17. Evans, *op. cit.*

18. *Ibid.*

19. Letter to Bertrand Russell from an unidentified Russian Jewish correspondent in "Soviet Anti-Semitism: An Exchange," *Commentary*, January 1965, page 1 of reprint.

20. *Ibid.*

21. On March 13, 1966, the American Jewish Orthodox organizations appealed to the Soviet authorities to "fulfill their pledge" to permit baking of matzoth throughout the USSR. *New York Times*, p. 12.

22. *New York Times*, February 11, 1966.

23. *Ibid.*, October 23, 1965.

24. *Ibid.*, July 16, 1965.

25. *Ibid.*, April 14, 1965.

26. *Jewish Daily Morning Freiheit*, May 29, 1966.

27. *New York Times*, March 22, 1966.

28. *Jewish Currents*, June 1966.

29. Speech of Israeli Foreign Minister Abba Eban to the General Assembly of the United Nations, June 19, 1967. *New York Times*, June 20, 1967, p. 17.

30. *Egypt's Liberation: The Philosophy of the Revolution* (Washington, D.C.: Public Affairs Press, 1955).

31. *Barron's*, May 29, 1967, "Legacy of Suez," p. 1.

32. *New York Times*, June 20, 1967, p. 17.

33. *Life*, June 16, 1967, "In 60 Hours a New Middle East," p. 4.

34. The left-wing Arab "intellectual," like his counterpart in other backward areas, is frequently the product of an exclusively verbal education who sees all issues in narrow, legalistic terms. Lacking those practical skills of which his country has desperate need, he is prone to dismiss them as mere technology. Frequently, he prides himself on possessing a higher education which in actual fact is mere cultural veneer and consists of little more than an ability to expound the real or fancied grievances of his country at the hands of foreign states in fluent language.

CHAPTER 16

1. Goodwin Watson, "The Problem of Evaluation," *Annals of the American Academy of Political and Social Science*, Vol. 244 (1946), p. 18.

2. *Social Psychology* (New York: Henry Holt, 1940), pp.

395 ff. Isacque Graeber expressed similar views, but in a less narrow economic context, in "An Examination of Theories of Race Prejudice," *Social Research*, Vol. 20, No. 3 (August 1953), pp. 267–281.

3. Hazel Gaudet Erskine, "The Polls: Religious Prejudice, Part 2: Anti-Semitism," *Public Opinion Quarterly*, Winter 1965–66, pp. 649–664.

4. *Ibid.*, p. 660.

5. *Ibid.*, pp. 658–659.

6. *Ibid.*, p. 659.

7. *Ibid.*, p. 661.

8. "The Quarter's Polls," *Public Opinion Quarterly*, Winter 1946, p. 620.

9. Erskine, *op. cit.*, p. 662.

10. Robert Bowers, "Anti-Semitism in Labor," an unpublished study available for inspection at the New York headquarters of the Anti-Defamation League. The quotation is from the summary in Melvin M. Tumin, *An Inventory and Appraisal of Research on American Anti-Semitism* (New York: Freedom Books, 1961), p. 173. Just as Erskine is the basic repository of polls on American anti-Semitism, so is Tumin the main analytical bibliography of studies on the subject.

11. *Public Opinion Quarterly*, Spring 1943, pp. 161–179.

12. Peter G. J. Pulzer, *The Rise of Political Anti-Semitism in Germany and Austria* (New York: Wiley, 1964), p. 281.

13. Even though the Pan-German League was only "half inside" the anti-Semitic camp, Pulzer regards this example as typical.

14. Bruno Bettelheim and Morris Janowitz, *Dynamics of Prejudice* (New York: Harper & Brothers, 1950). Summarized in Tumin, *op. cit.*, p. 57.

15. Gordon W. Allport and Bernard M. Kramer, "Some Roots of Prejudice," *Journal of Psychology*, Vol. 22, No. 1 (July 1946), pp. 9–39.

16. Prejudice is not necessarily reduced by contacts in which the Jews and non-Jews have markedly different status.

17. Harrison G. Gough, *Journal of Social Psychology*, Vol. 33, No. 2 (May 1951), pp. 247–255.

18. Joseph Greenblum and Leonard I. Pearlin in *Class, Status and Power*, edited by Reinhardt Bendix and Seymour M. Lipset (Glencoe: Free Press, 1953), 723 pp. Also Peter M. Blau in *American Sociological Review*, Vol. 21 (June 1956), pp. 290–295.

19. *Op. cit.*

20. Tumin, *op. cit.*, p. 58.

21. Angus Campbell, "Factors Associated with Attitudes Toward Jews," in *Readings in Social Psychology*, edited by Swanson, Newcomb and Hartley (New York: Henry Holt, 1952), pp. 603–612.

22. Tumin, *op. cit.*, pp. 38–39. Quotations are from Tumin's summaries, but the inner quotations are from Gough.

23. T. W. Adorno. E. Frenkel-Brunswik, D. J. Levinson and R. N. Sanford, *The Authoritarian Personality* (New York: Harper & Brothers, 1950).

24. *Ibid.*, p. 971.

25. Quoted from Adorno by Tumin, *op. cit.*, p. 9.

26. To give an example, Else Frenkel-Brunswik, one of the Adorno team of authors, writes ("Interaction of Psychological and Social Factors in Political Behavior," *American Political Science Review*, Vol. XLVI, No. 1, pp. 44–65): "There is reason to speak of a sexual marginality of the ethnocentric man and to recall also the sexual deviations observed in the Nazi elite."

27. William Peters, "Why Did They Do It?," *Good Housekeeping*, June 1962, unpaginated reprint.

28. *Ibid.*

29. *Ibid.* Emphasis supplied.

30. Bruno Bettelheim, "Dynamism of Anti-Semitism in Gentile and Jew," *Journal of Abnormal and Social Psychology*, Vol. 42, No. 2 (April 1947), pp. 153–168. The quoted material is from the summary in Tumin, *op. cit.*, p. 18.

31. "A Note on Anti-Semitism," *Psychiatry*, Vol. 9, No. 2 (May 1946), pp. 131–132.

32. Judd Teller, *Scapegoat of Revolution* (New York: Scribner's, 1954).

33. Albert Jay Nock, "The Jewish Problem in America (Part 1)," *Atlantic Monthly*, Vol. 167, No. 6 (June 1941), pp. 699–706.

CHAPTER 17

1. *Miami Herald*, June 3, 1965.

2. At the time, President William Howard Taft expressed the prevalent white American attitude toward Negroes when he told colored students at Biddle University in North Carolina: "Your race is adapted to be a race of farmers, first, last, and for all times." Quoted by Rayford W. Logan, *The Negro in the United States* (New York: Anvil, 1957), p. 66.

3. *Corrigan v. Buckley*, 271 U.S. 323 (1926). Direct residential segregation by state or local ordinance had been outlawed by the Supreme Court as early as 1917.

4. *Shelley v. Kraemer*, 334 U.S. 1 (1948).

5. Jerome Himmelhoch, "Tolerance and Personality Needs: A Study of the Liberalization of Ethnic Attitudes Among Minority Group College Students," *American Sociological Review*, Vol. 15, No. 1 (February 1950), pp. 79–88.

6. Peter P. Pompilo, "The Relationship between Projection and Prejudice with a Factor Analysis of Anti-Semitic and Anti-Negro Attitudes," unpublished Ph.D. dissertation, Catholic University (Washington, D.C., 1957).

7. *Dynamics of Prejudice*, Vol. II in *Studies in Prejudice*, edited by Max Horkheimer and Samuel H. Flowerman (New York: Harper & Brothers, 1950), 227 pp. The quotation is from Melvin H. Tumin, *An Inventory and Appraisal of Research on American Anti-Semitism* (New York: Freedom Books), p. 57.

8. *Public Opinion Quarterly*, Vol. IV, No. 1 (Spring 1940), pp. 94–95.

9. *Ibid.*, Vol. X, No. 1 (Spring 1946), pp. 122–124.

10. Irving Crespi, "Public Reaction to the Eichmann Trial,"

Public Opinion Quarterly, Vol. XXVIII, No. 1 (Spring 1964), pp. 91–104.

11. *Brown v. Board of Education,* 347 U.S. 483 (1954).

12. Misleading testimony was given by Dr. K. B. Clark, a Negro employee of the NAACP. Clark testified that, in segregated Southern schools, Negro children rejected brown dolls in favor of white dolls which they characterized as "nice." Professor Clark attributed this preference to a confusion of identity and self-hatred caused by segregation. What he failed to tell the Court was that, when he had applied the same test to Negro children in Northern integrated schools, "their preference for and identification with the white dolls was more marked." *Stell v. Board of Education,* U.S. District Court for Southern Georgia, 1963, testimony of Dr. Ernest van den Haag, R. 234–236.

13. *Columbia College Today,* Fall 1964, p. 19.

14. James Burnham, *Suicide of the West* (New York: John Day, 1964), p. 197.

15. Monroe W. Karmin, "Broader Integration Push?," *Wall Street Journal,* May 31, 1966.

16. Norman Podhoretz, "My Negro Problem—and Ours," *Commentary,* Vol. 35, No. 2 (February 1963), p. 64.

17. The tension would not necessarily vanish because gradations in color and race would persist. In mulatto countries, social status is generally determined by degree of visible race mixture and this causes envy, hostility and constant preoccupation with color.

18. Podhoretz, *op. cit.,* pp. 63–64.

19. Carleton S. Coon, *The Living Races of Man* (New York: Alfred A. Knopf, 1965).

20. John Buettner-Janusch, *Origins of Man* (New York: John Wiley & Sons, 1966), pp. 612–623.

21. Geoffrey M. Morant, *The Significance of Racial Differences* (Paris: UNESCO, 1952), p. 42.

22. Thomas Meehan, "Moynihan of the Moynihan Report," *New York Times Magazine,* July 31, 1966, pp. 5–49.

23. Curt Stern, "Genes and People," September 9, 1966.

24. "Possible Transfer of Metallurgical and Astronomical Approaches to the Problem of Environment vs. Ethnic Heredity," Paper delivered at a National Academy of Sciences meeting, October 15, 1966.

25. Meehan, *op. cit.*, p. 50.

26. Cambridge, Mass.: M.I.T. Press and Harvard University Press, 1963.

27. "Eugenics in Evolutionary Perspective," *Perspectives in Biology and Medicine*, University of Chicago, Vol. VI, No. 2 (Winter 1963), footnote pp. 165–166.

28. Audrey M. Shuey, *The Testing of Negro Intelligence* (Lynchburg, Va.: Bell, 1958).

29. *Ibid.*, p. 308.

30. Nathaniel Weyl, *The Negro in American Civilization*, *op. cit.*, p. 182.

31. Frank C. McGurk's important study is on microcards. It is summarized in Shuey, *op. cit.*, pp. 151–153, and Weyl, *op. cit.*, pp. 184–185.

32. "67.5% of Negroes Fail Draft Test," *New York Times*, October 2, 1966.

33. "Mental Tests for Millions in U.S.—What They Show," *U.S. News & World Report*, October 17, 1966, pp. 78–79.

34. *Ibid.*

35. *Ibid.*

36. Manheim S. Shapiro, *The Negro Revolution and Jews*, reprinted from *Council Woman* by the American Jewish Committee, 2nd printing, November 1964.

37. The existence of an organization called the Congress of Racial Equality does not invalidate this statement.

38. Podhoretz, *op. cit.*, p. 63.

39. *Idem*, p. 64.

40. American Jewish Committee, *A Selected Bibliography of Books, Pamphlets and Articles on Negro-Jewish Relations*.

41. James Baldwin, "The Harlem Ghetto—Winter 1948: The Vicious Circle of Frustration and Prejudice," *Commentary*, February 1948, pp. 165–170.

42. C. Belazel, *Jewish Frontier*, July 1964, pp. 16–18.

43. Shad Polier, "The Jew and the Racial Crisis," *Congress Bi-Weekly*, September 1964, pp. 5–8.

44. Judd L. Teller, "Negro and Jew," *Jewish Frontier*, September 1963, pp. 9–13.

45. Eugene B. Brody and Robert L. Derbyshire, "Prejudice in American Negro College Students," *Archives of General Psychiatry*, December 1963, pp. 619–628.

46. James A. Wilson, *Negro Politics* (Glencoe: Free Press, 1960), p. 155.

47. *Ibid.*, p. 157.

48. *Ibid.*, p. 156.

49. Quoted by Rabbi Richard C. Hertz, "Rising Tide of Negro-Jewish Tensions," *Ebony*, December 1964, p. 120. Emphasis supplied.

50. Sherman, *op. cit.*, p. 17.

51. *Ibid.*, p. 18.

52. Nathan Glazer, "Negroes and Jews: the New Challenge," *Commentary*, undated reprint.

53. Max Geltman, "The Negro-Jewish Confrontation," *National Review*, June 28, 1966, p. 621.

54. The punctuation and capitalization are in the original.

55. *New York Times*, February 9, 1966.

56. *Ibid.*, February 9, 1966.

57. Glazer, *op. cit.*

58. "When White Girls Go South as Civil Rights Workers," *U.S. News & World Report*, May 30, 1966, p. 10.

59. Eric Hoffer, "The Negro Is Prejudiced Against Himself," *New York Times Magazine*, November 29, 1964, p. 27.

CHAPTER 18

1. Eliezer Livneh, *State and Diaspora*, Jerusalem, 1953, p. 15. Quoted by Samuel Halperin, *The Political World of American Zionism* (Detroit: Wayne University Press, 1961), p. 316.

2. *Jewish Daily Forward*, January 9, 1959.

3. Diaspora means dispersion. In Jewish history, it refers to the successive scatterings of Jewry from its Palestinian base.

4. *In Vigilant Brotherhood: the American Jewish Committee's Relationship to Palestine and Israel* (New York: American Jewish Committee, 1964), p. 57.

5. *Ibid.*, pp. 54–55.

6. J. Robert Moskin, "Prejudice in Israel," *Look*, October 5, 1965, p. 67.

7. Joseph B. Schechtman, "Is There Discrimination in Israel?" *Alliance Review*, March 1952 and January 1953.

8. M. Smilansky and L. Adar, editors, *Schooling in Israel* (Paris: UNESCO, 1961), pp. 6, 10.

9. Moskin, *op. cit.*, pp. 70–72.

10. Weyl, *The Creative Elite in America, op. cit.*, pp. 130–198.

11. Sir Julian Huxley, "Eugenics in Evolutionary Perspective," *Perspectives in Biology and Medicine*, Vol. VI, No. 2 (Winter 1963), pp. 165–166, ftn. 2. Sir Julian assumes that genetic intelligence is polygenetically determined and "that its distribution follows a normal symmetrical curve." Sir Cyril suggests that some kinds of high intelligence may be determined by single genes.

12. The Negroes would never completely disappear by this process, but Podhoretz probably shares with most social scientists and literati who discuss the subject of race a profound ignorance of genetics.

13. Thomas B. Morgan, "The Vanishing American Jew," *Look*, May 5, 1964. (Reprinted by the American Jewish Committee.)

14. *Op. cit.*, p. 160.

15. Marshall Sklare, "Intermarriage and the Jewish Future," *Commentary*, April 1964, quoting *The Jew Within American Society*.

16. *Social Class and Mental Illness: A Community Study*, cited by Sklare, *op. cit.*

17. Morgan, *op. cit.*

CHAPTER 19

1. *Friends of the court.* Where powerful and wealthy organizations are involved, these briefs often involve a great deal of legal scholarship and keen constitutional analysis and may provide the kernel of the case for the plaintiffs which the appellate courts will consider.

2. Quoted in Gilbert, *op. cit.*, p. 151.

3. *New York Times*, December 2, 1966.

4. The quotation is from Legislative Reference Service, Library of Congress, Edward S. Corwin, editor, *The Constitution of the United States of America* (Washington, D.C.: Government Printing Office, 1953), p. 758.

5. Joseph Story, *Commentaries on the Constitution*, 1833 (3rd edition, 1898), pp. 224–225.

6. *Gitlow v. New York*, 268 U.S. 652 (1925). This did not mean that Gitlow's conviction was set aside; it was upheld and he served time.

7. *Everson v. Board of Education*, 333 U.S. 203 (1947), p. 212.

8. *McCollum v. Board of Education*, 333 U.S. 203 (1948) and *Zorach v. Clauson*, 343 U.S. 306 (1952).

9. For the court in the Zorach case.

10. Quoted in Gilbert, *op. cit.*, p. 95, an invaluable source on the development of American Jewish positions on this issue.

11. This account is distilled from the *American Jewish Year Book 1963*, pp. 88–102, an admirably objective and factual source.

12. *Engels v. Vitale*, 370 U.S. 421 (1962).

13. June 30, 1962.

14. Lucy S. Dawidowicz, "Church and State," *AJYB 1965*, p. 222.

15. The chief organizations testifying in support of the Amendment were the Catholic War Veterans, U.S. Junior Chamber of Commerce, American Farm Bureau Federation

and local branches of the American Legion, Daughters of the American Revolution, Veterans of Foreign Wars and General Federation of Women's Clubs. Dawidowicz, *op. cit.*, p. 223.

16. "Jews and the Crucifixion of Christ," *The Wanderer*, November 24, 1966. Condensed from Fr. Klyber's article in *The Liguorian*, April 1966.

17. Gilbert, *op. cit.*, p. 34.

18. ._.*d.*, p. 141. "Now" means 1965–1966.

19. A word deriving from the Greek and meaning "without norms," first popularized by Emile Durkheim, the French sociologist.

20. An excellent example is the pair of murderers whose grisly activities were delineated in Truman Capote's "anti-novel," *In Cold Blood*.

21. Quoted by Dawidowicz, *op. cit.*, pp. 211–212.

22. Quoted by Gilbert, *op. cit.*, p. 147.

23. *Idem.*

24. *Op. cit.*, pp. 231–235.

CHAPTER 20

1. Except for wage differentials based on productivity and even these are supposed to be temporary. The declared ultimate Communist objective is "from each according to his abilities, to each according to his needs."

2. Nathaniel and Sylvia Weyl, *The Reconquest of Mexico* (New York: Oxford University Press, 1939), p. 15.

3. Jeffrey Hart, *The American Dissent* (Garden City: Doubleday & Company, 1966), p. 110.

4. *Partisan Review*, Winter 1965, pp. 150–151. Quoted by Hart, *op. cit.*, p. 111.

5. Milorad Drachkovitch, "The 'New Left' in the United States: a Critical Appraisal," *Western Politica*, Vol. 1, No. 1 (Spring 1966), p. 10.

6. *Liberator*, New York, March 1966, p. 6. Quoted by Drachkovitch, *op. cit.*, p. 20.

INDEX

Abolitionism and anti-Semitism, 42–43
Acton, Lord, 4
Adams, John, 35
Adorno, T. W., 242–44
Afro-Asian Jews, I. Q. shortfall of, 297–300
Allinsmith, Wesley and Beverly, 6–8
Alter, Victor, 207
America, 316–17
America First Committee, 134–37
American Civil Liberties Union (ACLU), 306, 313
American Colonies and Jewry, 31–34
American Jewish Congress:
 and Vietnam appeasement, 169–71
 and Church and State, 305–08
American Revolution, Jewish role in, 34–35
Anarchists, 200

Anti-Defamation League, 85–87, 142
Anti-Semitism:
 and radicalism, 18–19
 in Spain, 20–27
 in Portugal, 27–28
 and utopian Socialists, 43–46
 and Union generals, 57–60
 a lower-class attitude, 81–83
 and Leo Frank case, 87–92
 and Ku Klux Klan, 96–99
 and Socialist Party, 96–101
 and Communist Party (U.S.A.), 119–21
 and Huey Long, 125–29
 and Coughlin movement, 130–31
 and Charles A. Lindbergh, 136–37
 and McCarthy movement, 138–41
 and the "Radical Right", 143–44
 and Christian anti-Communism Crusade, 144–48

and John Birch Society, 153–55

imputed to Goldwater movement, 166

under Lenin, 201–05

and Zionism, 201–02

purges of Jews under Stalin, 206

Nazi terror in Russia, 206–08

roots of Soviet, 208–11

under Stalin, 212–14

purges under Khrushchev, 214–20

in Poland, 223

and "Arab socialism", 229–30

class basis of in U.S., 235–36

and educational level, 237–39

by regions, 239

among "downstarts", 240–41

as a product of revolution, 245–47

and attitudes toward Negroes, 253–54

lack of in U.S. South, 254–56

of Negroes, 280–86

impact on Jewry of, 329–30

and Socialist authoritarian systems, 330–31

Arab-Israeli War, 220, 225–30, 286

Aristocracy and Jewry in Spain, 21–24

Arnold, Benedict, 103, 105

Arnoni, M. S., 334

Assimilation and class, 302–03

Attwood, William, 173

Baath Party, 230

Badeau, John, 226

Balabanova, Angelica, 197

Baldwin, James, 280

Baruch, Bernard, 54

Beard, Charles A., 70

Bebel, August, 246

Beecher, Henry Ward, 67

Ben-Gurion, David, 292–96

Benjamin, Judah P., 48, 50–54

Berger, Victor, 112, 114–16

Bettelheim, Bruno, 238, 240, 254

Biro-Bidzhan, 205

Black Muslim anti-Semitism, 284–85

Black Nazis, 285–86

Blaustein, Jacob, 294–95

B'nai B'rith, 41, 85, 314

Bodin, Jean, 27

Brandeis, Louis Dembitz, 57, 95

British Guiana, 147

Brown, Clifford A., 286

Bryan, William Jennings, 70, 72, 106

Buckle, Henry Thomas, 23

Bullitt, William C., 103

Bunin, Amos, 306

Burnham, James, 260

Butler, Erich, 156

Cabeza de Vaca, Alvar Nuñez, 22

Caesar's Column, 74

Cameron, W. J., 104, 107, 109

Carr, Edward Hallett, 202

Carrel, Alexis, 135

Castro, Américo, 15, 21

Christian anti-Communism Crusade, sources of support of, 146

Christian Front, 130

Christians, George W., 131

Clark, Colin, 172

Clark, Tom C., 118

Clerical celibacy, 11–12

Cleveland, Grover, 74

Columbus, Christopher, 25–26

Commons, John R., 79

Communist Party (U.S.A.), 116–23, 162
Conley, Jim, 88, 91
Coolidge, Calvin, 95, 107
Corporate hiring and U.S. Jews, 179–83
Coughlin, Charles E., 126–31
"Crimes against Property" (USSR), 217–18
Cromwell, Oliver, 30
Cuba, Jews in, 224

Damascus ritual murder affair, 37–38
Dana, Charles A., 44–46
Danger on the Right, 144–47
Davis, Jefferson, 53, 55, 60
Davis, John W., 98–99
Debs, Eugene Victor, 92, 95, 115
Decembrists, 191
Decter, Moshe, 216
De Leon, Daniel, 66, 111
Democratic Party, 37–38, 42, 63–65, 93–96, 98–101, 159–66
Dennis, Lawrence, 126, 132, 136–37
Despised Elite, the, 332–34
Dewey, Thomas E., 7, 137
Dietzgen, Joseph, 48
Disraeli, Benjamin, 52, 75
"Doctors' Plot", 213–14
Dodd, Bella, 118
Donnelly, Ignatius, 68, 72, 74–76
Douglas, William O., 311–12
Draper, Theodore, 117
Dreyfus case, 75
DuBois, W. E. B., 264

Eban, Abba, 223
Edison, Thomas Alva, 103

Einhorn, David, 49
Eisendrath, Maurice N., 169
Eisenhower, Dwight D., 8, 163, 164–65
Emanuel, David, 50
Emerson, Ralph Waldo, 44, 47
Epstein, Benjamin R., 138, 145–47, 149
Erlich, Henryk, 207–08
Evans, Hiram, 97

Ferdinand of Aragon, 23
Fillmore, Millard, 51
Ford, Henry, 101–09
Forster, Arnold, 138, 145–47, 149
Forsyth, John, 38
Fourier, Charles, 43, 44–45
Francis I of France, 15
Frank, Leo M., 87–92
French Revolution, 4–5

German Jews, economic advance of, 61–63
Gesell, Silvio, 73–74
Gilbert, Arthur, 320
Glazer, Nathan, 117, 121, 284–85, 287
Golden, Harry, 88–89
Goldwater, Barry M., 2, 143, 166
Gompers, Samuel, 111
Grant, Ulysses Simpson, 58–60, 63
Greeley, Horace, 45, 47

Halleck, Henry W., 58, 60
Hamilton, Lord Douglas, 147
Handlin, Oscar, 81–82
Harby, Isaac, 38–39
Harding, Warren G., 95
Hart, Emanuel, 42
Hart, Jeffrey, 333

Hart, Merwin K., 155
Harvey, "Coin", 74
Hayden, Tom, 334
Hayes, Rutherford B., 63
Hearst, William Randolph, 91
Hendrick, Burton, 52–54, 55
Hershey, Lewis B., 170
Higham, John, 82–83
Hillquit, Morris, 110, 113, 115
Hitler, Adolf, 106, 108
Hoffer, Eric, 290
Hofstadter, Richard, 72
Holmes, Oliver Wendell, 90
Hoover, Herbert C., 99
Huarte, Juan, 15
Huxley, Sir Julian, 300

Iberian Jewry, 20–27
Ingle, Dwight J., 268
Intermarriage, 84–85
Isabella the Catholic, 23
Israel and White South Africa, 300–01

Jacobs, Arthur T., 301
Jefferson, Thomas, 35, 309
Jewish anti-Communists:
    in U.S.A., 119–21
    in Russia, 198–200
Jewish education, 12–13
Jewish trade unions, 112
Jewry, an anomalous elite, 327–29
Jewry and deicide, 319–21
Jews and Negroes, a contrast, 274–76
Jews (Russia):
    and early revolutionary movements, 190–93
    dejudaization of revolutionaries, 193
    reasons for revolutionary attitude, 193–96

and Soviet secret police, 198
anti-Communists, 198–200
purged, 206
as security risks, 216
Jews (U.S.):
    income of, 173–74
    occupations, 174–78
    in professions, 174, 176, 184–85
    in the military, 178
    in business leadership, 178–83
    and higher education, 183–86
    gifted among, 184
    contribution to American elite, 186–87
    and musicality, 187–88
    and Nobel scientists, 188
John Birch Society:
    class appeal of, 150–51
    and Populism, 152–53
    and anti-Semitism, 153–58
    Jewish support of, 153–54
Johnson, Hugh S., 128–29
Johnson, Lyndon B., 171
Jones, LeRoi, 285–86, 335
Judaism without Embellishment, 218–19

Kaganovich, Lazar M., 203, 206, 212
Kamenev, Lev (Rosenfeld), 198
Kaplan, Fanya, 199
Kennedy, John F., 165
Khrushchev, Nikita, 214–22, 225
Kichko, T. K., 218
Klineberg, Otto, 234
Klyber, Arthur B., 320
Know Nothing movement, 42
Kossuth, Louis, 41
Kosygin, Alexsei N., 223

Kremer, Arkady, 196
Ku Klux Klan, 96–98, 106

Lafollette, Robert M., 95
Lasky, Victor, 119
Latvians in OGPU and CPSU, 198
Lawrence, David, 119
Lazarus, Emma, 66
Lehman, Herbert, 100, 138, 155
Lelyveld, Arthur J., 170
Leo, John, 307
Levine, Isaac Don, 119
Levy, Hayman, 34
Lewis, Marx, 116
Liebold, Ernest, 104
Lincoln, Abraham, 59–60
Lincoln, Eric, 281
Lindbergh, Anne Morrow, 136
Lindbergh, Charles Augustus, 134–37
Lippmann, Walter, 323
Lipset, Seymour Martin, 97
Litvinov, Maxim, 202–03
Locke, John, 31
Long, Huey, 125–29
Lopez, Aaron, 32
Lowell, James Russell, 47
Lyons, Eugene, 119, 155
Lysenko, Trofim, 209

Madariaga, Salvador de, 25
Madison, James, 308
Magnes, Judah L., 291
Mailer, Norman, 333
Manin, Daniele, 41
Mapam Party (Israel), 214
Marcus, Jacob, 31
Marranos, 24–29
Marshall, Louis, 94, 107
Marx, Karl, 45–48
Mather, Cotton, 32
McAdoo, William G., 98

McCarthy, Joseph R., 137–41, 164
McCarthy and anti-Semitism, 138, 140–41
McCarthy supporters, 139–40
McGurk, Frank C., 273
McKissick, Floyd B., 249, 271
McWilliams, Carey, 81
Miller, Arthur, 219
Miller, Herman P., 173
Miscegenation, advocacy of, 262–63
Monetary reform, 69–74
Monroe, James, 36
Monsanto, Benjamin, 39
Montaigne, Michel de, 27
Morgenthau, Henry, 64–65
Moskowitz, Belle, 99
Mourant, A. E., 298
Moynihan, Daniel P., 268–72

Napoleon I, 194
Nassau, John Maurice of, 28
National Association for the Advancement of Colored People (NAACP), 251, 260, 315
National Catholic Reporter, 307
National Union for Social Justice, 129–30
Negro family, the, 269–72
Negro I.Q., 272–74
Negro self-hatred, 288–90
New Republic, 323–24
New York Tribune, 45–47
Nihilism and the Negro, 278–80
Nihilists, 192
Nilus, Serge, 105
Noah, Mordecai M., 35–37
Nock, Albert Jay, 247

Pegler, Westbrook, 155–56
Pelley, William Dudley, 127, 132

People's Will, 192
Pestel, Paul, 191
Petlura, Simeon, 204
Pfeffer, Leo, 307, 317, 325
Phagan, Mary, 87–91
Pobedonostsev, C. P., 194
Podhoretz, Norman, 262–63, 266, 277–80
Polier, Shad, 307–08
Polish Jews, income of, 223
Possony, Stefan T., 11, 16, 188
Pound, Ezra, 73
Poussaint, Alvin F., 288–89
Prinz, Joachim, 166, 317
Progressive Party, 161
Protocols of the Learned Elders of Zion, 105–08, 157
Puritans and Jews, 32–34

Rabbinate and celibacy, 11–15
Race discrimination (U.S.), 258–62
Race equality, Jewish attitudes toward, 266–67
Race equality, Moynihan on, 268–69
Racially restricted covenants, 251–52
Radek, Karl (Sobelsohn), 197
"Radical Right", 149–52
Reed, John, 102
Reformation, 11
Religion and voting behavior, 6–8
Religious tests, 35–36
Republican Party, 2, 56–57, 63–65, 93–96, 159–66
Revolutions of 1848, 41–42
Ribicoff, Abraham, 326
Riesel, Victor, 119
Rockefeller, Nelson, 315
Roosevelt, Franklin D., 8, 99–101, 128–30, 131, 156, 159–60

Roosevelt, Theodore, 94, 95
Rosenthal, Erich, 84–85, 302
Rosenwald, Lessing J., 136
Roth, Cecil, 30
Rousseau, Jean Jacques, 4–5
Rousselot, John, 156
Russell, Bertrand, 221
Russell, William H., 52
Russian Jewish immigration, 77–80, 110

Saint-Simon, 43–46
Salisbury, Harrison, 215
Sarton, George, 16
Savinkov, Boris, 199–200
Schary, Dore, 142–43, 149–50
Schiff, Jacob H., 94
Schwarz, Fred R., 144–48
Schwimmer, Rosika, 102–03
Scientists, medieval, 16–17
Seligman, Joseph, 67, 82
Shapiro, Leonard, 198
Sherer, Morris, 325
Sherman, C. B., 282–83
Sherman, William Tecumseh, 58, 60
Shockley, William B., 268
Shuey, Audrey M., 272
Shylock, 86–87
Slavery, Jewish attitudes toward, 42, 49–56
Slidell, John, 54–56
Smith, Alfred E., 98–99, 137
Smith, Gerald L. K., 127, 129
Socialists, 66, 96–98, 110–16
South (U.S.) and Jewry, 39, 50–55, 254–56
Spinoza, Benedict, 27, 75
Stalin, Joseph, 198, 200, 212–14
Stevens, Thaddeus, 43
Stevenson, Adlai E., 8, 162–65
Stewart, Potter, 314
Story, Joseph, 309
Straus, Nathan, 64, 89, 92

Straus, Oscar, 64, 94, 95
Students for a Democratic Society, 334
Stuyvesant, Peter, 21
Supreme Court, 5, 257–58, 307–12, 326
Surinam, 28–29
Sverdlov, Jacob, 197
Sward, Keith, 187–88
Syrian Socialism, 230

Taft, William Howard, 94, 95, 106
Taylor, Zachary, 51
Teller, Judd, 245
Terman, Lewis M., 184
Tilden, Samuel J., 65
Toledano, Ralph de, 119
Torquemada, 22
Townsend, Francis E., 129
Tri-Continental Conference (Havana), 224
Trotsky, Leon (Bronstein), 115, 197
Truman, Harry S., 160–62

Van Buren, Martin, 37

Wade, Ben, 51
Wallace, George C., 168
Wallace, Henry Agard, 161

Ward, Lewis B., 178–83
Washington, George, 35
Watson, Tom, 76, 89–92
Weber, Max, 187
Weinstein, Jacob, 168
Welch, Robert, 153–57
Wesley, John, 34
Willkie, Wendell L., 137
Wilson, Henry, 42
Wilson, James A., 281
Wilson, Woodrow, 86, 94–95, 106
Wise, Isaac M., 42, 61–62
Wolfe, Bertram D., 119, 202–03
World Council of Churches, 319

Yemenite Jews, blood types of, 298–99
Yiddish Art Theatre (USSR), 212
Yiddish press, 65–66
Yulee, David Levy, 50

Zacuto, Abraham, 26
Zinoviev, Gregory (Apfelbaum), 197
Zionism, 201–02, 205, 209–10, 291–96